In This Body

IN THIS BODY

KAQCHIKEL MAYA AND THE GROUNDING OF SPIRIT

SERVANDO Z. HINOJOSA

UNIVERSITY OF NEW MEXICO PRESS ▲ ALBUQUERQUE

LIBRARY OF CONGRESS CATALOGING-IN-PUBLICATION DATA

Hinojosa, Servando Z., 1968–

In this body : Kaqchikel Maya and the grounding of spirit / Servando Z. Hinojosa.

pages cm

Includes bibliographical references and index.

ISBN 978-0-8263-3523-4 (cloth : hardback) — ISBN 978-0-8263-3747-4 (electronic)

1. Cakchikel Indians—Guatemala—Comalapa--Social life and customs. 2. Cakchikel Indians—Guatemala—Comalapa—Religion. 3. Human body—Social aspects—Guatemala—Comalapa. 4. Human body—Guatemala—Comalapa—Religious aspects. 5. Mind and body—Guatemala—Comalapa. 6. Midwifery—Guatemala—Comalapa. 7. Mental healing—Guatemala—Comalapa. 8. Indian dance—Guatemala—Comalapa. 9. Community life—Guatemala—Comalapa. 10. Comalapa (Guatemala)—Social life and customs. I. Title.

F1465.2.C3H56 2015

972.81'61—dc23

2015002177

COVER ILLUSTRATIONS:

A kneeling woman holding a cross-shaped *k'al k'u'x*. Drawing by Servando G. Hinojosa. Cave ceremony at Pa Ya' depicting offerings being made to the local spirit-owner. Painting by Alejandro Chacach.

DESIGNED BY Lila Sanchez

COMPOSED IN Minion Pro, Scala OT, and Scala Sans OT

For Nihan and Asya Mia

CONTENTS

Figures

Map

Preface

IT WAS BY CHANCE THAT I first went to San Juan Comalapa. I had visited Guatemala in 1990 as a student in the language and field school hosted by Tulane University, and decided to return the following summer. One of my Kaqchikel Maya language teachers, Chuti' Hunahpu, invited me to Comalapa, his hometown, and having heard of the place from other people, I decided to go. I had not intended at that time to choose a place to do my later fieldwork, but Comalapa became that place. One visit led to another, and gradually the town became something of a second home. But as the years rolled by, and as I did research for my graduate degrees there, Comalapa never lost its mystery. The place and its people kept steadily revealing things to me, things that sometimes took years to begin disentangling. One of the things I noticed was how so many local Maya talked about the body when describing spiritual experiences. Some Maya, for example, described how people with fright sickness become pale because of their weakened blood. Others sensed the workings of spirit in the growing and restless fetus. Time and again, the body became their main reference point for spirit. This told me that to appreciate Maya understandings of spirit, I had to attend to the inner workings of the Maya body.

The 1990s proved a good time to learn about the Maya body. There was a certain openness that made it possible to talk about. Early that decade, I sensed that people felt a growing and perhaps reassuring distance between themselves and the pains of the early 1980s, when so much of the country had been racked by state violence. With the passage of time, it became safer for Maya to talk with foreigners, and about more things. A calmer political climate and the return to at least the appearance of electoral processes in 1985 and 1990 made it seem like Guatemalan society had more possibilities before it than in recent decades. Among these possibilities was a new public dialogue about Maya spirituality. Much of this dialogue occurred within the context of a Maya revitalization movement that, among other things, voiced the need for spiritual renewal and encouraged Maya to get to know their ancestral 260-day ritual calendar. Many Maya learned about the calendar for the first time because of this, and many calendar diviners became emboldened to work more openly. By the time the peace accords were signed in December 1996, officially ending the thirty-six-year civil war, Maya from many walks of life had already committed themselves to learning about a native spirituality that had not before been allowed to exist in its own right.

My stays in Guatemala coincided with this changing social climate that saw public apprehension thawing for the first time in years. And while people remained guarded about some topics, I found that most people in Comalapa were willing to talk about one thing: the body. They told me a lot about their bodies, much like they might tell a neighbor. As they educated me about the bodily basis of their spiritual knowing, I came away thinking that their knowledge, grounded in the lived body, could enrich public discussions of Maya spirituality that the revitalization movement had sparked.

In this work I have the modest goal of exploring how spiritual experience is rooted in less visible places, where its realization speaks through a bodily vocabulary. I want to consider the body and its operations not only as the theater of spirit but as its primary expression, as revealed to me by Kaqchikel Maya of Comalapa. Doing this, I hope to widen the space in which Maya spirituality is discussed and to encourage others to appreciate Maya spirituality where Maya themselves live it, in their bodies.

Acknowledgments

PROJECTS LIKE THIS GROW FROM the help of so many people that I cannot possibly thank them all. It is fair to say, though, that the first seeds of this research I owe to the late Brian Stross, who introduced me to the Maya at the University of Texas and, just as importantly, made it possible for me to meet Judith Maxwell of Tulane University. Judie offered me a lot of guidance during my many stays in Guatemala during the 1990s and early 2000s. And even though I was a graduate student at UCLA during part of this time, she kept a keen interest in my work, something that greatly sustained me in the field. When I eventually became her student at Tulane, I got to claim more of her time, which made all the difference as I did my fieldwork. Thank you for making it possible, Judie.

While at Tulane I was also very inspired by Victoria Bricker and Munro Edmonson. Vickie always impressed me with her broad knowledge of Maya and her very easy manner. I still remember her stories of Chiapas. Getting to know Ed was also a gift. Seldom have I seen such a magnificent memory at work in a person, even as age and declining health took their toll on him. He and his wife, Barbara, always showed me unfailing hospitality, and I'll never forget house-sitting for them that one summer. It was a real privilege to know you, Ed. To my other professors and friends at Tulane I say thank you, especially to Adeline Masquelier and John F. Chuchiak.

My earlier years at the University of Texas were made all the more meaningful thanks to don Américo Paredes. His stories introduced me to the Rio Grande Valley, where many years later I came to live, and he remains a strong influence on me. I'm so glad he liked the drawings of South Texas my father gave him. At UCLA I had the privilege of working with Susan Scrimshaw, Carole Browner, and Peter Hammond, who all added to my understanding of Latin America and public health.

There are untold numbers of people in Guatemala to recognize. I early on received significant library assistance and other kinds of support from the Centro de Investigaciones Regionales de Mesoamérica (CIRMA) in La Antigua. Together with Judith Maxwell, R. McKenna Brown introduced me to the Kaqchikel Maya language, for which I am grateful. My thanks go to Vincent Stanzione for those long hikes through the living landscape, and to Rob Hamrick, who introduced us. Living in Guatemala was never the same after that. I thoroughly appreciated the company of John Hawkins, Walter Adams, Ana Juárez, and Richard Adams, the first three of whom were kind enough to include me in a National Science Foundation Research Experience for Undergraduates grant that extended for several years and that included several of my students from the University of Texas–Pan American (UTPA).

My biggest debt, by far, is to Maya individuals and families in Guatemala, and in Comalapa in particular. From the beginning in Comalapa, I stayed in Chuti' Hunahpu's home, where his mother, Aurora, always made me feel welcome, like a second son in fact. This study simply would not have been possible without them and their extended family. *Matyox chiwe iwonojel.* I also had the good fortune of knowing Reyna Cutzal's warm and generous family. Her mother, grandfather, two brothers, and sister always brightened when I came by, making these visits well worth the long walk to their cluster of houses.

If the beauty and importance of Maya cultural traditions is somewhat better secured through this work, it is only because of the many people like them who opened their homes and their hearts to me. I learned so much directly from them, and through them I became aware of other individuals who would become instrumental in my study, and whose views I have presented very imperfectly in this book. I still wrestle with whether to disclose their names. Although Guatemala may be on the mend after decades of civil violence, it has since become mired in other kinds of social traumas affecting people in towns large and small. Amid the resulting feelings of insecurity, then, I think it more prudent to use pseudonyms for many of the Comalapans who helped me. In the interest of posterity, though, I have included the actual names of two individuals who died during the period of this study. One is Martín Chacach, a noted linguist and supporter of the Pan-Maya movement, and the other is Alejandro Chacach, a painter, bonesetter, and dear friend. I never understood them to be closely related, or related at all, but they were both sons of Comalapa who will be missed now that they have moved on to the heart of the sky.

My research was also made possible thanks to different funding bodies at different moments. I recognize the invaluable support provided by a National Science Foundation graduate fellowship, a Mellon Foundation grant, two Foundation for the Advancement of Mesoamerican Studies (FAMSI) grants, and a Faculty Research Council grant from the University of Texas–Pan American. The shortcomings of my work, of course, should in no way reflect upon these bodies. Colleagues at my home institution of UTPA have also been a steady source of support and encouragement over the years. These include Tom Pozorski and Shelia Pozorski, and my dear friends Mark Glazer and his wife, Diana.

I must also recognize the different editors and staff at University of New Mexico Press. The press gave the manuscript the chance that it needed and enlisted a great team to get it into shape. Jean Molesky-Poz and the other, anonymous, reviewers made a big difference in improving the text, and I deeply appreciate it. Other individuals assisted me at different moments, but none more so than the press director, John Byram, who stewarded me through the last legs of the process. To the other folks who had a hand in this project I also say, thank you, and reiterate that whatever errors or flaws this work may contain are my own. Deep appreciation also goes to Bodil Liljefors-Persson and Christer Lindberg for permission to use some materials previously published in the journal *Acta Americana*.

Lastly, there is my family. My mother, Petra Z. Hinojosa, and my father, Servando G. Hinojosa, were constant sources of encouragement, even if they would have preferred that I shortened my stays in Central America. I thank my father for his wonderful artwork that put onto paper what I could not put into words in this, our second book collaboration.

To say that I owe a large part of this work to my wife, Nihan Kayaardı, would be an immense understatement. Her imprint on me has found its way into every part of my life, and this book is no exception. And with the arrival of our daughter, Asya Mia, in 2006, I am reminded that the work that really, really counts never quite gets finished.

S. Z. H.
ISTANBUL

Introduction

JANUARY NIGHTS IN COMALAPA ARE cold. The sun hurries off to warmer climes each afternoon, making streets like the one I am standing in darker and chillier by the minute. The men with me look nervous, shifting their weight, as if they were going to a party where they had to break up with their girlfriends. A few draw on cigarettes. Some of us finally decide to move inside the house we have been leaning on, hoping to shiver a little less. The house belongs to someone we know, a man who is expecting us. But tonight, going indoors blunts the highland chill only a little, and only because the room we enter is packed with men, women, and children, each bundled in jackets or long wraps. Like them, I would rather be in here than out in the darkening street. Unlike most of them, though, I have no idea what the night will bring, of how people will suffer.

Moving to the center of the room, I find myself next to a large pot erupting with red bromeliads. One the other side of the bromeliads, a couple dozen faces stare fixedly at the ceiling, unblinking despite the copal smoke that splashes into the air above them every few seconds. Manolo Calí, our host, is waving a censer over tonight's honored guests. The smoke smarts our eyes, but what really saturates the air is a palpable sorrow. It is not hard to see that many guests wish this day had never come. They are marshaling all their strength to be here and to keep themselves together, even if the objects at the center of attention are but shiny pieces of wood.

Comalapa's dance performers have come to the *entrega*, the "turning-in" event where they formally bid good-bye to the masks, costumes, and spirits they have bound themselves to for the previous three months. For no dancer is the separation easy; for many it is downright painful. Some dancers want to hold their masks one last time. They cradle them and whisper promises to them. Others just wipe their eyes and look away. But most dancers stand quietly, observing the faces they have come to know so well becoming ever hazier beneath Manolo's fragrant cloud. If this is their first time at an entrega, they might be feeling surprised, not at their own emotional swell but at how they are keeping it in check. Everyone knew this day was coming, but no one could have predicted how he would personally react to the separation that feels more like a dismembering.

Don Manolo's house contains the kind of scene anthropologists like: private, ritualistic, multisensory. It appeals ethnographically because it provides a ready world of contours and textures to explore, and the vocabulary to describe it with. But as the emotional wrenching at this gathering suggests, there is much more going on beneath the surface than we can initially sense. What I am seeing is emblematic of the kind of devotion and connection forged between Kaqchikel Maya dancers and their costumes throughout Comalapa's dance season. I am beholding a side of the dance tradition that even few Comalapans get to see, but that reaches to the core of Maya dancing. Tonight there are no scripts or choreographed steps, no spectators or fundraising pauses, those elements so central to public performances. Tonight people are stepping back and taking stock of the depth of feeling they have lived, of the visceral flexibility they have achieved in recent days. They weep because they are separating from what used to be them, or at least an extension of them. At the same time, the spirits of the dance are withdrawing to the hills, letting their human stewards reestablish their conventional bodies, now that the spirits are no longer anchored there. The dancers are bringing a major life commitment to a close. They will return to community life tomorrow having experienced something that, while very colorful and kinetic when dancers express it, all Comalapans in some way participate in. They will have lived the bodily grounding of spirit.

What I try to do in this study is explore how, for Kaqchikel Maya, spirit not only expresses itself through the body, but comes into being through the body. The body makes spirit a palpable reality, and this reality is experienced differently in different arenas of work and ritual. To identify how Kaqchikel spirit is embodied and lived I explore the arenas or domains of midwifery, soul therapy, and ceremonial dance. Each of these three domains centers on different bodily operations that experiences of spirit hinge upon. As a result, each domain emerges as a very productive site of body-centered spiritual discourse. Each domain reveals how Kaqchikels understand spirit, and enact spirit, through a bodily medium.

When I was first deciding which domains to investigate spirit and body through, some choices seemed obvious. Midwifery stood out as something I should explore since it involved the emergence of new, ensouled bodies, and because local midwives might be, as reported in other Maya communities, technicians of the sacred. I also felt compelled to include the people I call soul therapists because these individuals, by ritually reintegrating Comalapan lives, are the people most familiar with the physical effects of spiritual fragmentation. When it came to selecting a third domain to explore, though, I was at a loss. I might have been drawn to a public divinatory cult in Comalapa, but there was none. And the bonesetters that I had started researching a couple of years earlier basically saw themselves as empirical workers. It was not until I chanced upon a group of men ritually preparing for an off-season dance that I realized that dance had a hidden spiritual side, as well as an overt physical one. For the first time, I saw Maya ceremonial dance as relevant for my study, and I researched it shortly afterward during the 1995–1996 dance season. It turned out to be a good fit with the other two domains because, whereas the domains of midwifery and soul therapy are quite female centered and tend to involve older people in their purview, the domain of dance is heavily male centered and involves somewhat younger persons. The three domains also encompass a range of local religious experience, with the first two domains including many Catholics and evangelical Protestants, and the last one featuring a more traditionalist Catholic membership.

My choice of domains was also affected by the many people I had met over the years in Comalapa. Since first visiting the town in 1991 and then returning to it in 1992, 1993, and 1994, I had come to know numerous midwives and soul therapists, sometimes through my host family, sometimes through the good graces of other people. By the time I began my fieldwork in 1995, I had developed a strong sense of how midwives and soul therapists attended both spiritual and physical needs, and I knew I had to reach out to them again. I kept up with many of these individuals in the years after the main research was done, making several return visits to Comalapa between 1997 and 2007. These stays and visits gave me a good working exposure to the three domains over the years and slowly attuned me to the larger lessons of the lived body.

Midwifery, soul therapy, and ceremonial dance offer different vantage points for viewing the enactment of spirit through the lived body, whether a pregnant body, a distressed body, or a danced body. Taken together, the three domains provide a partial lens into Kaqchikel Maya spiritual experience, first in the way Comalapans conflate ideas of "soul" and "spirit," and then in how they articulate them using a bodily language. To more closely reflect local ways of talking about spiritual experience, then, in this study I use the terms "soul" and "spirit" interchangeably, like Comalapans do, although I respect the use of particular Kaqchikel and Spanish inflections of these. On the other hand, when I offer wider formulations on the non-visible components of human life and vitality, I usually use the terms "spirit" or "animating essence." But whatever the terms Comalapans favor, when they voice their understandings of soul, spirit, or animation in general, their accounts almost always move through idioms of bodily processes and sensations. More often than not, conversations about spirit turn to descriptions of things like fetal movement, weak blood, or facial pallor. The more time I have spent with Comalapans, actually, the clearer it seems that not only do they conflate soul and spirit, but they also consider the boundaries between spirit and body themselves to be very hazy, and sometimes absent. My tendency to distinguish the two stems more from my exposure to Cartesian reasoning than from local categories of experience. If there is a prevailing Kaqchikel Maya view of spirit and body, I have come to understand it more in terms of operational convergence than of outright differentiation.

Two observations have fed my interest in the grounding of spirit. The first is quite basic: the body is easily talked about. In a place like Guatemala where many topics are taboo, even the most reserved persons seem fairly willing to discuss their health problems with a stranger. Discussing sickness is, in fact, a good way to get potentially useful health information among Guatemalans. This is not to say that Guatemalans are not sometimes guarded about their bodies; they are. But since chronic illness is endemic to many peoples' lives, and perhaps because some Guatemalans feel they can benefit by talking about what ails them, I have found most people willing to talk about their bodies and health.

The second observation is that the body forms the touchstone for spiritual knowledge among Comalapa Maya. This means that when people talk about spirit, their narratives hinge on the idiom of bodily experience. For some areas of interest, like midwifery and soul therapy, this seems logical enough. I did not, however, expect that ceremonial dance would also implicate the body to the degree it does. Comalapans rely upon a bodily platform to engage these domains and other daily activities. Their bodies also guide them in achieving balanced relationships with the spirit-owners of the earth, relationships essential to life in Mesoamerica (Monaghan 2000; Molesky-Poz 2006). The continual reference to the body in daily life reaffirms that the body is the primary vehicle for apprehending the physical and nonphysical aspects of reality. As the frame of reference for conceiving spiritual reality, the body operates as the primary field of signification and as the medium through which a spiritual discourse takes shape.

However, for Comalapa Maya, the body is not a passive surface upon which volition is inscribed or into which externally derived signs simply force their way. It is not even the body recognized by Western physiology. The local body is an expression of ongoing processes binding the physical and nonphysical worlds. Its binding to worlds beyond its physical boundaries is evident every time a person suffers soul loss and every time birth organs influence the persons they were once connected to. From the time a fetal body is animated and thereafter, the existence of a "living" physical body is predicated on a nonphysical reality, together enabling ensoulment. Even stillborn babies' bodies are seen to have earlier manifested this ensoulment. Nonphysical reality needs the body, also, for making its agency accessible to human sensory perception. The body makes the intangible tangible for culture.

This book is organized into four parts. Part 1 introduces soul and place in Mesoamerica. It first addresses how the construct of soul has attracted the interest of many people over the years. Then, drawing from local stores of knowledge and what others have written, it introduces Maya folk syndromes as expressions of spiritual affliction, and blood divination practices as revealing of embodied soul. Part 1 then presents some of the ways that Comalapans refer to soul in its different permutations, including how they make conceptual linkages between soul and things like emotions, pain, and the physical heart. I then connect to the way that Kaqchikels understand the landscape to be an animistic terrain to be lived amid and to be very careful with. This is because spiritual life in Comalapa hinges on negotiating close relationships with spirit-owners of the hinterlands upon whom humans depend.

Following this, I present the reader to San Juan Comalapa itself, where soul is still conceptualized and lived, and where it now shows the influences of different church congregations. I discuss townspaces and lifeways to set the stage for viewing Comalapa as a place with locally meaningful categories of experience. Reaffirming the body as the primary vehicle of spiritual agency and as the necessary ground for full vocational expression, the section next explores some expressions of embodiment theory and how they partially frame Comalapan experiences of the body. At the close of part 1, I then revisit a native concept, k'u'x. Recognizing how this idiomatic complex encases several oscillations of embodied soul, I articulate its usefulness for bridging spiritual and physical dimensions of Maya life.

Comalapan categories of experience come into focus as parts 2, 3, and 4 reach into more specialized areas of life. Part 2, for example, centers on midwifery and the emergence of spirit. It walks through how pregnancy is seen as a family event and how midwives care for women's bodies during and after fetal gestation. Their attention to pregnant bodies gives them unique insights into fetal growth, animation, and even gendering, and underscores how their work is as much about spirit as about body. The midwives' knowledge of birth organs and blood, moreover, broadens our understanding of how soul strength registers as physical phenomena like movement, heartbeat, and circulation.

Some of the midwives' therapeutic responsibilities are shared by the subjects of part 3, Kaqchikel soul therapists. But these individuals place much more emphasis on diagnosing and treating spiritual maladies that afflict Comalapans. Soul therapists know how people have different spiritual components and how people can lose them, at times to spiritual beings of the countryside. In many cases soul therapists apply their signature ritual, the oyonïk (calling), to reintegrate their clients, and sometimes they use spiritually imprinted ritual surrogates for these. Soul therapy reveals that spirit is anchored in bodies and expressed through bodies, and that physical measures can fortify both spirit and body.

Part 4 spotlights ceremonial dance performers and examines how they take on enormous challenges and risks during the dance season. By becoming dancers, they not only agree to feed the dance spirits in their masks and costumes but also to bring the dance spirits into their bodies. The dancers must feed their masks well, for this will keep their own bodies strong and will make them suitable hosts for the visiting dance spirits. If a dancer does his job well, the season will go well for him, but if he does not, the spirit of the dance might visit misfortune upon him. Kaqchikel dancing shows how transactions with spiritual earth lords are governed by bodily parameters and have very physical outcomes. And as I indicated at the start of this introduction, these transactions usually end in a very painful separation.

Parts 2, 3, and 4 of the book, then, explore how Kaqchikel Maya enact spiritual awareness and experience through the body. I probe the worlds of meaning of each group of ritual specialists and underline moments of synonymy between spirit and body. This allows a look at how human bodies "initiate" a spiritual existence and maintain this existence, at times through close ties with nonhuman entities like dance spirits. It also highlights the role of the body as a vehicle of knowing. I would argue, in fact, that whatever resilience Maya spirit may encase, it is owed to a deep resilience of Maya body as the starting point for spiritual knowing. This has implications for the colonial enterprise.

If a prime objective of the Spaniards was to fashion Maya souls into Western souls, then we must conclude that they failed. This book, in a sense, addresses part of the reason why they failed: they failed to change the body, or at least change it completely. The documented characteristics of Mesoamerican souls that have resisted five centuries of acculturation attest to this enduring body. Although we cannot say that native souls of today are identical to pre-Columbian souls, native souls today do differ from the Western soul in ways that reveal their non-Western bases. For example, native souls are not primarily concerned with "salvation" (Farriss 1984:328), nor are they thought to be completely unified. Even when they have incorporated Western soul elements, native souls have resisted being completely reinvented along European lines. For this, it appears, native bodies deserve some credit.

I begin part 1 by reviewing concepts of soul in Mesoamerica, a topic that has long captivated Westerners. The discussion begins this way because soul is lodged within a history of mischaracterization and defamation that in many ways continues to this day. The way soul has been appraised has long been subject to vagaries of power, making it necessary to review part of its background before trying to discern its living soil, the body.

Part One

SOUL AND PLACE IN MESOAMERICA

CHAPTER ONE

Approaching Soul in Mesoamerica

THE HIGHEST FEATURE IN COMALAPA'S vicinity is Chuwi Kupilaj, a mountain looming over the town from the northwest. While occupiers have entered and left the region, and as languages, dress, and religions have changed, Chuwi Kupilaj has stood fast even as it surrenders more of its woodland edges to farmed fields, and as new cults use its sacred summit. Like Chuwi Kupilaj, the Comalapa soul has had different tenants, from Maya, to Catholic, to evangelical Protestant, and it has inevitably been shaped by each passing mantle. Like the sentinel mountain, though, the Comalapa soul is still very recognizable. Its lasting Maya qualities attest to a local, bodily grounding that has eluded centuries of forced acculturation. But the effects of those centuries are still felt, and the story of the Maya soul is still marked by the heavy hands that have impacted Maya bodies.

When Europeans imposed Christianity on the New World natives, they set a slow and painful encounter into motion. Spanish clerics wanted to extirpate all non-Christian elements from native religions and replace them with foreign religious concepts. Since the newcomers believed the Indians were little more than animals living in a state of diabolical deceit, they felt free to force religious changes on them and to usurp their wealth (Cervantes 1994). Different things hastened the natives' outward acceptance of the new religion. They were forcibly baptized and gathered into new residential-administrative settlements called *congregaciones*. Many of those lucky enough to survive the initial onslaught of foreign diseases found themselves bound to a life of work under the encomienda system, whereby natives were required to supply goods and labor to Spaniards who had received estates in recognition of their services to the Crown. But as

hard as these developments were for natives, complex spiritual transformations still lay ahead for them.

From the start, misconceptions about the American natives drove European social practices. While many Europeans admired how the natives
looked (Frost 1993), they disagreed over what they could not see: the natives'
souls. Many Spaniards claimed that American natives lacked souls or only
had souls like those of animals, perceptions that worsened life for the
natives. On the other hand, prominent "defenders" of the Indians like the
Dominican fray Bartolomé de Las Casas argued that the natives indeed had
souls like those of Europeans (Las Casas 1992a:19–20). The disagreement
actually centered on whether the natives had the higher faculties of soul
that "enabled them to hold beliefs, opinions, and convictions, and so to be
capable of the reasoning necessary for receiving the gift of faith" (Furst
1995:8). By attributing reason and intelligence to the natives, Las Casas
(1992a) argued that the natives were very capable of the Christian spiritual
aspirations the Spaniards espoused but rarely exhibited.

It was not until 1537 that the pope agreed with him. Paul III's papal bull
Sublimis Deus declared the Indians worthy of receiving the Holy Sacra-
ments of the church, confirming their full, if misled, humanity (Zavala
1991). Nonetheless, the Spanish emperor Charles rescinded parts of the
bull that would have brought ecclesiastical penalties against those who
ignored the decree. The papal bull fueled Las Casas's campaigns against
Spanish injustices but did not end them (Las Casas 1992b). The injustices
eventually prompted the New Laws of 1542, which decreed that Indians
were subjects of Castile and could not be enslaved or mistreated. When
the Crown summoned Las Casas to the Council of Valladolid in 1551, he
again defended the Indians against the plunder and encomiendas of the
Spaniards (Las Casas 1992a).

The encomienda system would yet take many more Indian lives. The
battle over the Indian's soul, meanwhile, shifted from characterizing it, to
"saving" it. Natives holding to their cosmology now had to contend with
the idea of salvation that intruded along with the idea of soul as a singular,
indivisible entity stained with "original sin." But clergymen intensified their
work among the Indians and enacted many enforcement mechanisms
meant to Hispanicize the Indians' spiritual practices and conceptions
of soul. Clerics forced Indians to stop using "idols" and to disavow any

spiritual connections with natural forces, including the ability to perform divination or shape-shift into animals (Greenleaf 1961:51–53). With these measures came the expectation that the natives of New Spain would come to realize their heresies and embrace Christianity, accepting God alone as the master of their one irreplaceable soul.

This mission had limited success, however. In many places the ostensibly Christian soul remained multiple and divisible (Ortiz de Montellano 1989:18). That it kept this quality so tenaciously suggests that religious authorities either thought it was not as problematic as other native beliefs, such as nagualism (Brinton 1894), and did not warrant censure, or that they largely overlooked it. The church may simply have tolerated it because it was so embedded in sickness complexes. At any rate, the idea that soul could fragment persisted, suggesting that native ideas of soul rest on bases outside the reach of civil and ecclesiastical authorities, bases hinging on non-Western understandings of body and even place.

Scholars like Evon Vogt (1965, 1969, 1976) and John Watanabe (1989, 1992) have shown not only that Maya souls often have non-Western features but that these features vary from place to place. In his classic example of how Mesoamerican souls differ from European ones, Vogt (1965, 1969) related how the Zinacanteco Tzotzil Maya's thirteen-part *ch'ulel*, or body soul, is located in the heart and blood. The ch'ulel could fragment and be ritually reintegrated. It would then rejoin a "pool" of souls after the person's death and be used by another human (1969:369–70). Vogt also detailed the *chanul*, or animal-spirit familiar, that shared a soul and life outcome with each Tzotzil Maya. The chanul dwells with other spiritual animals in a volcano guarded by the ancestral gods (1969:371). Vogt demonstrated that, even though Tzotzil Maya profess some Christian principles, their core spiritual concepts remain decidedly non-Western.

In Watanabe's complex portrait of the Maya soul, he revealed that some Maya souls root people of specific communities to specific ethnic places or "ancestral locales" (1989:273). Among the Mam Maya of Santiago Chimaltenango, the soul-like entity that did this was the *naab'l*. The naab'l does not simply animate the body as the Western soul is often said to do. Rather, it connotes "an interpersonal 'common sense' that abides in particular places," manifesting in people as a given "way of being" (1992:86). The naab'l evokes a sense of community membership requiring people to adhere to local norms. For these Mam Maya, another soul, the *aanma*, is more like the Christian soul, surviving the body after death (1992:87). Watanabe (1992:89) emphasized the lived importance of both entities, stating that "[f]ar from arbitrary mystifications, naab'l and aanma pertain directly to the 'rightness' of feeling, reasoning, acting, praying—in short, of living—in Chimalteco ways." Unlike the Western soul, the Mam soul matters most in the course of living, rather than of dying.

The connection between soul and lived experience resurfaces among Tzeltal Maya in Cancuc where many but not all of the multiple soul elements that Vogt reports among Tzotzils are found. In this locality, reports Pedro Pitarch (2010), while soul is understood in terms of the "bird of the heart," the heart- and mountain-dwelling ch'ulel, and the diverse and mainly body-external *lab*, it can also be framed in another way. For Pitarch, the Tzeltal recognition of soul hinges on a reconstruction of the past and of the world of the outsider, the Castilian or *kaxlan*. This understanding of soul acknowledges the basic way that soul, since the end of the body's fetal stage, folds the "other" into itself, much like the Maya community encloses the church and municipal authority into its geographical heart (2010:203, 208). Pitarch echoes much of what Vogt said about soul multiplicity, and refracts what Watanabe said about soul rootedness in place. It should not be surprising, then, that Maya souls still draw the attention of researchers interested in what makes these souls native, Western, or neither (García et al. 1999; Groark 2009), often to the frustration of those most interested in "saving" souls, like clergymen.

By insisting on the lived soul as a construct of daily importance, American natives deflected the European stress on salvation. Highland Maya made room for salvation in their emerging Spanish vocabulary, but the concept remained too abstract and removed from daily life to anchor their lives around. They valued local cults of soul, which for Chimalteco Mam Maya provided "an epistemology of afflictions, not a means of salvation" (Watanabe 1992:192). The Mam soul and its suffering remained more important for understanding social imbalance than for reaching a desired afterlife. While Tzotzil Maya had similar views of soul (Vogt 1969:373–74), Mam Maya put more stock in actualizing the "soul" intrinsic to responsible and conscientious community life than in saving it with church help.

Despite opposition from colonial authorities, these Maya and other native people kept many of their earlier soul ideas. When they accepted Christian ideas, they usually shaped them to fit their existing spiritual frameworks, although this is not always visible on the surface. Still, Western and non-Western spiritual concepts coexisted and sometimes combined. These amalgamations characterize most Mesoamerican soul thought today.

Discovering what soul means to Mesoamericans still requires more than just asking people about soul. Someone interested in soul must spend time with people, listen to their stories, watch them raise their children, and go about their daily lives with them. People do talk about soul, but more often they embed knowledge of soul into everyday activities. When researching Kaqchikel Maya soul, then, I have tried to see how people enact knowledge of soul in unspoken ways. This has meant observing how people regard their bodies, interpret their bodies, and treat their bodies. The body emerges as a central vehicle for understanding and actuating soul. This holds true for Comalapa Maya in general, but the body's centrality as a field of meaning is especially vivid among midwives, soul therapists, and ritual dancers, prompting this research into how soul is revealed and instantiated through these people with such specialized knowledge of the body. It works with the recognition that, as among Maya of other places, afflictions of the local Maya soul make themselves known through the body (García et al. 1999:161). And since so much about soul is revealed through the body, a useful starting point for discussing soul is a cluster of problems that beset the body, and a bodily means to diagnose them.

LOCAL FOLK SYNDROMES

Virtually every Comalapan knows about fright sickness, either by witnessing it in others or by suffering it personally. Kaqchikel Maya call this affliction *xib'iril*, a word derived from the root *xib'* (fear), but like many other Guatemalans they sometimes refer to it as *susto*. Xib'iril and its analogs have been identified in many Mesoamerican places and around Latin America.[1] Comalapa soul therapists diagnose and treat xib'iril on a regular basis, and few people find it strange that this service is sometimes needed. After all, Comalapans live in an often frightening world.

Like the term "xib'iril" suggests, frightening experiences can cause this condition. An animal can frighten a person. Street dogs and snakes are the usual offenders, but even horses or cattle can get unruly and startle someone. Participating in or witnessing a fight between men or spouses can cause xib'iril, especially among children. A child might also get xib'iril if an angry adult chides him, or if he sees a drunk, disorderly man. Many people get xib'iril when they slip, trip, or fall, although these mishaps will more likely produce xib'iril if they occur on a country path. Falling from a truck or bus can also cause fright, as can simply receiving a piece of bad news. Other studies in the Maya region have pointed out that sexual intercourse can precipitate xib'iril, since the soul can temporarily "drop out" of the body (Guiteras Holmes 1961a:297; Vogt 1969:370).

Importantly, supernatural agents cause some xib'iril cases. One most often hears about how rural spirit-owners can cause partial soul loss among those who either trip or fall in the woods, or who take resources from their domains without first asking permission, as I discuss below. Encounters with other spiritual entities can also cause xib'iril. For instance, men might encounter the *ya' son* or *siguanaba*, a female apparition, late at night on the trails. Drunk, wayward men are especially likely to see her, and those who survive the confrontation typically suffer a severe fright.

Pregnant women have to be especially careful about xib'iril. Although pregnancy produces a "hot" and strong personal state in women, pregnant women need to shield themselves from experiences that might distress their unborn.[2] For this reason, pregnant women are told not to look at things like cadavers and eclipses; they must also avoid domestic quarrels. Fetuses are connected to their mother's emotions, and they experience her trauma at such times. The midwife Eva explains that a pregnant woman can feel so much trauma when fighting with her husband that it can jeopardize her fetus.[3]

While many xib'iril cases are tied to accidents, encounters with supernaturals, and emotional hardships, Comalapans are just as likely to blame natural calamities and national events for chronic xib'iril cases. Many point to the human toll of the 1976 earthquake. Others recall the terrifying early 1980s when state forces, including death squads, took Comalapans from their homes and brought suspicion and fear into hundreds of Maya communities. These traumas left very deep marks on the collective Comalapa soul.

Soul fright produces serious bodily effects that can be directly witnessed, like a miscarriage, but more often it manifests in other ways. Persons with xib'iril often exhibit listlessness, loss of appetite, and general introversion. Lola, who is an *oyonel*, a soul "caller," says that xib'iril is a "cold" condition and lists diarrhea, nausea, noise in the stomach, cold sweats, and "cold blood" as its main symptoms. Xib'iril interrupts normal sleep patterns, making people feel sleepy in the daytime and lethargic on hot evenings. Gabriela, a midwife, says that the xib'iril sufferer sleeps too much, does not eat, and quarrels constantly with others, like a cat. She adds that, if the sun is out, the xib'iril sufferer will sit alone outside to warm herself, also like a cat.

Striking changes in physical appearance can accompany changes in a person's spiritual state. The oyonel Lencha says that xib'iril turns the victim's face yellow, for lack of blood, and makes his eyes look sleepy and fatigued. She also says xib'iril makes the victim's neck become skinny, even if he is obese. Xib'iril can be evidenced by a swollen stomach and by rapid breathing, says the oyonel Julia. The oyonel Sarita, on the other hand, points to facial and leg swelling and adds that the sufferer's hair stands on end. The pallor of many xib'iril sufferers reinforces the idea that xib'iril frightens, debilitates, and even thins the blood, entwining soul fright with concerns about anemia.

Anemia, in fact, is the most frequently stated physiological rationalization of xib'iril, next to *nervios*, roughly glossed as "jittery nerves." Anemia either produces or is produced by xib'iril, but is usually involved in the blood weakening that accompanies it. Curers who see nervios at work in xib'iril cases closely link nervios with embodied emotions. The oyonel Julia thus explains: "Xib'iril is nervios. For example, if I'm here [indoors], and it's night outside, it gives fright to leave the house . . . these are nervios." Fear, located in the blood, feeds nervios. Xib'iril can also be communicable, relates Sarita, for if a nursing mother gets xib'iril, she can transmit it to her infant through her breast milk.[4]

Oyonela' who diagnose with their hands can detect very physical signs in the xib'iril sufferer's body. Lencha says that she can palpate and detect an irregularity like a vanilla pod in the xib'iril sufferer's belly, as occurred with a girl she once treated. Probing the belly, Tencha likewise diagnoses xib'iril when she hears a watery noise coming from the upper left side of the abdomen. Xib'iril thus manifests itself physically throughout the body, including through certain organs, limbs, and bodily fluids.

Many of these physical and behavioral symptoms move the sufferer out of normal social activities, making him seem uninterested in being with others. When this happens, it can strain personal bonds. Families grow worried when they see this and seek oyonela' to restore their members to normal physical and social states of being. These strains may be what ultimately prompt families to reach out to oyonela'.

The most integral understanding of xib'iril, however, hinges on how fear affects spirit. While Comalapans do not often speak explicitly of xib'iril as soul loss, the way they handle xib'iril cases shows that they understand this ailment in terms of soul fragmentation, as chapter 7 discusses. The soul's multiplicity comes as no surprise to them, since even the God of Catholicism expresses a tripartite quality. Soul fragmentation and loss are also plausible, since most believe that some agency in the animistic landscape can "spirit away" easy targets. Moreover, human souls are considered inquisitive and fickle. Their curiosity lures them across the land during dreams, and their sensitivity jolts them out of the body during a shock. They are prone to lasting injury that is expressed as the body's debility. This vulnerability becomes more apparent when taking *ruwa winäq*, another folk syndrome, into account.

Ruwa winäq, literally "the eye of (the) person," is endemic to Comalapa, but it is linked to very distant cultures. Scholars have traced the ancestry of a related condition, "evil eye," to Indo-European and Semitic peoples, whose descendants brought it in varying forms to the New World (Dundes 1992:259). Latin American peoples then assimilated and reformulated it, giving it many local expressions (Maloney 1976). Although Comalapans sometimes call the condition *mal de ojo* or *ojo*, implying that it comes from an ill-intentioned gaze, they seldom attribute ruwa winäq to personal maliciousness. It is usually thought of as unintentional and involving admiration.

In Comalapa, ruwa winäq primarily affects children, since they often attract attention and because they are considered inherently "weaker" than adults.[5] Being admired by a stranger, or even a relative, can cause the condition. Kaqchikel Maya mothers are especially wary of ruwa winäq. They shield their infants and young children from the admiring glances of people from outside the household, family, and community, in ascending order of importance, to prevent it. Infants, especially, can be afflicted with this condition if someone simply looks at them. Even in places as innocuous as a church, or as necessary as the market, children can receive a glance later blamed for ruwa winäq.

Pregnant women are very dangerous in this regard. Their suspected desire for children and their *ruq'aq'al ri k'ik'* (strong, hot blood) can upset the delicately balanced life-force within a child and sicken him. Elsewhere in the Kaqchikel region, menstruating women have been viewed with similar distrust (Adams 1952:34). The "hot" blood of drunk men and of men who are tired and perspiring at the end of the workday can also cause ruwa winäq. Men returning from the fields are told to rest and cool down before coming near children, even their own. Work-weary men and pregnant women cannot help their "hot" states, but they are supposed to be careful around the young and vulnerable so as to not put their weaker souls and bodies at risk.[6]

Parents also shield small children from ruwa winäq by dressing them in red garments and wraps when in public. The color red, through its own "hot" qualities, counteracts the "hot" qualities of ruwa winäq. Tiny red cloth pouches containing pungent herbs are sometimes worn by children and others for this protection. Red pouches containing rue (*Ruta graveolens*, Kaq. *rora*) and wormseed (*Chenopodium ambrosioides*, Kaq. *sikyäj*) are also placed on K'iche' children in Momostenango to shield them from *uwach winak* (Tedlock 1987:1074).[7]

Ruwa winäq manifests in various ways, but Comalapans look for certain bodily signs. An afflicted child becomes unusually listless and cries a lot. If he develops a fever, which is likely, or if his countenance turns red, his family might retrace their steps and try to remember who gave the child the unwanted glance. That person will probably be asked to touch the child to undo the harm. If the child's condition does not improve, his mother, grandmother, or another person prays over him with eggs, salves, and massage to reduce the child's body heat, the ailment's main expression. The child is taken to a ruwa winäq specialist if his condition persists or worsens.

Since ruwa winäq is widely recognized in Comalapa, almost anyone in town can point out the home of someone who can treat it. Persons who treat ruwa winäq are usually healers in a broader sense, also working as oyonela' or, in many cases, as midwives.[8] Oyonela' and midwives both treat this condition, but oyonela' are more often sought either when treatment for both ruwa winäq and xib'iril is needed or when a diagnosis of either is still pending. Overall, oyonela' also enjoy greater public confidence than do midwives when it comes to diagnosing and treating the bodily effects of spiritual injury. This is probably because oyonela' tend to be older and more removed from modern medicine than are midwives.

When an oyonel treats a child for ruwa winäq, the child's mother should participate. The oyonel and mother kneel before a home altar and pray several Lord's Prayers and invocations to the Virgin Mary. Some oyonela' apply commercial salves to the child's belly and feet. Most oyonela' rub an egg over the child's entire body, marking small crosses on the head, torso, and limbs, praying all the while. The oyonel Tencha carefully breaks the egg into a bowl of water, inspects it for any signs confirming ruwa winäq, and discards it. Some curers use a lemon or a sprig of rue in place of an egg. Many oyonela' also bathe the child. Oyonel Lola, for instance, prepares a foot bath of five sprigs of rue, three sprigs of wormseed, lemon juice, rubbing alcohol, and a small quantity of baby's urine. The bath draws heat down from the child's head and upper body, restoring his temperature balance.

Ritual knowledge of ruwa winäq reaches across lines of specialization, residing among oyonela', midwives, and laypersons. This is not the case with ritual knowledge of xib'iril. Fewer people know how to deal with xib'iril and are able to perform the treatments. This is because soul therapy requires specialized ways of knowing the totality of soul and body and how these react to jolting experiences. Pragmatic handling of the afflicted body begins with knowing the soul's expressions.

Comalapans size up the soul's condition by observing physical signs. Some of these signs, which I discuss later in the book, can be noticed by laypersons, while others need a more practiced eye or hand to detect. And for those who can read it, blood reveals the embodied soul.

MESSAGES IN THE BLOOD: PULSING

Kaqchikel Maya make a connection between blood, soul, and vitalizing qualities like *chuq'a'* (soul strength) or heat. So closely do they ally the blood with the soul and these qualities that curers sometimes pulse the blood to diagnose the soul. Mesoamericans who "pulse" as part of their curing practices usually place one or both of their hands on different parts of their client's body, concentrate deeply, and let the client's body speak directly to them through their hands. What to a layperson might feel like a throbbing blood vessel, to a pulser might be a manifestation of soul distress. For Kaqchikel Maya pulsers, the blood becomes not only the medium of the soul and its vitalizing qualities, but a direct expression of these, which can vary in movement and color according to their state.

Pulsing specialists work in Comalapa, but there are very few of them. According to Hugo Icú Perén, a local physician, some curers probe the body to feel if the malady is centered on one of the organs, muscles, nerves, or other body parts (Hugo Icú Perén, personal communication). These curers are very discreet about pulsing, however. This may be because their pulsing takes readings of clients' spiritual states, something that might draw censure from more judgmental persons than Icú Perén. I never sought out pulsers in Comalapa and so did not knowingly speak with any. Still, if their pulsing tries to reveal the spiritual and bodily dimensions of illness, this would be consistent with what Maya pulsers do elsewhere.

Yucatec Maya healers of Campeche, for instance, palpate the body to "listen" for sounds that reveal the nature of the illness. In this way, a tympanic sound reveals "stagnant blood" that can be treated by drawing out a few drops (García et al. 1999:66–67). The Tzeltal Maya pulser in Chiapas similarly feels for the "words" in his client's body that reveal the sickness's origin (Pitarch 2010:72–73). The idea of listening to the blood is quite pronounced among Maya in Mexico, where audible messages reportedly move in the blood of suffering bodies.[9]

Maya pulsers in Guatemala are likewise attuned to finding information in the blood. For example, Mam Maya curers of Todos Santos Cuchumatán (Oakes 1951:184; Villatoro and Acevedo 1989:6) and Poqomam Maya curers of San Luís Jilotepeque (Gillin 1948:389) reportedly pulsed to elucidate the inner life of the body. Tz'utujiil Maya healers in Santiago Atitlán (Douglas 1969:155–56), meanwhile, pulsed clients' wrists and bodies to specifically locate "bad blood." If we take the attentiveness with which K'iche' Maya daykeepers of Momostenango observe the movement of their own blood and tissues as a form of pulsing (Tedlock 1992), then we can include these ritualists in this group as well. The way that K'iche' daykeepers report bodily sensations as "lightning in the blood" may be unique among Maya, but it shows how the body, including the ritualist's own, can "speak" to the perceptive listener.

Pulsing abilities are imperative for many Maya healers. They make knowable the animating essence acting through, and embodying through, the medium of blood. Pulsing is a bodily lens into a person's inner states, but while pulsing is not the main diagnostic method used by most healers in Comalapa, the quality of a person's blood is still considered key to any diagnosis of soul. This is because, at a practical level, Kaqchikels see blood not only as a body product but as a direct expression of the vitality and strength of what in Comalapa goes by different names.

COMALAPAN PERMUTATIONS OF SOUL

Comalapans use several words to convey the idea of human "soul" or "spirit." When speaking Spanish, they usually speak of *alma* and *espíritu*, words roughly equivalent to "soul" and "spirit," respectively. In Kaqchikel, the words *wanima* and *xamanil* are somewhat analogous to "soul" and "spirit." Wanima, meaning, "my *anima*," derives from the Spanish word *ánima*, "soul," itself seldom used in Comalapa. Wanima most often refers to a personal, interior essence, akin to a "soul" in Western thought. Xamanil can refer to the interior soul of a person, but it can also refer to an extrasomatic entity like the Holy Spirit. One oyonel points to this aspect of xamanil by asserting "Ri espiritu atk'äs richin ri Dios," "the espíritu is alive unto God." Another oyonel attests, "The espíritu is an espíritu, it is xamanil. . . . It can't be seen, nor can it be touched," emphasizing the invisibility of xamanil. Either wanima or xamanil can be "fractured" or "lost" due to fright sickness, although wanima is most often spoken of in this respect. While local healers and others do explain some differences between alma, espíritu, wanima (or *ranima*), and xamanil, in popular usage Comalapans frequently interchange the terms.[10]

Comalapan Kaqchikel Maya do not seem to recognize an animal-spirit companion as part of the soul, unlike Tzotzil Maya (Gossen 1975:451–54; Eber 1995:156), Tzeltal Maya (Pitarch 2010:40–41), and, to a lesser degree, Tz'utujiil Maya (Douglas 1969:92). It bears noting, though, that the seventeenth-century cleric Thomas Gage (1958:234) wrote of how the Guatemalan Maya he encountered believed in a beastly "familiar spirit."

Whether or not such a belief ever existed in Comalapa, the closest thing there today to zoomorphic spirits or beings that influence human life are the *dueños* or *rajawala'* (spirit-owners). As I discuss below, these "owners" of geographical features and classes of animals are sometimes the very features and animals themselves. They can frighten people who tread upon or encounter them. The spirit-owner of any given place or animal category exists as spirit and matter, although of a different order of reality than human spirit and matter.

To complicate things further, Comalapans also use the Spanish term *corazón* when referring to emotional, spiritual, and even animistic matters. But while the word "corazón" literally refers to the physical heart, it is also tied to the notion of soul and of being alive. In fact, Comalapans often use this term when describing how they feel pain in the depths of the soul, particularly with reference to wanima. Locals sigh and say, "Janila' niq'axon ri wanima," which one woman explains means, "My corazón hurts greatly." An elderly man agrees and explains what corazón and wanima mean to townfolk: "In Kaqchikel there isn't a difference between corazón and *anma*. . . . [We say,] 'q'axom wanma,' 'my corazón hurts.'" An oyonel concurs, adding, "The *awanma*, for me, is the corazón." The practical usage of "corazón" makes it a seat of the emotions, but this cannot be fully appreciated until we consider the more inclusive term "k'u'x."

K'u'x is allied to the above ideas of "soul" and means, at once, the physical heart, an animating spirit, an animistic center, the seat of human sensibility, and even the human placenta (Hinojosa 2002b). Kaqchikels directly link it to certain soul concepts, as in the phrase "Niq'axon pa ak'u'x, niq'axon pa awanima, xe junan," "Your k'u'x is in pain, your ánima is in pain, this means the same thing." The woman who utters this says that, inasmuch as k'u'x and ánima experience pain, they are the same entity. Indeed, a Comalapan Catholic priest (a Kaqchikel) says that locals refer to their k'u'x "when something pains their corazón." He goes on to explain that this is because "[when] something ails their alma, they feel a physical pain." K'u'x conveys soul distress through the heart, foregrounding its quality as the seat of the soul and emotions (see Hill and Fischer 1999). At other times, it is suggestive of an animating essence or animistic center (López Austin 1988, vol. 1:181), usually situated in the chest.[11] In colonial texts like the *Pop Wuj* and, more recently, in the invocations of

K'iche' and Kaqchikel daykeepers, *ruk'u'x kaj, ruk'u'x ulew* also refers to the godhead residing in heaven and earth (Tedlock 1985:75, 341).

The k'u'x concept usefully encapsulates different aspects of the animating essence in relation to physical matter, which we especially see in the way that Comalapans blur the boundaries between soul and the physical corazón. This will become more apparent later. For now we can appreciate that k'u'x is both multiple and singular, invisible and visible, and divine and organically human. To a great degree, it encompasses all the soul concepts introduced thus far, while allowing for the operational presence of individual soul aspects.

For Comalapans, the soul manifests gradations of ensoulment, or degrees of soul strength, in contrast to the Western soul, which is typically characterized by its presence or absence. The Comalapan soul's strength is usually expressed in terms of chuq'a'. This is a quality of the soul and of the body: that of having or being chuq'a'. It is a condition of strength or vitality, so its presence in human life connotes health and well-being. A midwife describes the healthy ranima in those terms: "k'o ruchuq'a' ri ranima," "the ranima has strength." A soul that has *ruchuq'a'* (in possessed form), and is thus very strong, resists soul debilities more than souls whose ruchuq'a' is low.

Comalapans distinguish between the ruchuq'a' of men's and women's souls by talking about their respective bodily features and behavior. Many curers and laypersons say that because men and women get sick equally often, their souls must be equally strong. One midwife reasons that if the body temperature of both men and women is the same, then their almas' strength must also be the same. Another midwife disagrees and says that, based on how aborted fetuses look, male souls are stronger, because male fetuses look more developed than female ones early in gestation. Offering a different perspective, one oyonel argues that women's almas are stronger than men's because men will drink when faced with problems, but women will not. Women can resist drink even if they get beaten, he says, because "women are strong in their thoughts." The relative physical constitution and strengths of male and female bodies index attendant soul strength and vitality, chuq'a', in each of these cases.

Not surprisingly, human blood is closely associated with chuq'a'. When blood is spilled, it is said that ruchuq'a' is being lost. Midwives especially fear this and warn that when a child's umbilical cord bleeds, his chuq'a' is being spilled. As the pathway for blood, nourishment, and strength, the cord is an extremely important conduit of ruchuq'a' for the infant and must not be allowed to bleed. Tzotzil Maya of San Andrés Larraínzar also recognized great synonymy between blood and spirit and considered that "[a]s the spirit and the blood are practically synonymous, any great loss of blood may be interpreted as damage or destruction of the spirit" (Holland 1961:223).

Comalapans show most concern for the blood and chuq'a' when discussing xib'iril. Xib'iril can severely weaken, thin, and dilute the blood, making its sufferers pale. A midwife says of xib'iril, "It gives them anemia. . . . When they are really malnourished, they have anemia." Xib'iril more often afflicts persons already weakened by sickness or malnutrition. A weakened nutritional state precipitates the soul-loss condition, in turn exacerbating the weakened state. A physically strong and healthy person, in contrast, can better deflect xib'iril. An elderly curer says that people with "good blood" are *k'owiläj winäq*, tough, strong people who are not easily frightened. On the other hand, he says, "anemics are easily dominated by those beliefs [of spiritual danger]," making them vulnerable to xib'iril. K'iche' Maya of Momostenango with healthy blood and bodies are likewise said to be *co (winak)*, "strong people" (Tedlock 1987:1074).

Curers voice different understandings of the interplay between blood chuq'a' and xib'iril. One oyonel explains, "When we are healthy, we have red blood cells, but when the red blood cells are weakened . . . the blood weakens," making the person lose sleep and appetite. He says that physicians will diagnose the person with anemia, but that vitamins will not alleviate the condition. Then, the person's face and feet will swell, he warns. While this curer emphasizes the normative nutritive quality of blood, a midwife emphasizes its normative hot quality. She says of the healthy person that "when the blood is thick, the blood helps us to get heated up." But when the person gets frightened, she says, "the blood becomes like water . . . it gets cold." Each curer underscores the blood's physical weakening tied to the onset of xib'iril.

One oyonel brings together popular understandings of soul, heat, and blood. He calls the alma *meq'enal*, a word derived from the Kaqchikel word *meq'en* (hot). God's breath produces this soul heat. He explains,

"When God gave life to Adam, he blew into him . . . it is an *aire* . . . it is something invisible." For him, "Blood is the *heat* that is given to the body; it is when the blood weakens that the body becomes cold." The breath of God, according to this oyonel, is the invisible heat ensouling the body and expressed through the blood. A reduction of this heat amounts to a weakening of the original breath of life in a person. His words reiterate that when the soul is intact and strong and possesses chuq'a', the blood is also strong. But when the soul is jarred and fragmented, so too does blood lose vitality; it lacks redness, heat, and thus chuq'a'.

A comparable relationship between soul, blood, and heat appears in Santiago Chimaltenango, Guatemala. As mentioned earlier, naab'l is a soul-like entity that binds people to a local moral consciousness. Naab'l invokes a socially and community-grounded aspect of personhood, a way of being necessary to operate among others who share a set of expectations and responsibilities (Watanabe 1992). Aanma, meanwhile, is the inner soul that can leave the body during dreams or as a result of shocks. Each of these entities relates very closely to the blood. For the Chimalteco soul to be restored following fright sickness, the patient's body must be doused with a special liquid to "'heat' the patient's blood and so induce the soul to return" (Watanabe 1992:88). Blood without heat will deflect the reintegration of the aanma, so the heat restoration is needed. In Comalapa, similarly, heat and chuq'a' must be restored ritually to the blood following xib'iril.

Chuq'a' is important in Comalapa in a way analogous to heat among Tzotzil Maya of Chamula (Gossen 1974, 1989; see Groark 1997:45). In Comalapa, one's chuq'a' increases from childhood to adulthood, just as heat accrues during the Chamulan's life-span (Gossen 1974:37). Old age and natural death accompany a decline in these qualities in both places.[12] Although its chuq'a' or heat valence may change over time, blood remains critical throughout the Maya life-span for robust life, and for what it reveals about soul.

Oyonela' do what they can to keep Comalapans spiritually strong, and they must be very diligent about this because Comalapans live surrounded by a countryside that on the one hand sustains them but on the other hand can endanger them. They and other local ritualists know that powerful animistic forces operate in the hinterlands. These forces might go unnoticed most of the time, but when humans encounter them or even seek them out, lives and livelihoods may be at stake. Comalapans cannot risk being unaware of the town's surroundings and its perils.

THE SACRED LANDSCAPE AND SPIRIT-OWNERS

Beyond Comalapa's town limits lies a world of deeply contoured surfaces, and the entity called the dueño is closely bound to these. Townspeople conflate him with the rajawal, and he remains an active spiritual agency despite the influence of Christianity. The dueño and the complex of spirit-ownership intertwine with local life at many levels. He is a manifestation of, and steward of, the natural realms, and in this role he makes himself known to people who live in close contact with his domain. Comalapans often blame the dueño for seizing souls and causing fright sickness, and for this reason they consider the hills and forests to be somewhat danger-ous to human soul-body integrity.

The dueño is known by various names, according to the language being used and depending on which of his aspects is being stressed. His names point to different domains of influence and control. For instance, the spirit-owner of the countryside and of specific mountains may be called in Spanish *dueño de la tierra* or *dueño del cerro*. In Kaqchikel, he might be called *rajawal ruwäch ulew* or *rajawal juyu'*. In Kaqchikel, *ajaw* refers to owner or lord, and the *r(u)-* possessive prefix makes the ajaw in question owner or lord of the term following the word "rajawal." Hence, "rajawal juyu'" refers to owner or lord of the juyu', the hills or woods. Likewise, when K'iche' Maya refer to the *rajaw juyub*, it is understood that he "owns the land and everything on its surface" (Molesky-Poz 2006:97).[13] For Kaqchikels, this being also owns the different classes of animals and takes on different names accordingly. The spirit-owner of coyotes, for example, is known as the *rajawal utiw*, and the spirit-owner of cattle is called the *rajawal vakx*. Ritual dancers invoke the *rajawal tzyaq* or *dueño del traje*, the spirit-owner of the dance costumes who is also called the *rajawal moro*.

It is unclear whether the dueño/rajawal is a single or multiple entity. The oyonel Mela told me that there are several dueños, but that they are all the same. Another oyonel, Everilda, said there is only one dueño but that he transforms himself into several. Importantly, locals comment upon the dueño's unity or multiplicity only when I ask them explicitly about this. Otherwise, they do not bring up his numerical fluidity. The dueño exists as an intrinsic, immanent part of the local animistic world, following Garrett Cook.

Discussing the folk theology of Momostenango, Cook (1986) describes local K'iche' Maya as animists. He discusses how spiritual agents act through the local landscape and ceremonialism and sketches some of the relationships these agents sustain with humans. Cook (1986:139) says of the K'iche', "They live in an inherited world which it is their job to maintain." What they maintain is the complex of relationships between humans and other beings. Humans offer *costumbre* (ritual acts) in exchange for and in recognition of assistance from the spiritual world, whether it is explicitly spiritual help or tied to material needs. These ties were begun in mythical times by earlier Momostecans. Many of these ancestral Momostecans, especially dead sodality members and dancers, still influence the lives of residents today and form part of the spiritual community that humans interact with (Cook 2000:102). Momostecan life depends upon these interactions linking human needs and sacrificial acts with spiritual mandates and control over natural bounty.

Relations between humans and other local beings in this town hinge on the notion of balance. Humans must remember the spiritual owners of the hills, fields, and animals and compensate them for the resources taken from them. Humans satisfy the dueños through prayers and burnt offerings of candles, incense, liquor, and other gifts. In turn, spirit-owners provide the rain, food, and health necessary to human life. They might also withhold calamities like the hailstorms and strong winds that plague farmers. And if humans ask first for permission, as Jean Molesky-Poz (2006:97, 106) points out, the earth lords might even tolerate it when people make deep intrusions into the earth, like when they build houses or highways. All undertakings that make use of the natural realms must be undergirded by a sense of reciprocity, one reminding people to show gratitude for the earth's gifts and to safeguard where they come from.

This is also the order of the day in Comalapa. Locals must offer a sacrifice, or, in the case of Protestants, a prayer, in the fields before sowing and during the harvest. They direct these sacrifices to a dueño, rajawal, God, or to an assortment of beings. Kaqchikels must also remember their deceased relatives, especially on the first two days of November, when graves are cleaned and adorned. Protestants, although claiming disinterest in community remembrances of the dead, also find ways to participate in them.[14]

The importance placed on balanced spiritual relations is very evident in xib'iril care. Serious xib'iril cases are thought to be best handled by oyonela' with proven track records for retrieving lost soul portions and for placating the rajawala' responsible. Oyonela' with heavier workloads, consequently, are those who implicate the rajawala' in soul loss. These oyonela' remind us that "ri juyu' ek'äs," "the countryside and hills are alive," inhabited by, if not actually defined by, sentient beings.

Comalapans pursue pragmatic relationships with their animistic environment and attend closely to the spiritual qualities of the world. This is true for locals of different formal religious backgrounds, who generally share the idea not only that divinity exists in the world but that it may exist in ways beyond what their congregations teach them. This is why an elderly evangelical Protestant man says of maize and other plants: "They have espíritu, that's why they are born, that's why they grow." People, animals, places, and natural forces like rain, wind, and earthquakes are all viewed through an animistic lens, especially by older Comalapans. As for the source of this world view, Comalapans explain that "es costumbre de los abuelos," "it is a legacy from the ancestors."

BEHOLDING THE RAJAWAL

Generations of Comalapans have developed strong ideas about how the rajawal looks and acts. Most people describe him as a well-dressed, fair-skinned man, looking like either a Ladino or a gringo. Some say that he can transform himself into any person. If a Comalapan encounters him on an isolated trail, he might invite the surprised person to his sumptuous home, offer him wealth, or admonish him for hunting too many animals. The rajawal might appear to a farmer and ask for a tortilla; if the farmer complies, he has a bountiful harvest. The oyonel Everilda speaks of the rajawal as a collective and says that they might take the form of an elegant woman: "They are the ones who transform into humans, they talk with people, but, when you get slightly distracted, say, and just look to the side, this gentleman or lady disappears." When the person realizes with whom they are speaking, or just before they do, the apparition vanishes.

Most people say that the rajawal speaks fluent Spanish (the sign of a privileged background), but a few say he addresses Maya in their native Kaqchikel. The traits Comalapans ascribe to the rajawal, in any case, place him in a social category far removed from the depressed economic conditions of most Maya. For this reason, Maya from around the region associate the rajawal with the foreigners' purported world of riches and corruption. They are wary of urban Ladinos and foreigners (including anthropologists) who visit or live in their towns, unsure of these peoples' nature or purposes.[15]

Just as Comalapans impute human behaviors upon rajawala', they also give them human names. For instance, the oyonel Patricia calls the rajawal presiding over the hilly Tz'an Juyu' precinct of town Manuel, and calls the spirit-owners of Q'eq' Ulew and Sarima', Fermín and Fernando, respectively. The oyonel Linda, however, says that the rajawal of Sarima' is named Sulumán, a name of unclear origin. Some people, like the oyonel Tencha, refer to all rajawala' by a single name, usually Diego Martín, a being often referred to as *padre de la tierra* and honored on November 11–12 (see Christenson 2001:174). His name comes in part from San Diego, to whom the church has assigned these days; locals honor him by eating and praying in the fields. At other times, the rajawal of a given locality is simply referred to by the corresponding toponym. The hills Chuwi Kupilaj, Xenimache', and Sarima' are thus presided over by rajawala' named Kupilaj, Xenimache', and Sarima', respectively.

Certain spirit-owners, such as Sarima', are assigned military identities. He rides a white charger and trains his unseen armies on the slopes of Sarima'. And, like the Guatemalan army, he has established a base just outside of town. People on trails sometimes hear him shout commands to his men from atop his horse, accompanied by a military band. On Tasbalaj hill south of town, another rajawal, a collective one, moves about with a warlike aspect. A Comalapan named Miguel connects this hill to the stone jaguars located near the town square:

> Long ago, each town had its protectors, say, an army. The feline [tenoned] heads that you see in the Comalapa town square, those *tigres*, were like the army of the town, the guardians of Comalapa. One day,

they were discovered and exposed on a hilltop called Tasbalaj south of town. It was anthropologists or archaeologists who discovered them. They brought them out of the ground and lifted them to the town square by helicopter. Since there was a paved road, the stone tigres were going to be taken out by truck, but they couldn't lift them, even with helicopters. But they did take two of the tigres by very powerful helicopters; one is at Universidad de San Carlos. In Kaqchikel, these tigres are called *b'alam*. There aren't any like these in other towns. These tigres were taken out of where the army garrison is now. The garrison was built at the place the tigres were dug up. Once, when Zaragoza wanted to invade Comalapa, the tigres turned into real animals and defended Comalapa.

Mounted barely a foot off the ground, the stone faces of Tasbalaj still keep watch over the town square. Time has eroded the jaguars' snarl, but the Tasbalaj spirit-owners remain vigilant both there and on Tasbalaj itself. Since Tasbalaj overlooks the main road leading into and out of Comalapa, its rajawala' are well placed to defend the town again, should the need arise.

The rajawala' of hills like Sarima' and Tasbalaj, not surprisingly, often have a military title. Some people extend this ranked naming to the rajawala' of all locations. The oyonel Linda, for instance, says that each hill is inhabited by a caporal (corporal). Other hills, like Sarima', are patrolled by higher-ranking rajawala'. In Santiago Atitlán, likewise, the spirit-owners of different geographic and occupational domains are ranked in sibling terms or according to the Tz'utujiil civil government hierarchy (Douglas 1969:88).

The oyonel Victor understands spirit-owners differently than most people, calling them *mundos*. He says that three of the most important *cerros* (hills) of Comalapa—Chuwi Kupilaj, Sarima', and Xenimache'—are all powerful mundos, although he also calls them *caballeros* (knights or gentlemen). The designation "mundos" for spirit-owners is more often used in the K'iche' area. Maya there liken mundos to kings, presidents, ministers, mayors, and *principales* (town elders) (Cook 1986:140–41; Bunzel 1952:148–51). And, like powerful humans, powerful cerros in places like Santa María Chiquimula can be asked to work together when responding to petitions (Molesky-Poz 2006:112).

SEIZING THE SOUL

Comalapa's rajawala' are blamed for many xib'iril cases. Spirit-owners are said to exact vengeance upon those who flout their rules of natural resource use. People who take from the land's bounty without ritually acknowledging the rajawala' court misfortune, sickness, and even disaster, and they risk having part of their soul seized by a spirit-owner. This can happen especially when a person trips, slips, or falls out in the bush (Wilson 1991:55). The rainy season from May to October, when trails are slippery, thus sees an increase in xib'iril cases. As Tencha stresses, "By way of him [the rajawal] is how people return. . . . If you are running, and you fall, it is *he* who is pulling you down." Oyonela' say that the rajawal that "pulls" a person to the ground, seizing his soul, must be invoked and supplicated to return the soul. And when the rajawala' of certain hills develop a reputation for causing xib'iril, people call those hills "very strong." One must tread lightly in those places.

Local earth lords are suspected of causing fright sickness in many other parts of the Maya area as well.[16] Maya wariness about spirit-owners and soul capture, and the use of compensatory ritual, has been documented at least as far back as the colonial period.[17]

Maya also blame soul mishaps on discontented ancestors. Among Tzeltals of Tzo'ontahal, ancestors could "grab the soul" of a person, sickening him. This happened when the ancestors feared that the person would become a witch (Nash 1967:138). Past Comalapan curers would reportedly tell the families of sick children that their *abuelos*, deceased grandparents or ancestors, were unhappy with them and were coming to take the children away. But today, when Comalapans attribute xib'iril to spiritual agency, they usually hold spirit-owners responsible, not ancestors.

Spirit-owners cause many episodes of xib'iril because there are so many places a person can cross paths with them. As elsewhere in the Maya area, Comalapan rajawala' focus their energies outside the settled townspace, where people are far from the relative safety of home. And since some locales in the countryside have become known for rajawala' activity, Comalapans try to keep very alert when they venture into the hills.

Particularly "strong" hills not only bear the imprint of spiritual risk, but they also attract people seeking the power of such places for divination or *trabajos*, a term referring to hexes or other dubious invocations. Victor explains how this works. He says that *zanjorines* (diviners or prayer makers) go to a strong cerro and "call forth the caballero of each cerro." The zanjorín beckons the caballeros of the three important hills, Chuwi Kupilaj, Sarima', and Xenimache', to converge at the hill from which he invokes them. To see whether the caballeros are responding, he looks into his divinatory portal, such as his scissors or a *guacal* (gourd), and says something like, "Ah, the Kupilaj is here, the Sarima' is coming." If one of the caballeros is not in agreement and does not come, however, the effectiveness of the divination or trabajo is lost, says Victor.[18]

One hill in particular is considered a locus of danger, veneration, and natural resources. Many Comalapans report that Chuwi Kupilaj, northwest of town, has long been home to many spiritual dramas. From sightings of the rajawal and his sumptuous home, to soul seizures, to the deployment of coyotes before the 1980s civil crisis, the hill and its spirit-owner have supplied years of living narratives. The reputation of Chuwi Kupilaj's rajawal today looms as large in popular experience as does the hill itself, standing some 430 meters above the town. It is such a strong hill, the oyonel David confides, that "some people go to pray there, others go to do an act of witchcraft there." Comalapans steer toward the former option, though, especially when the annual rains are late.

When sufficient rain has not fallen by June 24, the day of San Juan Bautista, practice dictates that the patron saint's image should be carried from San Juan Church all the way to the top of Chuwi Kupilaj, where mass is celebrated. In this way, some say, San Juan is directly beseeched for rain. Others insist that the supplications go to Kupilaj himself, by whose whims the rain is released or withheld. The curer Fermín states, "According to the beliefs of the people, over there is the source of the rains, when it starts to rain, that over there is the source of the rains. . . . Chuwi Kupilaj ruxe'el ya'," from Chuwi Kupilaj issues the water/rain. Another curer, Alejandro Chacach, concurs: "The water is stored over there. . . . Chuwi Kupilaj is like as though it had a vein . . . and it drains out to [the gorge] Las Delicias." The day Chuwi Kupilaj bursts open, he muses, all Comalapa will be washed away.

Alejandro does not think that Comalapa will soon face a deluge, but, as he suggests by linking Chuwi Kupilaj and Las Delicias, gorges are also spiritually active places. Las Delicias, in particular, bears notoriety not only as the receptacle into which Chuwi Kupilaj drains but as the abode of dance patron spirits. As I discuss in the chapters on moros dancers, moros spirits take shape as dwarf-like men dressed in lavish dance costumes. The little dancing moros can be so immanent in the gorge that some dancers can even smell their costumes. A vigil inaugurating the dance season is thus held at Las Delicias. The oyonel Patricia stresses how important this costumbre is for moros costume stewardship. She warns that if the dance troupe does not do the rituals, one of the dancers must die. She adds of Las Delicias, "His alma will go there to that place," where the dancers' debt will be collected. The smaller gorge Chuwa Burro is another important site for moros dancers. It is here that the moros costumes and their rajawala' must be first welcomed into Comalapa.

Gorges are also engrained in the spiritual topography through a notorious female entity, the ya' son, mentioned above. This apparition waits near bodies of water and presents herself to people, usually drunk men wandering around late at night. She is said to entice men, perhaps with the voice of their spouse or paramour, to walk with her. She may then reveal her hideous aspect to them or trick them into pursuing her into a gorge. Severe xib'iril befalls the men, assuming they do not die of fright on the spot or in the gorge. This temptress is also known as the siguanaba throughout the region.[19]

Like other bodies of water, rivers are considered spiritually active places. Perhaps because of the murmuring current, the year-round moisture, and the presence of wildlife, rivers evoke a sense of life allied with spiritual sentience. They are places where the rajawal resides and where he sometimes inflicts injury. But rivers are also places where the rajawal listens. Oyonela' like Alicia respect this and seek out rivers for conclusive oyonïk (calling rituals). Although the element of water alone might seem the focus of riverside oyonïk, water movement is of greater interest to oyonïk participants there. Flowing water can "wash away" and "carry away" spiritual ills as well as "return" the strength of the blood, making riversides ideal for healing prayers.

Like the tenoned feline heads from Tasbalaj, lithic monuments often command attention as focuses of spirit-ownership, and prominent among the in situ lithic features of the hinterlands is B'alab'aj, "stone of the jaguar."

Called Piedra Iglesia, "church stone," by some and Iglesia Ab'aj, "stone church," by others, it stands six or seven meters high and is embedded in a flank of Chuwi Kupilaj. Scattered colored candle stubs and embers litter its base, recalling frequent visits by persons invoking the local rajawal. An artist points out that young people sometimes inscribe the name of their love interest on the stone and leave an offering for the rajawal, hoping that he will ignite a spark with that person. Others say that, when the proper prayers are uttered at the stone, a door opens, inviting people to unknown things within. One man describes the risky side of the stone:

> When they made the church bells at Pa Minix [a former quarry], some men were enlisted to carry a bell from there all the way to town. The men, big and strong, weren't supposed to stop and put the bell down, but to go straight to town. The bell carriers passed by Piedra Iglesia and put the bell down on the ground there, against orders. When they tried to lift the bell up again, it wouldn't budge, so it stayed there at Piedra Iglesia. Now, every Good Friday, the bell tolls three times at midday. If someone happens to be passing near the place and he hears it, he will die within seven days. The person will get increasingly sicker over a seven-day period and will die. That sound of the bells steals one's espíritu.

West of Comalapa, near the settlement called Pa Ya', "at the water," is a hill with a large cave. As with other local features, the cave, also called Pa Ya', has a mixed reputation. The persons who introduced me to the cave, the curer Alejandro Chacach and his family, approach the place with a knowing respect. We reach the cave mouth following a short climb up an overgrown slope, and, once inside, a bell-shaped chamber marked by a small aperture of sunlight at its apex becomes clear. The ground is lunar, with a thick layer of dust. Alejandro sacrifices a chicken to the cave's rajawal and leaves an offering of candles in the form of a cross at the innermost part of the cave, where we find candle stubs of previous visitors. One of our companions places the leftover food in wall crevices as we leave.

Not all Comalapans look favorably upon the cave and its alleged spirit-owner, though. Some visitors disparage it. Evangelical Protestants like Delicia, for example, consider the cave a curiosity, albeit a dubious one.

FIGURE 1.1

Cave ceremony at Pa Ya' depicting offerings being made to the local spirit-owner.
Painting by Alejandro Chacach.

She describes how she and members of her Bible study group, while once visiting Pa Ya' village, decided to visit the cave. They approached the cave with mock fear and trepidation, linking hands, muttering prayers, and suppressing laughter. By her description, even these visitors were impressed by a spiritual presence in the cave. Interestingly, the owners of the land where the cave is situated are Jehovah's Witnesses. They nevertheless let people visit and pray in the cave, and, in fact, one member of this family, a local physician, once eagerly took me to the cave himself.

Stands of trees also have spirit-owners, although stands are approached less often than other features of the landscape. The oyonel David recounts that certain brujos, ritualists with ostensibly dark motives, used to seek certain tree groves, and "there, they would speak with the rajawal ruwäch ulew." These groves, though, have long been cut down, he says. Although forest is rapidly disappearing around Comalapa, there remain many stands of regrowth forests, making yet feasible this type of rajawal interaction. Trees have long been reported to be animated and to interact spiritually with Maya.[20]

Features like these populate the Comalapan spiritual landscape. Spiritual agents also leave their mark at crosses, roads, urban shrines, and other spots. But to better understand place-specific spirituality, we must visit what enclosures and *ganado* mean for Comalapans.

CORRALS AND THE *GANADO*

The motif of enclosures or corrals surfaces throughout the Maya area. It can relate to physical features in the landscape, such as gorges or caves (Tedlock 1992:149), or, as in Chiapas, to spiritual enclosures in hills where human spirits (Pitarch 2010:25) or humans' animal-spirit familiars are kept (Eber 1995:156; Gossen 1975:451). Physical and spiritual enclosures are likewise found in Comalapa. Gorges like Chuwa Burro and Las Delicias and Pa Ya' cave exemplify the physical kind. But although these take physical form, they enclose spiritual entities, ones that reveal themselves to people near these places or inside them. Spiritual enclosures, meanwhile, appear often in Comalapan narrative. People reportedly find themselves within chambers where animals, dance costumes, or other riches are guarded by a spirit-owner. Humans must somehow first enter through the "door" of these physical or spiritual enclosures to see what is within. The door may look like a large rock. The recurrent theme is that the rajawal is protecting something from careless use or predation by people. A man named Jesús gives an example of this experience.

Jesús describes how a rajawal made contact with his relative Rafael. About a year ago, says Jesús, Rafael encountered a large snake near his house, but he did not kill it. He simply shooed it away, and it went up the hill. Then Rafael found himself "summoned" to the hill, and there he saw a corral completely full of wild animals. It was "a world of animals," says Jesús. A man in the hill, the rajawal of the animals, told Rafael, "These are my animals; sometimes they leave and cause trouble; sometimes they come back bruised up." The animals were under his protection. The rajawal thanked Rafael for not killing the snake. Jesús says that Rafael sometimes tells this story when he sees someone about to hurt a snake.

Comalapans create corrals to enact certain mythical and ritual activities. A gorge-like corral, adorned like a chapel, is built at Las Delicias for welcoming dance costumes to the community. Moros dancers also erect corrals in which to perform their dances. People recall when the public would build a corral in the town *parque* in which bulls would be "fought." At the domestic level, most local Catholic homes have a rectangular room dominated by an altar at one end bearing chromolithographs, statuary, candles, and flowers. Families use this room to receive guests and to hold group prayers. Busy curers set aside a small room where they can assemble their ritual objects and separate their clients. The curers Lencha and Rolando have made such enclosures in their homes. These recall the in-house enclosures reported by Thomas Hart (2008:117–18) and Maud Oakes (1951:107) in which Maya ritualists channel spirits for clients.

In the figurative corrals of the hills and in the constructed ones of the townspace, Kaqchikels demarcate space for engaging sacred time. Profane time is momentarily set aside, and human perceptions of time shift. Indeed, many people returning from a rajawal's corral say that their memory has blurred and that time has greatly elapsed since they first entered the corral. Sacred-time observance may help explain how moros dancers can withstand ten or more hours of near-continuous dancing. Their temporal frame of reference differs strikingly from that of the spectator standing outside the corral.

The second motif found in sacred-landscape narratives is that of ganado. In Spanish, "ganado" usually translates as "cattle" or domesticated herd animals. In Comalapa, ganado can mean a state of being "won over" or captured, in a different way than that implied by the Spanish verb *ganar*, to "win" or "earn." Indeed, ganado signifies a succumbing to a rajawal's machinations or wishes. A person can become ganado in an encounter with the rajawal in one of three ways: (1) when the rajawal seizes the person and spirits away his soul and body; (2) when the rajawal seizes part of a person's soul and indebts the person to him; or (3) when the rajawal claims a person's soul through a pact. In the first two cases, a severe fright may be involved, and the rajawal will try to bring the person to his corral. Some Comalapans say that the rajawal will thereafter enslave the human there. From this we can see how a person who is captured, herded, and controlled like an animal indeed becomes animal-like and ganado in both senses of the word.

The oyonel Lela explains that, since most spirit-owners are señores (male lords), they make ganado out of many local men. She feels that rajawala' have more use for male labor than female labor in their spiritual *fincas* (estates). That is why, Lela says, many men enter the forest and later emerge unable to talk, without speech, having encountered the rajawal and become ganado. She reiterates that moros dancers run a high risk of becoming ganado.

The risk is high because dancers become stewards of the costume and mask, vowing to sustain their rajawala' with food and drink. In return, the spirit-owners allow the dancers to step into their mysteries and reenact part of Comalapa's mythical past. For a dancer to renege on his feeding obligations constitutes a breach of contract that can invite retribution by the costume rajawal. As David puts it, if the dancer fails to feed his costume and mask properly, "the clothes or the mask can take control of one"; they can "ganar" him. When a dancer collapses from fatigue during a dance, some say that he is being ganado. So dangerous is moros dancing in this way that Comalapans say that each year one of the moros participants has to die.[21]

Both dancers and nondancers enter agreements with spirit-owners, but nondancers do not put themselves in the spiritual cross fire that dancers do, nor do they really want to. Moros dancers take their feeding duties seriously because to fail at this could trap them in the rajawal's service as ganado. If dancers are not careful, their fate can be like that of other people who make inescapable pacts with rajawala'.

THE PACT, PACT MAKERS, AND THE DREAM ENCOUNTER

The more profitable kinds of pacts are also the riskiest. In a well-known kind of pact, a rajawal grants a person great wealth in return for the person's later servitude. The oyonel Pablo says that such pacts explain the dramatic increase in disposable wealth in Comalapa. In the early to mid-1980s, he says, there were few cars in town. In the 1990s and later, people suddenly acquired vehicles and large houses, something that initially puzzled him. Pablo argues that people with a fast-growing net worth must be getting their money from some spirit or rajawal. He even names specific people he thinks have struck a deal with a rajawal, people I know.

Getting a "gift" from a spirit-owner is not entirely straightforward, though. Reyna Cutzal, a Protestant woman, relates that once a rajawal is petitioned for money, the petitioner must surrender later to the rajawal, even if the person decides not to accept the wealth.[22] Maya in other places are also said to make pacts with spirit-owners to meet their daily needs or to acquire sudden wealth (Hart 2008:82–83; Warren 1989:80). Accounts of these are often offered as cautionary tales.[23]

Comalapa's hills harbor dangers for people seeking to make a pact with the dueño and for those trying to avoid him. But even people who do not walk into the hills can fall victim to their powers. A person can court danger by simply dreaming. This is because dreams enable the soul to leave the body and wander the hinterlands, a view held by many Maya (Fabrega and Silver 1973:232; Pitarch 2010:36).[24]

When a person dreams, "one's espíritu is observing things, be they present or future," the oyonel David stresses. The ability to collapse and traverse time is shared with dreams among Yucatec Maya of Chan Kom, for whom dreams reveal future events and calamities (Redfield and Villa Rojas 1971:211). The dreaming faculty also helps reveal if and where a person has suffered soul loss (Hart 2008:126). Since the soul wanders the countryside during dreams, visiting favorite places and abodes of rajawala', a xib'iril sufferer's dream can reveal exactly where his soul portion is lingering.

The midwife Gabriela says that when a person dreams that she is in a certain place, it is because she has passed through there and come back. But if a person really likes a place, or if she has been frightened there, Gabriela says, "one's ánima stays there, one begins to dream over there." The oyonel Tencha agrees that people "dream and they see where they have been *asustados* [frightened], like in water." Once the xib'iril and its location are confirmed, the soul can be entreated to return.

When xib'iril is due to soul capture by a rajawal, this being must be appeased to gain the soul's release. The healing rituals are considered most effective when the final ritual takes place where the fright occurred. Oyonela' listen for descriptions of this revealed topography when xib'iril sufferers describe their dreams, and they try to do the final healing ritual there. When the rituals are finished, the rajawal might visit the sufferer in a dream and say that he accepts the reparations. David explains that a man who got xib'iril by falling into a river remained ill even after several oyonela' tried helping him. Then, an oyonel did three soul recovery rituals at the river and sacrificed three chickens there. On the night of the final ritual, the sufferer dreamed of a gentleman telling him, "Many thanks, because you served me on some occasions, you behaved well, go now to your home."

Just as dreams relay information from rajawala' to people, they can also relay it from the ancestors or ancestral gods to the living, sometimes to disentangle cases of disease.[25] Many Maya also value dreams as vehicles that reveal and support specialized vocations (Hart 2008:130, 197).[26] In the initiatory dreams I describe in chapters 4 and 7, I sketch out how spiritual entities reach out to Comalapans and how Comalapans respond. These dreams launch a dialogue based on mutual obligations between humans and particular rajawala'. Oyonela' can use these dream reports to restore spirit while engaging those entities with whom they share the earth.

CHAPTER TWO

The Human Landscape in Comalapa

COMALAPANS LIKE TO POINT OUT the tenoned heads in the little park next to the town center. The heads' features are barely visible today, just a few running contours in low relief. But with a little squinting and imagination, one can make out the feline faces that once scowled from them. No one knows exactly who they once scowled at, though, or even who made them. Some say the tenoned heads came from Tasbalaj, a hill south of town where the area's first inhabitants are said to have settled. This makes the felines the community's first guardians and helps explain why Comalapans today look fondly on them.

But even before Comalapans placed these tenoned heads on their low concrete pedestals next to the park, they knew that people had been living in the area for a long time. Many farmers turn up small artifacts in their fields, and most children grow up listening to their grandparents' stories of when the town was already old. In repurposing the stone heads as park monuments, we see the town reclaiming not so much its founders as its authenticity of place. In an age when government officials, teachers, clergy, and health workers all emerge from Spanish-speaking institutions and represent those institutions, the felines remind locals that a part of Comalapa will always be Chi Xot, what the community was called before the outsider kaxlanes came.[1] And although the town has grown and changed immensely since it was Chi Xot, and an army outpost now occupies the hilltop where the stone heads were found, Comalapans have adapted themselves to the new material and social conditions. They have made the most of new technologies and crops and have identified new ways of being as Comalapan ways of being. As a result, the stone felines have borne witness to a very incomplete project of Spanish acculturation.

Comalapa today remains strongly identified with Kaqchikel Maya. A government estimate of the 2010 population indicates that over 79 percent of the municipality is indigenous, with the remainder being "nonindigenous" or Ladino (Guatemalans who do not identify as Maya).[2] But since the demographic estimates exclude the ethnic background of at least 4,000 Comalapans who were part of this population projection, the percentage of Kaqchikels is likely much larger. Approximately 42,226 persons live in the municipality, with 25,394 of them in the town center and 16,831 living in the surrounding fourteen villages (*aldeas*) and some thirteen hamlets (*caseríos*). In the late 1970s, 54 percent of Comalapans were reported to be monolingual speakers of Kaqchikel (Farber 1978:33). The use of Spanish at the time was probably greater than this, though, because many of the women listed in the survey as Kaqchikel-only speakers likely also had a working knowledge of Spanish (Garzon et al. 1998:141). That women were the ones listed as Kaqchikel-only speakers is still telling, since this points to how women in Maya communities have historically had fewer opportunities to learn Spanish than men. But whatever the distribution of language abilities among men and women in previous decades, in recent years the picture has changed.

More Comalapans have moved toward bilingualism since then, as suggested by how older Maya women, the group with the highest rates of Maya monolingualism in Guatemala, are frequently heard speaking Spanish in the market and when interacting with visitors. And while many young Maya in Comalapa remain actively bilingual in Kaqchikel and Spanish, the combined effect of schooling pressures, a growing preference for Spanish in the home, and the need to interact with Guatemalan society outside of Comalapa has meant a decline in Kaqchikel usage (Garzon et al. 1998:140). As Spanish usage is bolstered through classrooms, business transactions, and work-related travel, the ancestral language of the home is heard less often in the street, but it is still present at every turn. It remains to be seen whether Spanish will entirely displace Kaqchikel among Comalapa youth, and whether this will happen at the pace witnessed in other Kaqchikel towns. But judging by how the Kaqchikel language still forms the basis of a rich oral tradition, local people still value it as a chief vehicle of their values and beliefs (Carey 2001:27). Comalapan Kaqchikel speakers today form part of a Kaqchikel-speaking community numbering at least 450,000 (Kaufman 1990:63).

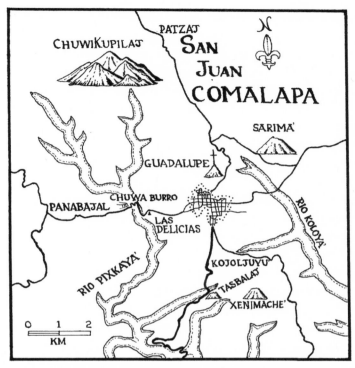

Map of San Juan Comalapa and its surrounding geographical features.
Map by Servando G. Hinojosa.

The Comalapa town center, or *cabecera*, is situated in an uneven valley
at 2,110 meters above sea level. The municipality of Comalapa extends
across seventy-six square kilometers of the Department of Chimaltenango,
under whose jurisdiction Comalapa has been since 1839, the year the
department was itself created (Asturias de Barrios 1985:13; Villatoro 1987).
Imposing hills, deep gorges, and rolling valleys characterize the municipality's topography. The four most prominent cerros (hills) around the
town center are Chuwi Kupilaj, Tasbalaj, Sarima', and Xenimache'.[3] On the
western flank of the municipality runs the Pixkaya' River and its tributar-
ies, while the Koloya' River runs east of the town center. Comalapans often
perform rituals atop Chuwi Kupilaj and in the valley of the Pixkaya', as
well as in a few caves and other landforms throughout the municipality, in
keeping with highland Maya practice (Scott 2009).

Comalapa shares boundaries with the municipalities of Zaragoza, Santa Cruz Balanya', Tecpán Guatemala, Santa Apolonia, San José Poaquil (a former dependency of Comalapa), San Martín Jilotepeque, and Chimaltenango. Tecpán Guatemala (sixteen kilometers away) is reached by dirt road through Panabajal village (six kilometers away), and San José Poaquil (eleven kilometers away) is reached by dirt road via Patzaj village (seven kilometers away). Comalapans going to Guatemala City must journey eighty-two kilometers, sixty-three of these on paved roads in the mid-1990s. Road construction crews were hard at work widening and asphalting the remaining nineteen unpaved kilometers between Comalapa and Zaragoza on the Inter-American Highway by 1998.

This newly paved roadway is the main access road to Comalapa. A large white cross marks the entrance into townspace proper, and just past this, the road bisects the town cemetery. The Calvario Chapel sits on a rise on the eastern half of the cemetery, facing north toward town. This chapel stood damaged for many years following the 1976 earthquake, but it was restored in the 1990s and is now opened during Holy Week. The flagstoned thoroughfare continues on past the Nazareno Chapel and the Sagrado Corazón Church on the east side of the street and leads to the town parque. Facing west on the parque stands the town landmark, the colonial San Juan Church, a structure dating to the early seventeenth century (Farber 1978:44) and also severely damaged in the 1976 earthquake. During this church's rehabilitation, Comalapans built a new San Juan Church next door, which became the seat of traditionalist Catholic-Maya devotions. Beyond a creek at the northern end of the town's thoroughfare stands the Guadalupe Chapel, on the Cerro de Guadalupe. It is opened only during the Virgin of Guadalupe celebratory weekend around December 12 of each year. A cross marking the northern edge of the townspace once stood in this area.

Few architectural features mark the east-west axis of town. The Sangre de Cristo Chapel is one, located two blocks east of the parque, facing south. Another is a small blue-green cross at the easternmost end of this street. At the street's western end is the Placita de Mayo, a town quarter said to have once had a cross that defended the town against a plague in the early twentieth century (Asturias de Barrios 1994:204). The day of San Bernardino is celebrated there every May 20 with children's festivities. Locals say that in addition to the crosses once posted at each of the four town entrances, a wall once enclosed the entire inhabited townspace. The wall, like the crosses, protected the town from pestilence, sickness, and unwanted people. Some older Comalapans insist that when an earthquake destroyed the wall in the early twentieth century, sicknesses immediately ravaged the town. But the wall was not rebuilt.

Comalapan townspace is no longer encircled by a wall, but it is still highly organized. At least three spatial systems operate. For many years the town was divided into eight districts or *cantones*. Still earlier, and contemporary with the cantón system, the town center was organized into some forty-five barrios (Asturias de Barrios 1994:202). These barrios were sometimes named after a local resident, or after an urban feature like a washtrough or a cross. Comalapans used the cantón and barrio systems for residential purposes until 1991, when the national government declared that Comalapa's four quadrants marked off by the two main roads in town were now four official zones and would supplant earlier spatial systems. Although the postal service encouraged users to learn locations by the newly numbered zones and streets, most older Comalapans still refer to places in town by their cantón and barrio names.

Residential practice persists in another way. Anne Farber (1978:41) noticed in the mid-1970s that Maya in Comalapa lived throughout the entire cabecera and municipality, but that Ladino residents tended to live close to the parque and along the town thoroughfare. This pattern continued into the early 2000s.

LIFEWAYS AND VESTMENT

Comalapans retain many elements of centuries-old ways of life, and this is especially true when it comes to food production. With small-scale agriculture the mainstay of most people, land ownership is highly valued. Those who do not own land often hire out their labor for day wages, about four dollars a day during the mid-1990s. Locals who farm usually use a hoe and stick and must often walk several hours to reach their parcels. When the rains arrive by May, Comalapans start planting maize, which, when harvested at year's end, will supply most of their food the following year. Locally grown black beans and squash are the second-most abundant staples. Farmers grow

other New and Old World cultivars like cauliflower, tomatoes, potatoes, rad-
ishes, fig-leaf gourds, broccoli, cabbage, beets, chilies, wheat, fava beans, and
onions for both the local and export markets. Rice, coffee, and sugarcane,
meanwhile, are trucked into town for the Tuesday, Friday, and Sunday
markets. Local and nearby growers supply fruits like apples, peaches, straw-
berries, hog plums, watermelons, avocados, cantaloupes, and quinces to
Comalapa, and lowland producers bring bananas, plantains, and pineapples
to the market. Many people, especially poorer ones, supplement their diet
with semicultivated herbs. And those lucky enough to find them or afford
them eat wild mushrooms during the rainy season.

Motorized mills, and not stone mortars, grind most maize today, but
maize is still prepared for grinding by being boiled for several hours in a
lime-infused bath. Tortillas are still patted by hand and cooked atop
comales (clay griddles) placed over wood-burning stoves or cooking fires.
Maize is prepared into a wide array of foods, including *atol de ceniza* and
atol de elote (maize porridge), *tamalitos* (steamed maize cakes), *elotes* (corn
on the cob), tamales, and *chuchitos* (steamed maize and meat cakes). Even
the most acculturated Maya households in the town center rely fundamentally on maize.

Several butcher shops tied to the covered market area, as well as pork
handlers, serve the local appetite for meat. Many households also raise
chickens for eggs and poultry, and some also keep *chompipes* (turkeys) and
ducks for this reason. People often raise poultry and swine as living capital, for ready sale to meet sudden medical or travel costs. Egg-laying chickens and milk cows also bring extra money to some households. Dried fish
is often sold on market days and becomes very popular during Holy Week,
when meat restrictions apply. Exotic meats like dried shrimp and fresh-
water crabs from Lake Atitlán often appear in the markets, although they
are too costly for most people.

Many Comalapans are in the business of transshipping different commercial products. If a person is resourceful enough to buy a truck, large or
small, and carefully maintains it, it can become key to his family's capital
accumulation. Outside markets became much more accessible to Comalapans when the road between Comalapa and Zaragoza was opened during
the Jorge Ubico presidency (1930–1944). Today, with ride hitchers moving
constantly between towns, truck owners have another source of money,

which, at the very least, defrays fuel costs. Interurban busing entrepreneurs (usually non-Maya) enjoy what is probably the most lucrative, and dangerous, of all transportation markets.

The production sector centered on weaving and handicrafts is both large and vital to local identity. Comalapan women who identify as *naturales* (*indigenes*) are expected to wear the local costume consisting of a distinctive *po't* (woven blouse), *uq* (wraparound skirt), and *pas* (sash). An indigenous woman who stops wearing the uq and becomes *de falda* (a skirt wearer) might get silently rebuked by other naturales who have kept their dress. The same is true for those who stop wearing the local po't. Today, though, more females wear embroidered blouses, especially local students and Maya who have moved to Guatemala City. In addition, increasing numbers of younger women use po't from other Maya communities on a daily basis (Hendrickson 1995). This is sometimes motivated by the growth of pan-Maya consciousness or, more often, by questions of style.

While the local ethos prescribes "native" dress for women, it does not do so for men. Only a few of the oldest Kaqchikel men in the town and villages still wear the local male dress consisting of *wex* (white cotton trousers), *kamxa* (button-down shirt), *koton* (blazer), *xerka* (knee guard / apron), and *ximb'äl* (sash). A straw hat or fedora completes the costume. Most Maya men and all boys now wear Western clothing, except during displays of "native pride" like the annual San Juan Day parade, during some school events, and during *cofradía* activities. Male and female Ladino clothing choices are typified by Western attire.

Maya women and girls put such a premium on wearing native garments that many Maya girls are encouraged from a very early age to learn how to weave. Girls typically learn to use the backstrap loom from their mothers and other older womenfolk. Local po't (Sp. *huipiles*) and sashes are always woven on the backstrap loom, whereas uq (Sp. *cortes*) are made on standing looms. The making of women's clothes shows a marked sexual division of labor: whereas women weave huipiles on backstrap looms, men are generally the ones who weave cortes on footlooms. These male weavers make cortes in the towns of San Cristóbal Totonicapán and Salcajá, then have itinerant merchants sell them in different highland markets. Some Comalapan artisans use footlooms, but most often to produce items like change purses and tablecloths that are exported through various brokers.

A HOUSE DIVIDED: RELIGIOUS FISSURE

For many Comalapans, the most important division in town is not one overlaid by costume use but one stemming from fissures in the Catholic community. Many Comalapans say that for most of the town's history, local residents all basically considered themselves the same kind of Catholics. But things changed dramatically in the twentieth century. Protestant groups began making inroads into many communities. One response by the Catholic Church in the 1950s was to place renewed emphasis on group Bible study, lay leadership, and engagement with social concerns. This project, known as Catholic Action, focused on themes of Christian renewal and reaffirmation of Catholic orthodoxy. It was intended not only to stem what the church saw as loss of members to Protestant groups called *evangélicos*, but to redirect Catholics away from local forms of veneration that had developed during the colonial period. These local forms of veneration brought Spanish Catholic and indigenous elements together into a system usually referred to as costumbre by Maya, or as traditionalist religion by anthropologists. Catholic Action especially took issue with how many Catholic practices had taken on a Maya character, as exemplified by religious sodalities called cofradías. The church claimed that these groups, which took primary responsibility for saint cults and town celebrations, were misrepresenting Catholicism and corrupting the church's purpose. According to the church, cofradías promoted wasteful spending and alcohol abuse. Still worse, claimed the church, cofradía practices validated non-Christian, Maya outlooks. From the cofradía point of view, meanwhile, adherents of the Catholic Action movement were simply an aloof clique trying to sow divisions in the church and town.

The Catholic Action movement took root in Comalapa, though, and more prayer groups identifying themselves as *catequistas* began meeting in peoples' homes. Gradually, local support for the cofradía and its syncretic, traditionalist practices began to erode. The two Catholic wings grew increasingly different in their venerative styles, and they came to take positions against each other. Tensions between these camps peaked in December 1967, and they physically collided in the colonial San Juan Church. Hundreds of people clashed, wielding machetes, sticks, and stones, in a fight for control of the San Juan Church. Among the many things at stake were the use of church space, control over its finances, and, most importantly, the question of which Catholic world view would prevail locally (Carey 2006:158–59). Adherents of the different camps became virtual enemies after this confrontation. Family heads reportedly drew lines in the sand and demanded to know where their children stood. Some children were disowned as a result. In the uneasy years that followed, the catequista group intensified its organizing and raised money for a separate church building. The cofradía loyalists, meanwhile, staked out the colonial church building as their own. But even as the camps were settling into their separate philosophical domains and dividing their space, disaster struck.

On February 4, 1976, an early-morning earthquake struck Comalapa, leveling almost every home and structure in the town (Asturias Montenegro and Gatica Trejo 1976:117). It left the colonial church in near ruins and buried thousands in their homes. Comalapans recall that the earthquake hurt all people, irrespective of their religious affiliations. As a result, many Catholics put their animosities aside during the town's reconstruction efforts. But this period also spurred the catequistas' plans to build their own church, the Sagrado Corazón. For its part, the cofradía camp determined to construct a new, sturdier San Juan Church next to the old one. Even in the wake of the common disaster, then, the divided Church remained divided.

Starting in the early 1980s, the local diocese assigned priests considered "conciliatory" to Comalapa to ease the town's religious conflicts. The priests reminded Comalapans that there was still only one *parroquia de Comalapa*, "Comalapa Parish," and not two. Gradually, tensions eased between the two Catholic camps, and they reached a more tolerant coexistence by the 1990s. For example, although the two Catholic congregations maintain their own litters used for Holy Week and other seasonal processions, the cofradía members often walk in Sagrado Corazón processions, and catequista leaders often accompany San Juan processions. Some Catholic Action events are even held in the San Juan Church. The two local parish priests made strong calls for unity among Comalapa's Catholics in the 1990s. They took pains in calling for brotherhood, but they also admonished behaviors commonly associated with the cofradía.

Even though the cofradía is closely identified with Comalapa traditional culture, it does not sit well with many people, and its future is in peril. The nine cofradía members take responsibility for caring for the specific saints and virgins in the San Juan Church. They are complemented by the nine *texela'*, or *capitanas*, a religious sisterhood whose members also care for specific saints and virgins. Texela' spend a lot of time cleaning the church and embellishing and dressing the statuary. Cofradía members and their mayordomo assistants must ring the church bells on the hour and keep guard over their staves of office and other church valuables kept in a vault in the sacristy. The large silver-headed staves, some of colonial manufacture, are carried by the cofradía members in their processions and bear the emblem of the saint or virgin to whom they are dedicated. The texela' also carry staves of office bearing saintly icons. Known as *candelas* (candles), these staves consist of a baroque, metallic leaf and flower crest set atop a short ribbon-wrapped staff.

Each cofrade and texel is supposed to occupy his or her office for a year, and then pass along their staves and offices to new persons. But they have had an increasingly difficult time attracting new people to fill their positions. One reason for this is that cofrades and texela' are expected to give generously of their time and money. In addition, the drinking at many cofradía and texela' functions makes participation still less appealing to many Comalapans. Members of these groups have had to keep their positions beyond their allotted time when they cannot find replacements. When a young person gets inducted into the cofradía, then, it creates quite a stir in town. But the occasional outbursts of interest in these groups may not be enough to carry them beyond the dedication of their current aging members.

While the traditionalist cofradía and texela' try to keep active, or at least intact, catequista Catholics face a different kind of problem, seemingly having much in common with evangélicos. Both catequistas and evangélicos disapprove of heavy drinking, or of drinking altogether. This pits both groups against the common perception that San Juan Church members drink. Both groups also emphasize scripture and disapprove of lavish festival spending. Catequistas know that their people might come to sympathize with evangélicos, and this worries some of them. Evangélicos, though, tend to view all Catholics, including catequistas, as being categorically different from them, as irresponsible spenders with a penchant for alcohol and graven images. What evangélicos and their leaders find still worse are what they consider dangerous alliances between Catholic worship and "pagan" Maya religious practices (as I discuss later).

FIGURE 2.1
Cofradía and *texela'* in a procession, bearing their crests. Photo by author.

Proselytizing Protestantism is still relatively young in Comalapa, but it has been through many episodes of fissure. Of the dozen or so town-based Protestant temples resulting from local splintering, a few show great institutional momentum or high membership. Iglesia Betlehem is the most significant of these. It was founded in 1918 by Iglesia Centroamericana, the first major Protestant mission to Guatemala. Situated directly north of the colonial San Juan Church on the parque, this temple makes a striking counterpoint to the Catholic authority of the town center. Another major congregation is Iglesia Elim, also with US missionary roots. This temple professes Pentecostalism, however, making it quite different from Iglesia Betlehem. Many Comalapan evangélicos, in fact, consider Iglesia Elim the ecstatic extreme among Protestants and disagree with its emotional devotional style. The remaining evangélico churches in the cabecera and villages occupy different points on the continuum between Iglesia Betlehem's relative solemnity and Iglesia Elim's charisma.

Some congregations are harder to fit among local Protestants, namely Jehovah's Witnesses and the Church of Jesus Christ of Latter-day Saints. It is unclear when they began their ministries in Comalapa, but at least two families trace their identity as Jehovah's Witnesses to the early 1980s. Mormon missionaries are often visible in Comalapa, but these missionaries say there are only two converted Mormon families in town, along with a few other inactive members. These two groups maintain small meeting halls in the town center. Unlike with most evangélico temples, though, their halls lack sermon-projecting loudspeakers.

The last three decades in Comalapa have witnessed other changes in Maya religiosity, ones closely tied to the Maya revitalization movement that took form starting in the late 1980s and early 1990s. This movement called attention to how many key features of Maya life had been under assault since the beginning of the colonial period, asserting that it was time to give them renewed respect. It sparked discussions among Maya about their relationship with Christianity (Pop Caal 1992:37–42) and with other Ladino-dominated institutions like schools and the university (Cojtí Cuxil 1994:66–67; Garzon et al. 1998:174). That the movement's inception coincided with the 1992 International Year of Indigenous Peoples and with the five-hundredth-year commemoration of the Spanish invasion of the Americas encouraged a sense of historical vindication among Guatemalan Maya. This fueled the growing interest in using and teaching Maya languages, something that became a signature part of the movement (Garzon et al. 1998). Different individuals and groups also promoted the study of Maya weaving and other arts (Hendrickson 1995; Otzoy 1996). And for those interested in Maya forms of worship, the movement provided an opening to revisit assumptions about native spirituality, even calling into question the very meaning of Maya religiosity.

In line with the general tenor of the movement, many emergent forms of

Maya spirituality invited Maya to reflect on their collective past. They encouraged Maya to seek an understanding of how their ancestors saw the world, and then to rebuild personal linkages to those world views (Molesky-Poz 2006:35–38). To arrive at these understandings, Maya had to attune themselves to the cosmos, in part by cultivating a close sense of reciprocity with nature (Molesky-Poz 2006:44, 102) and by studying texts like the *Pop Wuj*. Many voices took this a step further and stressed that Maya should learn the 260-day ritual calendar, the *cholq'ij*, and use it in their own lives (MacKenzie 1999:42–43). On one level, and as we see today among different Maya, becoming initiated in the calendar would enable Maya to make ritual requests for things like wisdom, health, and money on auspicious days (Hart 2008:39–40). On a deeper level, though, by reclaiming the calendar as a birthright and by letting it guide their relationship with the Earth, it could awaken ancestral knowledge in the initiated and help anchor them in a Maya present of their own making.

Before long, though, these antisyncretic forms of Maya spirituality diverged ever further from the traditionalist forms that had long set the pace of life in many Maya towns. The renewed emphasis on ancient texts and the calendar, for instance, contrasted with the kind of cofradía-centered practices that in many places were simply struggling to survive (Cook and Offit 2013:157; Stanzione 2003:251). The contrast was not absolute, however. Some of what Maya spirituality encouraged, like understanding spirituality to be a felt experience (i.e., attending to dreams, intuitions, and body movements), in fact overlapped with what traditionalists had long observed (Molesky-Poz 2006:47–48). But the antisyncretic Maya spirituality program differed fundamentally from traditionalist thinking in that it set out to incubate a kind of spirituality completely free of Christian influences. Whereas traditionalist Maya religion had long incorporated Catholic elements and even situated itself largely in churches, the new Maya spirituality tried to reconstitute ancient Maya practice by distancing it from Christianity (MacKenzie 2009:371), liberating it, in effect, from the conqueror's imposed world view. By purging it of outside influences, cultural activists hoped to shape a more "authentic" spiritual option for Maya.

The newly articulated Maya spirituality thus emerges in counterpoint to syncretic traditionalist practice. In advocating a Maya path strictly rooted in the local and not the European, antisyncretic Maya spirituality maps uncomfortably onto previous Maya spiritual outlooks, especially those identified with the cofradía. To the extent that these changes are affecting local cultural dynamics, C. James MacKenzie (1999:42–44), and Garrett Cook and Thomas Offit (2013:158), have shown that this situation really amounts to a confrontation between the syncretic tendencies of costumbre and the antisyncretic views of Maya spirituality. Working convergences between these two expressive modes are probably still in the making (Cook and Offit 2013:159–60).

Like elsewhere in the highlands, Maya spirituality in Comalapa remains more appealing to young people than cofradía service does, and it is also much likelier to involve women at different levels of participation and leadership (Cook and Offit 2008:55). Perhaps not surprisingly given their senior status, the ritualists I have worked with most closely in Comalapa do not openly identify with the Maya spirituality movement. And while Comalapans are not of one mind when it comes to identifying with either traditionalist religion or Maya spirituality, traditionalist religion still holds sway in most spaces where Maya-centered ritual is carried out. Costumbre still colors most ritual transactions in Comalapa, and for the moment this means that oyonela' and other kinds of diviners and healers continue to live and work like their parents and grandparents did.[4] But even though local ritualists are not defined by Maya spirituality, this tendency has made inroads into town.

Diviners in Comalapa, locally called "people who know things," normally operate independently of each other, but in the mid-1990s a small number of them aligned with the revitalization movement and became organized as the Asociación de Aj Q'ijab' de Comalapa. A reputed principal of this group, a former Comalapa politician, happened to be someone I often spoke with. Although he never acknowledged that there was an actual association of Maya priests, he intimated that he was very involved in Maya religious activities, including divination. He even showed me a hand-drawn Gregorian calendar with days marked in Maya day glyphs, extending back several years. In later years this group, or an outgrowth of it, further developed its sense of spiritual mission at the same time that it grew its national political outlook. When its core membership expanded to a handful of people in 2005 and decided it was time to go public, it made itself formally known as the Asociación de Sacerdotes Maya Oxlajuj B'atz (Esquit 2007:255).

The existence of this group shows how local people can reframe their spiritual outlook to the point of aligning themselves with national movements, even if the actual number of local converts remains small. What it does not show is that the religious climate of the town is still quite unfriendly and even hostile to those whose religious practices fall outside of official institutions. Comalapans in groups like these have learned to keep a low profile because they fear rebukes from religious leaders and townspeople. The fears are real. Catholic and Protestant leaders cast Maya spiritual activities, both traditionalist and antisyncretic, as misleading and paganistic. Pulpits chastise people accused of promoting non-Christian practices, calling them *esos brujos*, "those witches." But Comalapans still seek them out. What is more, some local diviners and Maya priests, as the above organization names indicate, are referred to as *ajq'ij*, "he of the day," a term elsewhere reserved for Maya calendrical specialists or priests (Tedlock 1992). Significantly, except for persons influenced by the pan-Maya movement, local diviners do not base themselves on the 260-day Maya calendar, as the title ajq'ij would imply. Locals do distinguish the ajq'ij from *ajitz*, however, the latter being persons involved in a darker side of Maya spiritual practice. Maya often use the term "ajitz" to denote a witch, but Maya who are deeply invested in any form of Christianity typically consider anyone involved in non-Christian spirituality an ajitz. These reproaches have made local Maya diviners and priests more discreet and cautious.

Still, different kinds of ajq'ijab' (pl.) practice with more openness than before in many Guatemalan towns (Hart 2008; Molesky-Poz 2006). But while more Maya than ever identify with antisyncretic spirituality, understanding this development requires that we take a broader view of how Maya have tried to keep their culture and religion intact in the past. This will illustrate not only that Maya have deployed their own ideas and principles before, but that these are rooted in local experience.

ANTISYNCRETIC SPIRITUALITY IN THE CONTEXT OF CORE MAYA PRINCIPLES

It is tempting to see the emergence of antisyncretic Maya spirituality as conclusively proving that Maya cultural ideas are resilient, but the story of Maya resilience actually begins much earlier. Different scholars have identified distinct Maya ways of being in different places and times going back to the Spanish colonial era, ways of being traceable to some underlying creative and tenacious structures that have endured years of acculturative forces. Without these structures, which have also been called core Maya principles or recurrent schema, Maya would not have been able to creatively adapt to Spanish culture and its successors. And by adapting as they have, Maya have shown themselves able to see their changing world through a Maya lens and able to make that world fit their needs.

Over the past several decades, scholars have taken different approaches to argue that Maya religion is organized around some very enduring core principles. One of these approaches, for example, focuses on the late calendrical system of the "Short Count" and centers on the idea that Maya attend to events unfolding around them with an eye to how history occurs in cycles. Victoria Bricker (1981) has argued that since Maya saw history as repetitive, with events in one twenty-year Katun period repeating themselves in later cycles, past events could be used to predict the future. Another exponent of this view, Nancy Farriss (1984), detailed how awareness of the cyclical nature of time explains how Maya adapted and survived during the eighteenth century. By viewing the presence of Spanish people in terms of the Katun cycle, Maya could see the conquest as part of a pattern of events that would periodically occur, and that would subsequently be undone.

The model proposed by Bricker and Farriss, also known as the millenarian myth model, sees the attention to cycles as a kind of "armature" of Maya culture, to use a term favored by Patricia McAnany (1995) and Garrett Cook (2000). An armature is a deep structure that helps maintain ideational continuity in a culture even when that culture is threatened. The basic strength of an armature like this one is that, while newer elements can get organized around it, it bears up under the weight of these accretions and provides a stable framework for the culture. This, in turn, makes it possible for Maya cultural forms to remain identifiably Maya even after centuries of domination by other cultures. But there is another strength to the idea of armatures. By stressing that Maya expressive culture has been structured around different kinds of armatures, Cook (2000:188) alerts us not only to the operational importance of these structures but to how they are rooted in the physical world in which Maya live. The most convincing models of core Maya principles, in my view, take both of these considerations into account.

In light of this, two of the most important models discussed in Maya ethnographic accounts center on world renewal and on the living landscape. These provide good ways to chart how humans and divinities interact, and to observe Maya in what John Watanabe (1989:273) calls their ancestral locales. These are places where people live out a local sense of identity and propriety anchored in devotions to the town saint, making them a key stage for enacting core Maya principles.

The first of these models foregrounds the need for periodic renewal of the world. In one of its framings, it considers the way that Maya identify the workings of (re)generative principles. Tz'utujiils of Santiago Atitlán do this by deploying an awareness of vegetative growth and replacement linking ritual and daily activities to creation events. Documented by Robert Carlsen and Martin Prechtel (1991), this complex, which they call *jaloj-k'exoj*, centers on different operations of change. One type involves the change of something in its "individual life cycle," and the other type centers on generational change (Carlsen and Prechtel 1991:26). Both types are embedded in local domains of experience, from farming to the "replacement" of grandparents with grandchildren. Other scholars working in Atitlán have also found local residents heavily invested in world renewal. They have pointed to the central role that cofradías play in this and have showcased how their members carefully maintain the Martín and Mam bundles to keep the world intact (Christenson 2001; Mendelson 1958; Stanzione 2003).

In another locality, Momostenango, Cook (2000) and Cook and Offitt (2013) have analyzed how K'iche' ritualists perform annual costumbre to renew the community. Here, too, different sodalities have been responsible for carrying out renewal-centered activities that get staged in the countryside as much as in the town itself. One of the most important of these groups is a dance troupe whose members, at crucial moments, undergo changes in consciousness that signal their contact with spirit-owners. They reveal the key role that dance plays in renewal in ways that dovetail with Comalapan experience. The core symbolism of renewal is very evident among Comalapa moros dancers, who also set out to rekindle ties with spirit-owners. And in both places, although the dances are encased in a "Spanish" form, what validates the contact with supernaturals are changes in bodily experience. At the height of their dancing ordeals, the changes in Comalapa moros consciousness are akin to the animal-spirit awareness reported by monkey dancers in Momostenango (Cook and Offitt 2013:68, 72–74). That Comalapa commits to the dance in December and January, after most harvesting activities, is also telling, as it suggests the need to move the town out of agricultural dormancy, in line with how Holy Week activities of other towns take place just prior to the new agricultural year.

Across different ethnographic accounts there is also a sense that we can understand critical aspects of Maya experience by situating Maya within the living landscape (Gossen 1974; Vogt 1969). This approach explores not only how Maya view landforms like hills, caves, and gorges as animate but how they interact with them in ways that reveal an enduring sense of reciprocity with the earth and attention to the ancestors (Cook 2000; Tedlock 1992). While attention to the living landscape runs through many works on Maya life, it is most developed in highland accounts. The work of Gary Gossen (1974), Barbara Tedlock (1992), and Evon Vogt (1965, 1969) is foundational in this respect, but other scholars have since mapped out how Maya continue viewing their surrounding topography as spiritually alive and connected to them. Some, like Thomas Hart (2008), narrate how hills are spiritual mundos, living entities, and command respect. Others, like Jean Molesky-Poz (2006:75, 96, 111), stress that the land must be revered not only because it gives sustenance but because it awakens people to sacred vocations. Both reiterate that landforms and the shrines within them possess spirit-owners with their own narratives and temperaments.

Capricious spirit-owners are very familiar to Kaqchikels, Maya who regularly tie different human activities to operations of the sacred landscape. This is especially true for moros dancers and soul therapists, who steward relations between humans and spirit-owners. By tracing many human afflictions to earth lords, oyonela' in particular point to how Maya locate agency in the land. Spirit-owners can cause calamities as well as withhold them, and they can send and alleviate illness, but their importance goes well beyond this. Interacting with spirit-owners tethers people to those spirit-owners and their lands over time. So strong can ties become between a Maya group and its local earth lords, in fact, that when civil war has pushed people out of their home territory, as Richard Wilson (1991:44) reported among Q'eq'chi's, those people can lose access to their earth lords. Unable to pray to them, their planting rituals are compromised, worsening their crisis of displacement.

Moments like these threaten a group's anchoring in their home community. This ties into a current of work that examines how a group's moral framework is rooted in the place they call home, how people are anchored not only physically in their communities but morally as well. Gossen (1974:7, 29–30) makes the case, for example, that Tzotzils in Chamula, by orienting their daily life and ritual actions around primordial time-space concepts, morally anchor themselves in their town. Aware that destructive forces threaten to unravel the present creation, Chamulans maintain their actions within a very specific framework, guided by the Sun-Christ who confers ritual primacy to specific directions and movements. A sense of responsibility for keeping the physical and moral order also pervades Santiago Chimaltenango. There, as Watanabe (1990:132, 137–38) outlines, the community and the interactions it enables underpin a sense of social propriety. Locals bind themselves to the town saint, not as an intermediary before God but as an axis around which revolve mores of local conduct.

Among these Mams, as among Tzotzils, relationships with local earth lords run deep and effectively shape the very possibilities of being human, predicated on an abiding ethic lived by the whole group. For Q'eq'chi' Maya, likewise, so deep is the relationship with local earth lords that the mountains are said to "reach right down inside them, moulding their concept of personhood" (Wilson 1993:128). This relationship with earth lords can expose them to vulnerabilities, but they are necessary ones, for when these Maya leave the orbit of their earth lords, problems really begin. As with Tzotzils, people in Mam and Q'eq'chi' communities feel more vulnerable to destructive forces the further they venture from their homes, whether to coastal worksites, to unfamiliar forests, or to the far north. This recalls how in Comalapa, Kaqchikels often express fears of body predation when talking about going to work in the United States. For many of them, the north is where people operate with very different value systems, bordering on the nonhuman. These instances bear witness to a recurrent Maya idea that, far from their homes, corrosive forces will imperil their moral core as well as their bodies.

While these are not the only ways that scholars have talked about enduring Maya ways of being, they keep the focus on some stable ideas. Works like these advance what Cook (2000) calls the "continuity thesis" of Maya culture. This line of research sets out to "identify the central aboriginal elements and themes in ethnographically described village cultures, and to explain how fundamental cultural patterns persist within and give coherent structure to changing institutions" (Cook 2000:185). By stressing the need to look at community-based life, scholars like Cook reveal the local as a primary stage for the operation (and continuation) of core Maya principles.

Close observation of local culture has allowed researchers to chart how, as powerful forces challenged Maya religion over time, Maya religion did not change its principles, only the appearances and names of the actors through which those principles were played out. It did this by substituting newer elements for older ones, and by layering newer elements onto existing frameworks. So whether Maya were substituting Spaniards for other aggressors in different moments of ethnic conflict (Bricker 1981:180), or whether they were conventionalizing sociality through locally sovereign "saints" (Watanabe 1990:138), their basic structures accrued elements in ways that aligned with established native patterns. Maya thus reconciled changes to their culture with "preexisting cognitive schemas" to ensure continuity (Christenson 2001:12).

For centuries, then, Maya have adapted new symbols and elements from dominant forces like Christianity and creatively fitted them onto their core principles, accommodating new elements within existing structures. This accounts for how core Maya concepts remained stable even when their surface details changed, and even when their religious lexicon was rapidly shifting over to a Christian one during the colonial period. Although the process was never easy, Maya came to adopt Christianity on their own terms. They participated in public Christian religiosity while continuing many of their ritual observances at the household level, where Spanish authority was weakest (Farriss 1984:289–90). In this way, they maintained those private rituals of childbirth, illness, and death that spoke to abiding concerns of well-being where it mattered most, in the home and body. To these private spaces we can add fields, cenotes, and caves where, even if the language of devotions was Spanish, the inner structure of the activities was not.

As Maya continued adopting Christian symbols in later years, they kept working them onto their structural core. In the process, many Maya not only came to embrace cofradías and to craft local narratives about Christ's crucifixion, but to attribute them to their earliest ancestors (Warren 1989:37–38, 49). Similarly, Comalapa Kaqchikels and other Maya came to frame their towns' Christian patrons as akin to founding ancestors who still preside over the places where people keep their devotions (La Farge 1947:61–63; Watanabe 1990:135–41). An important thematic thread becomes visible here: many Maya see themselves as the keepers of old traditions, as being entrusted by the ancestors with their continuity (Bunzel 1952:160, 249–50; Carey 2001:77–79, 168; Montejo 2005:34). This features vividly in accounts of Santiago Atitlán, for example, where members of the San Juan and Santa Cruz cofradías curate sacred objects embodying the generative forces townspeople rely on (Carlsen 1997:81, 152; Christenson 2001:162). Many dancers and daykeepers in Momostenango likewise work with a sense that they must steward their costumbre just like their forebears, the *primeros*, did (Cook and Offit 2013:88). By safeguarding their ancestral inheritance, even when the risks are high and even when different mantles of authority press down on them, Maya have continued actualizing their core principles.

We can thus see that by the time antisyncretic forms of Maya spirituality emerged in the context of the Maya revitalization movement, core Maya principles had already shown their resilience many times over the centuries. The movement was not the first time that Maya were guided by core principles, but it was one of the few times that they actively identified and applied select principles to a program (Fischer and McKenna Brown 1996; Montejo 2005). As they did this, many Maya came to face questions about the place of Christianity in Maya religiosity (Wuqub' Iq' 1997). While conceding that different elements of Christianity had earlier been tolerated and even embraced by local groups, some movement-aligned expressions of Maya spirituality concluded that Christianity was an outright deviation from Maya spirituality (Pop Caal 1992). According to this view, the Christian layerings in Maya ritual have had less to do with a Christianity alignable with Maya spiritual schemas than with a Christianity whose primary purpose was to intrude into Maya life. At difference with the general view among scholars that Maya applied Christian elements to their cultural mainframe, new Maya spirituality advocates have downplayed the idea that tenets of Maya religion were conveyed primarily through Christianity. Likewise deemphasizing Christian elements as primary vehicles for transmitting Maya core principles, Molesky-Poz (2006) suggests that Maya beliefs endured largely intact the conversion efforts of

Christianity. In other words, Maya beliefs have continued for the most part despite Christianity, not with the inadvertent support of it.

As many Maya have set out to define their spirituality in non-Western terms, many have become interested in pre-Columbian Maya culture. This has prompted many to learn about Maya epigraphy, often through workshops conducted by international specialists. But while an important current in the pan-Maya movement has been a renewed embrace of pre-Columbian symbols, the picture at the local level has historically been quite different. Inhabitants of different towns orient themselves around immediate and familiar traditions. In Santiago Atitlán, for instance, what motivates local art and ritual is the local and ancestral (Christenson 2001:27), not the obscure and pre-Columbian. That Atitecos historically organized their religious life around cofradías and Holy Week observances reaffirms the operative importance of these cultural forms in defining what is local and ancestral, and, although for fewer and fewer people, what must be continued. It also suggests that, if there is a locally maintained system of core principles, it has until recently been outwardly characterized by the accretion of Christian elements.

This is largely true of many highland communities, including Comalapa. When describing what is unique about their town, many Comalapans point first to their colonial-era church and to their saint's feast in June. Even people who do not identify as any kind of Catholic show affinities for these town features because they are considered local and ancestral. It should come as no surprise, then, that a sense of local antiquity and rootedness pervades the way people talk about things like the cofradía, moros dancing, and the work of oyonela'. Representations of these are even staged in decorative "floats" paraded around town during the titular feast.

Valuing of the local is also seen in how the town's primitivist painters for decades depicted idyllic scenes of home life and costumbre. Painters saturated their works with nostalgic and ancestral themes, giving visual voice to local ways of doing things (Asturias de Barrios 1994). After the civil conflict began to subside, though, and some Maya began to evaluate and adopt pre-Columbian symbols, something happened. Pre-Columbian themes tied to the movement began appearing in the work of Comalapan painters. Some artists began incorporating classic Maya iconography into their works, while others put rather enigmatic elements like Maya "cosmic

DNA" on their canvases. Then, several years after the 1996 peace accords, a mural series in Comalapa that commemorated select aspects of local history also began giving a more prominent place to pre-Columbian images (Carey 2011:709). While this was not an altogether new subject of public art in town, the mural did mark a shift. There had already been paintings of pre-Columbian Maya figures around town, especially on watering troughs, but these had been mainly for Comalapans to see. By putting the new mural on the wall bordering the cemetery at the town's entrance, Comalapans set it where visitors would see it.

Even if in these cases Comalapans layered some pre-Columbian elements onto the local, the local continues guiding Comalapans in their daily interactions. It should, therefore, also guide the way researchers understand Comalapa Maya experience. Cook and Offit (2013:154) likewise stress how there is much to be learned from the local, from the creative encounters that underlie town life and that village-level ethnography draws out so well. My research partly speaks to their call for a sustained look at local ways of being, and agrees that this lets us see how core ideas get actualized, even under adverse conditions. The ethnographic focus on Comalapa, then, makes it possible to observe that while some of the core Maya concepts discussed above resonate with Comalapa experience, these organizing principles still have limited explanatory power. Ideas about renewal and the sacred landscape, for instance, are useful for framing the work of oyonela' and moros dancers, but they are less useful for understanding midwives. And the moral anchoring described earlier ties in better with some midwives' rituals than with those of other specialists. To the extent that local organizing principles operate in Comalapa, earlier ethnographic works do not fully account for them.

This brings me to look closely at life in Comalapa and to discern how Kaqchikel Maya pay close attention to the body as they articulate understandings of spirit. The lived experience of many Comalapans shows how key information about spirit comes from bodily experience, both from everyday oscillations in physical feelings as well as from more striking changes tied to pregnancy, soul loss, and dance. Since the main way that Kaqchikels narrate their spiritual states is in terms of blood quality, especially its temperature and color, it is clear that normative states of blood are a central concern to Comalapans and that these states are deeply implicated in their actualizing of spirit. To be sure, while no one set of principles speaks to the whole of Comalapa Kaqchikel experience, the operative importance of normative bodily states for understanding spirit may be another one of the armatures of Maya culture that Cook (2000:188) refers to.

The attention to states of body and blood among Kaqchikels is evocative of how other Maya spiritual complexes are also rooted in bodily experience. Barbara Tedlock's (1992:138–46) identification of lightning in the blood among K'iche' daykeepers was very revealing in this sense, and set the stage for understanding how later Maya who identified with the native spirituality movement continued regarding their blood as a ritual guide (Molesky-Poz 2006:75, 116). That the signaling power of blood operates in tandem with the primacy of heat in Maya experience is suggested by the work of Gossen (1974) and Watanabe (1992), who demonstrate that physical and ritual heat maps onto local conceptions of maturity and social belonging. Gossen (1974:36–37), for instance, outlines the need among Tzotzils to accumulate heat over a lifetime. With adulthood and cargo roles comes more mature heat, he argues, and more binding to the oral tradition that conveys local organizational principles. In the Mam community where Watanabe (1992) probes the lived experience of soul, meanwhile, blood and heat command attention because they together form the baseline for proper ways of being. There, socially normative states are grounded in normative states of blood hinging on heat (Watanabe 1992:83–84). The ways that Maya in these and other accounts structure key parts of their lives around core ideas of body and blood does not mean that they confine their thinking to these ideas. They do attest, though, to how guiding principles anchored in the body are particularly enduring and reach into many areas of local life. But as Kaqchikels in Comalapa can corroborate, knowing about normative bodily states does not always shield one's own body from infirmity. When this strikes, Comalapans turn first to a local group of skilled individuals.

HEALTH SPECIALISTS IN CHANGING TIMES

Long before local Catholics and Protestants first argued over the right way to be Comalapan, and before different Comalapans voiced what Maya spiritual practice should look like, townspeople have had a more pressing concern:

health. And there to deal with this concern has been a wide range of health specialists. Most work outside the purview of biomedicine, without licenses or official registry. Some of them are well established, though, and have built large clienteles. Their work, together with the work of formal health practitioners, is an outward expression of a deeper Comalapan interest in keeping a proper state of being. Since integral health for Comalapans means spiritual integrity as well as a functioning body, townspeople consult health specialists who can help them with each of these, even if a given health worker specializes in only one of these dimensions.

Physicians are the most visible formal health workers, and six of these worked in Comalapa in the late 1990s. Four of these physicians are Maya; the other two are Ladinos. Of the four Maya physicians, three are local Kaqchikels and one is a K'iche' speaker from another town. Three of the Maya physicians work out of private clinics in their homes or family businesses, whereas the fourth alternates between work at an agency in Chimaltenango and his Comalapa home on weekends. One of the two Ladino physicians operates from a home clinic, and the other one is the attending physician at the Comalapa Health Center. Aside from these six physicians, a local gynecological clinic schedules a visiting physician once or twice a week.

Local physicians typically aspire to operate their own private clinic, but before they can, they often work at one of two local clinics. One is Hospital K'aslen, a private hospital in the northeastern part of town. The other clinic is operated by the Christian Children's Fund and is located behind the town market. This agency maintains a small office and clinic in Panabajal village and periodically brings children from nearby villages in for checkups with visiting physicians and dentists. Two churches in the town center also offer weekend clinics. San Juan Church keeps a small clinic on its property and schedules a physician or two on Saturdays and Sundays. Iglesia Betlehem, meanwhile, makes affiliated physicians, sometimes from out of town, available to members on weekends. The Comalapa Health Center is the busiest of all local clinics and is the first stop for most people seeking medical care. But since local people have long been suspicious of hospital facilities, at times seeing them as "virtual halfway houses to death," as David Carey (2001:266) puts it, they prefer to try other options first, including consulting individual workers like health promoters.

Auxiliary personnel like health promoters and nurses help with patients at the hospital, the CCF clinic, and the health center. Trained health promoters usually offer basic diagnostic services and drug dispensation out of their homes. Locals also seek them for their injection services. Comalapan health promoters receive training from different sources, including local physicians, visiting physicians, and clinical staff. Some regularly visit out-of-town sites for training, such as the Behrhorst Clinic in Chimaltenango.

Other local people are equally important in health care. Midwives, soul therapists, bonesetters, herbalists, and diviners attend to many local people and sometimes attract people from out of town. Midwifery is especially vigorous in Comalapa, not only because nearly every family uses midwives but because it is adapting quickly to mounting biomedical pressures. For example, medical personnel require midwives to be trained in problem diagnosis and hygiene so that they can get an "authorization" to practice. Many midwives (*comadronas*) received this document starting in the 1990s, but many have dismissed the idea and work without it. The enactment of this regulation likely speaks more to the state's interest in discrediting Maya medicine (Berry 2006:1962; Carey 2006:32) than it does to actually improving the midwives' work. In recent years, midwives have responded by forming the Asociación de Comadronas de San Juan Comalapa to try to gain respect for their work from the formal sector, as well as to gain more local autonomy (Mignone et al. 2009).

Soul therapists are offered no such authorizations, however, since they work far outside standard medical parameters. Instead, oyonela' apply a strong spiritual mandate and alleviate cases of soul fright. People turn to them when accidents, scary encounters, apparitions, and even traumatic memories leave imprints that make daily life difficult. Soul therapists work out of their or their clients' homes and provide affordable, needed services that other persons cannot. I will discuss midwives and soul therapists in greater detail in parts 2 and 3, respectively.

Whereas dozens of midwives and soul therapists work in Comalapa, far fewer people work as bonesetters. Since first visiting the town in 1991, I have met and interacted with seven bonesetters and learned of an eighth. Given the physical demands of agrarian life and of an increasingly mechanized world, it is no surprise that Comalapans get injured. Fortunately, bonesetters are no strangers to injuries and apply their hands to bodies in pain almost every day. But like with cofradía members, Maya bonesetters are, on the whole, male and older, and others hesitate to take up this craft. They are the subject of separate study (Hinojosa 2002a, 2004a, 2004b).

Local herbalists work in Comalapa and sometimes operate openly in one of two *naturista* shops. These shops sell plant mixtures brought largely from outside town. Many more people than these have specialized herbal knowledge, of course, but they work largely behind the scenes in their homes. Comalapa's surrounding area provides many medicinal plants that most adults are familiar with, even if they also use store-bought medicines.

CHAPTER THREE

Embodying Spirit in Comalapa

DAILY LIFE IN COMALAPA IS a lot like life in other highland Maya towns. People tend their fields, weave in their patios, ride buses, and visit the market. They also send their kids to school, buy televisions when they can, and try not to get sick. Everyday pressures and demands shape their schedules. But Comalapa Maya live in a world in which daily activities often carry a heavy spiritual imprint, and even spiritual risk. This is especially true when it comes to activities tied to reproduction, healing, and ritual dance. These three areas reinforce the sense that lived, bodily experience is paramount for understanding spirit. They reveal the body as the primary vehicle of spiritual agency and as the necessary ground for full vocational expression. And the more closely one looks at the hidden life of the body in the work of midwives, oyonela', and moros, the harder it becomes to distinguish where body ends and spirit begins.

Spiritual grounding in Comalapa depends upon the physical medium not only for coming into being but for reaching its fullest expression. The animating essence destined for the fetus in utero will be of little consequence to human life until it enmeshes with the fetal body. Once it does, it can express itself as an ensouled human life. The spiritually grounded body still faces perils, though, and this is why the oyonel is needed. She will defend human ensoulment. In the moros dance, the spiritual grounding achieved by the dancers is coupled to the agency of the rajawal tzyaq. The lord of the costumes, normally manifesting through different facets of the natural world, reaches an especially vivid expression as it assumes the sparkling clothing and mask, and the dancers themselves, as its embodied terrain.

The examples from midwifery and oyonel work indicate spiritual grounding as the unmarked condition, something to be preserved. In moros dance, spiritual grounding assumes a marked quality, since dancers and rajawala' must actively try to manifest through human and nonhuman bodies. But in every case, bodies can manifest their connectedness to other orders of reality at key moments. This grounding takes shape through available media.

The grounding operations in the three domains also suggest that local Maya generally recognize no clear boundary between spirit and body, and that they operationally conjoin them (Manning and Fabrega 1973:266–67). Among Comalapa Maya, action taken on what we call the body is felt to act upon spirit itself, and action taken on what we call the spirit affects the body directly and even immediately. When I have spoken of spirit and body as separate entities, then, it has only been in an "as if" manner. The different domains challenge the idea of complete spirit and body individuality.

This is especially true with soul loss. When a soul fraction is off wandering, it does not necessarily evidence clear boundaries existing between soul and body. Even at this moment the body is not left without soul, otherwise the body could not survive. In oyonïk, the stimulation of the physical body and the surrogate body through shock demonstrates a linkage of the body's physical consciousness to a point outside the physical body. The continuum of consciousness, of which this linkage forms a part, does not stop at the limits of the body's nervous system but extends into an ambulatory sentience expressed as a wandering soul.

By the same token, when a body part gets separated from the rest of the body, the separated physical part is not necessarily separate from spirit. As I will explain when discussing placentas, umbilici, and even bodily emana-tions like perspiration, body parts whose physical connection with the body is cut retain affective relationships with the body. These affects bear likeness to spirit linkages. Blood, moreover, is often directly equated with soul and soul strength (chuq'a'), and spilled blood retains this property of the body. Even the placenta, and sometimes the womb, is referred to by its life-giving property, being given the same name used to denote the ani-mating essence and the source of all life, k'u'x. It remains to be seen whether midwives will come to understand soul and body as fully separate entities with their increasing exposure to biomedicine.

Spirit-body separateness is difficult to find in moros dance, as well. For two or three months, the dancers introject their bodies into objects, the costumes, which are in turn considered physical dimensions of a spiritual intelligence. The spirits underwriting the dance reveal their agency through intense physical manifestations in the dancer during convergences of bodily function and spiritual will. When this happens, dancers say they feel somewhat "themselves" and somewhat "other," indicating the permeability between self and other and the indeterminacy of all boundaries.

This is not to say that Maya conflate "spirit" with "body" in every possible way. After all, they have lived under a Christian regime lasting nearly five hundred years and have incorporated some Western views of spirit and body. Maya today generally recognize that something survives the terrestrial body. This "something" might dwell in several places, in the hills, in the cemetery, in the heavens, and it is just as unique as the body with which it once formed a continuum. This individuated spirit, if we can call it that, retains its uniqueness for around two or three generations after the person's death. Thereafter, the deceased person's spirit conflates with the abuelos, the "ancestors," and what was once personally unique about the spirit dissipates into the reaches of genealogical time.

Local Maya views of spirit and body occupy a tenuous space between credence in an undifferentiated spirit-body and recognition of the individuated operations of spirit and body. The idea of an undifferentiated spirit-body is probably rooted in pre-Columbian tenets of spirituality, and the second derives from Christian ideas of soul transmigration. Comalapa features both ideas, but in the activities covered in this study, it binds spirit closely to matter.

BODY AND THE STAGING GROUND OF SPIRIT

Spirit is coterminous with matter, and Comalapa Maya track the presence and agency of spirit through physical media in different ways. Some of these ways stand out in the three domains because the domains speak to the powerfully symbolic arenas of reproduction and spirituality, arenas that have been contentious battlegrounds and sites of rapid change. People thus think about these domains, and talk about them. When we take what everyday people say and couple it to the ideology and practical action of domain specialists, we see spiritual grounding taking place on uniquely physical stages.

Midwives, for one, interpret the spiritual dimensions of bodily signs,

starting with those in the womb. For them, the ensouled life usually begins
there, although a few midwives locate ensoulment at the moment of birth.
They usually articulate this as a soul "arrival," but not necessarily one that
happens at a single moment.[1] During gestation, the fetal animating essence
becomes manifest and leaves a bodily signature initially expressed only
through movement like the heartbeat, kicking, and growth. Early on, however, fetuses also begin to sense emotion. Fetal emotion begins as spiritual
grounding consolidates, usually two or three months into gestation. During
this time the fetus can begin transmitting food cravings to the mother and
becomes sensitive to soul perils existing outside the womb. It can feel fright.

The placenta and umbilical cord are unique windows for examining the
manifestations of the animating essence. Midwives and mothers see the
drops of blood in the cord as prechildren. They equate the drops, in turn,
with the vitalistic energy nourishing life, chuq'a', firmly linking physical
manifestations of human life with the spiritual strength behind it. Abiding
affective and spiritual relationships persist between the mother and the
placenta and between the child and its umbilicus. The animating essence
also reveals a signature through the birth organs. An amniotic shroud can
presage specific kinds of mental, emotional, and spiritual development in
the child. As for the midwife herself, a divine source awakens her hands'
innate knowledge of the body. This suggests the grounding of a sentience
in the hands, one that finds its supreme expression in fetal ensoulment.

Activities performed by oyonela' reveal that human spirit must retain
its contiguity with the body. This contiguity begins during gestation but is
formalized by Catholic baptism, which affixes the soul to the child's body.
If accidents or transgressions with rajawala' fraction off part of the soul
from a person's body, it must be coaxed back through calling rituals. In
more severe cases of xib'iril, several prayers and sacrifices may be done,
including sacrifices at the location of the fright, where the disembodied
soul might be wandering and listening. Oyonela' often strike the body during calling rituals to stimulate the corporality and physical senses of the
body, kindling the lost soul portion's body memory and inducing it to
return (Hinojosa 2011). These ritualists sometimes create ritual surrogates
for their clients, using the client's clothing to ground the person's soul in
the effigy, as I explain in chapter 8.

Spirit infuses all participating agents in the moros dance, and each agent's contiguous spirit must be acknowledged and propitiated. This means that the masks, costumes, dancers, marimba, spirit-owners, and the money-attracting brujito doll must each be fed and cared for. The dance ground itself is a participant and receives its nourishment. The spiritual agent at the heart of moros activities and paraphernalia is the rajawal tzyaq, a being that safeguards the world's natural resources. The rajawal tzyaq takes both physical and nonphysical forms and makes his presence directly felt in the dance corral, in the dancers' dreams, and in their bodies.

Dancers attend closely to their assigned masks, for it is through the masks that the rajawal tzyaq imparts vital messages to them. Moros feed their masks food and liquor and try to turn their otherwise pale complexion reddish. When masks turn red, the spirit of the mask has registered his satisfaction with the offered food. This redness signals the dancer's body's own nourishment, manifested by the dancer's reddening face. The dancer feels satiated, like the spirit of the mask, and can dance for long periods of time. To deny the mask's spirit its due nourishment can provoke physical-spiritual retribution against the dancer. The mask feeding and color attention instantiates a bodily index of the spiritual states of both rajawal tzyaq and dancer. The color of the mask and dancer corresponds directly with their state of spirit and body.

The dancers' work is very specialized, but some of it connects with the other domains. With midwifery, for example, dancing has much in common. In both domains, new bodies take form as a result of complex animation processes. The heightened sensorial states attributed to pregnant women also emerge among dancers. In the work of soul therapists, as in that of dancers, successful outcomes depend on group ritual participation. Clothing actuates spiritual and bodily transformation in both domains, as well.

Many bodily signs arise in these domains, and their interpretations can vary. At times, individuals assign meanings to signs and are fairly certain of their diagnosis, like when a jittery and sleepless person thinks that his symptoms point to xib'iril, or when a moro thinks that his mask is pale because the spirit of his costume is hungry. At other times, a specialist must distinguish finer shades of meaning in bodily signs. For instance, a midwife will decide whether the marks on a fetus's body are vocational omens, food-craving imprints, or just birthmarks. Similarly, an oyonel can judge whether someone's dreams of a distant place are visions of a wandering soul, previews into the future, or just dreams.

Comalapans ascribe meanings to bodily conditions and features, but not in a fixed way. Signs are mutable and vary widely in meaning according to their temporal and spatial context. Their meaning pivots upon highly situated factors in what can be called an intertextual mode of interpretation (Tedlock 1981). For instance, blood does not unequivocally signify an embodied child unless the blood is inside the umbilical cord following a live birth. Sleeplessness does not definitely signify soul loss if it is not accompanied by nervousness, diarrhea, and distant dreaming and if it does not follow a very distressing event. Likewise, a dancer's tiredness is not a sign of rajawal volition unless the dancer has fallen short in his mask-feeding duties.

The local system of meaning is generative and malleable and does not constrain interpretations to fixed molds. But when new factors enter the vortex of signification, chains of interpretation are produced that, while seemingly novel, may be guided by prior chains of interpretation. Consider the Maya midwife who is admonished by physicians that, to avoid infant blood deprivation, she must not permit umbilical bleeding. She will probably gladly heed the advice and will view the bleeding cord as a sign of danger to the infant, perhaps even thinking about the blood loss in terms of physical distress. But her willingness to view the bleeding cord as a sign of danger will be shaped by her previous understanding of blood as chuq'a' that can be lost as blood is lost. She will accept the new reading of the bleeding umbilical cord as a sign of danger insofar as it conforms to her current understanding of bleeding as a sign.

Emergent world paradigms like Christianity, Western philosophy, and biomedicine have made spirit and body anything but stable entities over the past few centuries. Taking the view that the body has yet many unexplored generative possibilities, the way some theorists have outlined the body's complex way of engaging with the world may be instructive.

THE ENGAGED BODY

In his framing of the body as the starting point of experience, Thomas Csordas (1990, 1993, 1994a, 1994b) begins by bridging ongoing analyses of the physical and social body (Scheper-Hughes and Lock 1987) with local embodied experience. He first distinguishes between research on the body and that on the strand of phenomenology concerned with embodiment (1993). Differentiating between body and embodiment, he says that "the body is a biological, material entity, while embodiment can be understood as an indeterminate methodological field defined by perceptual experience and the mode of presence and engagement in the world" (1993:135). In line with moves away from Cartesian dualism, he adds that a principal characteristic of embodiment is "the collapse of dualities between mind and body, subject and object" (1990:7), something earlier endorsed by Michael Jackson (1983:132). Csordas places the undifferentiated body at the center of analysis, but he takes the point further. He articulates the body as the existential ground of culture and self, the point through which the conditions for consciousness are laid (1994a:6). Insofar as embodiment grounds the human's being-in-the-world and forms the starting point for his consciousness, it is implicated in his construction and apprehension of objects.

In a way, Csordas exemplifies "thinking with the body," even if this "thinking" is involuntary and "preobjective." On the level of perception, mind and body cannot be distinguished (Csordas 1990:36) because perception is not about positing the existence of objects ready to be perceived by a mind. Citing Maurice Merleau-Ponty (1962), Csordas discusses how perception begins in the body and ends in the creation of objects. For this perception to take place, the perceiver must begin from a position of the body-in-the-world, a position of embodiment. To appreciate how being-in-the-world is the basis for all practice, including perception, Csordas draws from Pierre Bourdieu's (1977) effort to define the relationship between practices and the unspoken "sense" and "reason" that makes these practices perdure in a social context. For Bourdieu, the socially informed body was the generative source, and product, of these culturally appropriate dispositions. The system by which this works and continues is the "habitus."

Merleau-Ponty and Bourdieu together informed Csordas's idea of somatic modes of attention. A somatic mode of attention is an attention that is not bound up in subject-object differentiation (different from subject-object perception). It occurs in a bodily and multisensorial way, not in an objective, analytical way. As Csordas (1993:138) puts it, "Somatic modes of attention are culturally elaborated ways of attending to and with one's body in surroundings that include the embodied presence of others."

One's body pays attention to other bodies. In daily life, the somatic mode of attention can account for a person's involuntary visceral reactions to other people of certain body types, or the uncanny sense that one is being watched. In Deborah Gordon's (1990:278) application of a parallel concept, cancer patients experience a "somatic conviction" that something is wrong within their bodies, that malignant bodies, in effect, occupy their bodies.

In Comalapa, Csordas's somatic reasoning helps frame how expectant mothers feel the physical cravings of their fetuses within and how infants "sense" when their mothers lie down or awaken, prompting the infants to cry. It also helps frame how xib'iril victims and moros dancers feel involuntary changes in their bodies in response to an external presence. But while Csordas provides a literate way of discussing human embodiment and perception, his work does not speak as well to the whole of Comalapan life. To keep the analysis closer to local experience, his model would need to explicitly engage a discourse involving human and nonhuman bodies (see 1994b:278). This would be needed, for instance, to explain how moros achieve a deep engagement with their fully embodied costumes and masks. It would also better account for the embodied presence of other nonhuman entities like rajawala', animals, and the *k'al k'u'x*, a ritual bundle I will discuss in chapter 8.

An expanded spiritual idiom for embodiment is also needed when Maya manifest a consciousness directly through their bodies in spiritual contexts. In the K'iche' area, daykeepers experience a "lightning" soul moving through their blood, tissues, and muscles, conveying messages from the natural and supernatural worlds (Hart 2008:115; Tedlock 1992:53; Molesky-Poz 2006:116; Saler 1970:135–36). The Maya curers' and patients' bodies can also convey diagnostically useful spiritual messages through either twitches or pulses.[2]

Even outside of spiritual contexts, the body often reveals a consciousness based upon spiritual awareness. For instance, Comalapan midwives and weavers attribute knowledge to their hands. Maya midwives depend on their hands to palpate pregnant women, but their hands cannot be "taught" the art of massage. Midwives say that their hands' abilities come from either a divine source or from a knowledge implicit in the hands. Either way, the palpation must be done in recognition of the holy trust placed in them.

Comalapa Maya weavers locate knowledge and sentience in their hands, but they take a more active role in awakening this. Girls normally learn to weave from an early age, but if a mother thinks her daughter is not learning quickly enough, she may lightly strike her daughter's hands and call out, "Why can't you learn to weave? Why can't you learn to weave?" Then, the mother or another female relative will place some thread from the girl's loom in the hand of one or more specific statues in San Juan Church. Each of these (archangel) images is called *la madre de las tejedoras* (the mother of weavers) and is asked to grant weaving knowledge to the girl's hands (see also Pacheco 1985:85). But since it is believed that some girls are not destined to be weavers, their hands are not forced to show ability.

We can speak also of a bodily consciousness at work among local bonesetters, who rely heavily upon their hands' knowledge. However, Comalapan bonesetters work almost entirely as empirical, not spiritual, practitioners (Hinojosa 2002a). Only in a few places in Guatemala do bonesetters consider their bodily ability a divine gift (Paul 1976; Paul and McMahon 2001). And while it is possible that primitivist painters in Comalapa, of whom there are many, recognize a divine embodied knowledge in their hands, I have not verified this. As more young children learn painting as a viable vocation, this understanding of embodied knowledge may surface or strengthen.

Guatemala's decades of civil strife have strained the embodied experience of Comalapans. Linda Green (1998) has observed, in reference to the Guatemalan civil war, that bodies testify to and constitute social memories of violence. Elsewhere in Central America, others have also argued that war and civil distress are lived and embodied (Jenkins and Valiente 1994; Quesada 1998). These violent chapters of recent history make it necessary to assess how "low-intensity" warfare and displacement affect people like Comalapans, many of whom wrestle with traumatic memories. Many locals, in fact, blame their xib'iril cases on events of the early 1980s. Awakened bodily memories from that time constitute even bigger problems for Guatemalans more viscerally affected by state violence. Long the locus of torture and punishment in Mesoamerica, the body has been deliberately targeted by recent Guatemalan regimes endorsing Western capitalism (Klein 1990/1991; Simon 1987). Victims of harassment and torture, as Elaine Scarry (1985) suggests, undergo deep levels of fragmentation that affect their senses of reality and the world. Body violations alter the existential grounds of individuals, imperiling their spiritual integrity and adding more painful dimensions to the Guatemalan tragedy. And even though the more overt targeting of bodies by the government subsided following the 1996 peace accords, other forms of structural violence have become more prominent since then and have proven no less injurious to Maya people (Benson and Fischer 2009). If anything, the post-1996 period has revealed that state actors (and others allied with the state) are still very determined to maintain power over indigenous Guatemalans and to wield it using whatever economic, discursive, or physical means they can (Little and Smith 2009).

Of course, Comalapa Maya experience does not rest entirely upon tragedy. Day-to-day activities take precedence over most sad echoes from the past. Body-souls survive, as people survive, and enable local ways of being.

FIGURE 3.1
Alejandro Chacach, a noted local painter and manual medicine worker, on his rooftop.
Photo by author.

BODIES MADE, BORN, AND DANCED

Comalapan ways of being reveal a spiritual grounding discourse centered on clothing, birth organs, and spiritual morphology. These things supply information about reproductive and ritual life, but they also spotlight unique spiritual and experiential operations, reaffirming how material reality is the vehicle for spiritual grounding.

Clothing and the act of "dressing" can effectuate and formalize spiritual grounding. This has unfolded in many ways over time, from the way saint statues were adorned during the colonial period to the way ritual dance costumes are handled at present. With respect to saint statues, according to Archbishop Cortés y Larraz (1958, vol. 2:89; in Hill 1992), late eighteenth-century Comalapa Kaqchikels paid careful attention to the saint images in the local church, and dressed them like locals. As Robert Hill (1992:158) reported, "Even the saints became community members as they were adorned by their worshipers in the local costume." The archbishop detailed how the local Kaqchikel of around 1770 "dressed the saints with many garments and put *paños* (tzutes) on their heads, the same way that the men dressed" (Hill 1992:158). They even got rebuked by the local priest for doing this, but vowed to continue this ancestral practice.

The Comalapa Maya here included the saints in their communities by dressing them in local garments. The saint statues had long undergone this transformation, and no cleric could stop it. We can appreciate how the spiritual grounding of the saints is formalized and made meaningful to Comalapans by the act of dressing. Through dressing, these objects receive their material needs, like clothing, and probably other things like candles and incense that the account does not mention. Members of Comalapa's religious sodalities still pay much attention to these images, at times also dressing them like the community members that they are.[3]

Among the moros, meanwhile, clothing takes on and reveals spiritual agency in different ways. For example, by formally welcoming the costumes into Comalapa and by feeding them, the moros directly anchor the rajawal tzyaq, the spiritual lord of the costumes, in the clothing. Subsequently, clothing reveals this spiritual agency in the way that it emits *ruxla'* (its odor or emanation), which signals the presence of the spiritual lord in the garments. But to hear it from Paulino López, a moros organizer, the costumes' primary spiritual grounding takes place earlier, when they are still being stitched together. He explains, "The costumes are made of thread and material, but because of the rites to which they have been submitted, those . . . *chapines* [Guatemalans], ever since their fabrication, they are incorporated by espíritus." From their earliest moments on the costume storehouse sewing machines, the costumes have been imbued with the animating essence of the rajawal tzyaq. Paulino says that the dance costumes are *e k'aslike' taq tzyaq* (living clothing) due to both their fabrication and their later ritual treatment by dancers. In his view, the rajawala' fuse with the costumes long before the costumes ever leave their storehouse.

These cases show how human will, through the handling of clothing, actively furthers spiritual grounding, even into nonhuman bodies. Colonial-period Maya dressed their saints in local garments, formalizing their spiritual grounding as Comalapans. They became ensouled bodies capable of hearing supplicants. Moros dancers and organizers, in turn, locate the rajawal tzyaq's materialization in the costumes in the costumes' own feeding, odor emission, and manufacture. Clothing becomes the axis for spiritual grounding in these instances. It can be the catalyst of the grounding (as with the saints' clothing) or the medium through which the animating essence manifests (as with the moros costume). Clothing's pliability facilitates human involvement in spiritual grounding.

Keeping in mind that the hands of midwives, weavers, and bonesetters embody an innate capacity for exercising a vocation, it bears noting how another body part, the birth organ called the amniotic shroud, can also be tied to a child's future vocation. In this case, the animating essence predisposes a person's body to certain faculties and, through the amniotic shroud, physically imprints this on the child. For instance, many Comalapa Maya say that a shroud on a newborn girl signals her future as a midwife. The same caul on a boy presages his future work as a physician. The shroud makes these vocational messages manifest for the midwife.

An amniotic shroud on the newborn's body, at his moment of exposure, is the most forceful statement the vocational aspect of soul can make. But the sign alone does not guarantee a particular vocation. The child's parents and family must be open to it, and even help it unfold over the child's lifetime. The sign's veracity is confirmed only later when a person develops physical mastery of his or her vocation.[4]

The physical, amniotic expression of spiritual grounding points to how a person might foresee having certain capacities, but whether he can reach these depends on how his vocational soul aspect is allowed to develop physically. Social environment matters. This is akin to how calendrical birthday auguries elsewhere in Guatemala depend on personal and family intervention (Tedlock 1992). The birth organ aspect of soul thus speaks to a dimension of soul as a realizable vocational personhood, enmeshed in gender roles but not limited to them. Birth organs reveal an initial, bodily vector through which the animating essence manifests agency.

Moros dancing reveals a third dimension of spiritual grounding, relating to a kind of spiritual morphology. For moros, all physical and spatial elements of the dance are contiguous with the spirit of the dance, and they express this in bodily ways. The transembodiment of each dancer's body with the rajawal tzyaq's body, brought out through episodic feeding of the costumes and dancers, illustrates this.

Dance organizer Gabriel Miza helps me understand how dancers also feel bound to a greater visceral whole. He explains that when you dance as a moro, "you feel as though you were no longer a person, you feel like a Maya person." The moro feels transformed from an everyday person to an embodied spirit of the dance, awakened to the surrounding sacred geography in an unordinary time frame. He neither looks nor feels like he usually does; what he does feel is striking. Gabriel says that when he puts on the costume, he feels very different from those who are observing him: "It feels as though you were a *member* of the dueño de la tierra [an aspect of the rajawal tzyaq]" (original emphasis).

What does he mean by feeling like a "member" of a larger whole? The midwife Celedonia offers a clue. She says that moros give food and drink to their costumes "because they think that there once existed a body of theirs . . . from the time of the Maya." The notion of a collective dancer "body" resurfaces, and again, "Maya" refers to a removed, mythical reality, or to an originary set of practices safeguarded by the moros. By feeding, and by actively grounding the spirit of the dance, the moros acknowledge the "member"-ship of all human and nonhuman elements in the dance. They indeed morph into the body of the spiritual moro. This recalls what a K'iche' Achi dance director says he feels when he recites his lines during the dances: "[I]t is as though I am empowered by the great Man of Rabinal, or the Man of Quiche'—in my body" (Hutcheson 2003:274). For him, too, the dance instantiates an embodied linkage with the patrons of the dance, which also feature as its main characters. Notably, Lorna Marshall (1965:270) characterized Botswana !Kung trance ritual dance as "one concerted religious act of the !Kung [that] brings people into such union that they become like one organic being."

Comalapa moros achieve a parallel operation, although their collective body extends beyond its human participants. It extends into the different things they wear and brandish, into the spaces they inhabit, and apparently into earlier generations of Comalapans. Although the local moros do not speak of venerating dead dancers like dancers in other towns do, they do imply that they are carrying on an unbroken lineage of dance from the abuelos. Matthew Looper (2009:225) argues, in this respect, that the way that Maya dancers from Comalapa and elsewhere today regard the bodily, material, and spatial elements of dancing to be imbued with "ancestral presence" is consistent with how classic-period Maya themselves experienced these elements. Whether or not this is the case, local moros undoubtedly see themselves as stewards of a practice their ancestors set into motion, and that still bears their living imprint.

Material vectors come directly into play in these and other instances of spiritual grounding in Comalapa. Clothing, birth organs, and spiritual morphology recur as embodiment vehicles among Kaqchikels, but no material vehicle or idiom is more important than k'u'x. Conversations about birth, life, sickness, health, emotions, and spirit revolve around this idiomatic complex.

K'U'X AS A BINDING IDIOM

As mentioned in chapter 1, k'u'x is closely allied to different conceptions of soul, heart, emotions, birth organs, and divinity. This is very evident in the work of midwives, soul therapists, and ritual dancers, who firmly connect inflections of spirit to a bodily ground.

Midwives, for example, consider the placenta and, at times, the umbilical cord to be expressions of k'u'x. They call the placenta *ruk'u'x ak'wal* or *ruk'u'x ti ri ne'y*, the heart/k'u'x of the child, and say that it "suckles" and gives life to the child from inside the womb. Midwives also regard the fetal k'u'x as the fetus's physical heart, as the animating essence (ranima) ensouling the fetus, and as the place where this ensoulment occurs. They view the early fetus as an entity where human life is initially focused, and thus as something of an animistic center.

In oyonela' work, k'u'x manifests as the physical corazón and as an animating essence. It presents itself dramatically through the k'al k'u'x, an ensouled ritual bundle. With its rolled-up, *k'al* quality, this effigy exemplifies the grounding of soul through the union of cloth and ruxla' in a distaff interlocutor. Oyonela' also deal with k'u'x in its expression as spirit-owners of the hills, as with the ruk'u'x ulew, for it is in this aspect that nonhuman k'u'x can seize human k'u'x and cause xib'iril.

During moros activities, the godhead is invoked as "ruk'u'x kaj, ruk'u'x ulew" (heart of the sky, heart of the earth). Other aspects of the godhead reside in places sacred to the moros, such as Las Delicias. These aspects are called, among other things, *ruk'u'x ri ajmoro* and receive thanks during community *días de campo*, days for visiting and eating in the fields. Ruk'u'x kaj and ruk'u'x ulew intertwine fundamentally in concept and practice and cannot be fully separated. Members of progressive Maya groups today offer supplications to this expression of k'u'x.

In each domain, k'u'x serves the interests of the domain but keeps its polyvalent quality. Even when k'u'x means something as discrete as the physical heart, it transmutes the heart into an animistic entity. We can appreciate the corazón-k'u'x as the center of embodied life energy and sensibility when, as a midwife explains, if a person's corazón begins to beat quickly out of fear, it is because "the soul is upset" and may be warning him of danger. Here, the embodied corazón-k'u'x attends with a consciousness reaching past the body's boundaries, evoking Csordas's (1993) operation of somatic attention. This attention faculty expands still further when the soul aspects of k'u'x "leave" the body, surveil, and return during dreams.

The different domains of experience in Comalapa reveal two things. One, that spirit and body remain elusive constructs for Kaqchikel Maya, and that they resist clear delineation. Lived experience suggests a spirit-body continuum with supple, situation-relevant boundaries. And two, they reveal that the idiomatic complex "k'u'x" reaffirms the groundedness of spirit in each domain. By ascribing an organically pragmatic quality to spirit, k'u'x frames the animating essence in the bodily terms that make sense to Comalapans, and that only slowly came to make sense to me.

APPROACHING THE THREE DOMAINS

I was slow in grasping how Comalapans thought about spirit and body, mostly because I early on insisted on structuring the local world into discrete spiritual and physical parts. And while this allowed me to reach some of the outer contours of local experience, it was not enough for revealing how Comalapans understood spiritual experience. It was only after interacting with more midwives, soul therapists, and ceremonial dancers and witnessing their work that I saw how people frequently referred to bodily experience when voicing their understandings of spirit. Noticing this narrative pull, I became less interested in drawing boundaries between spiritual and physical reality and more interested in exploring the body as the primary vehicle for apprehending and enacting spirit.

Maya midwives, soul therapists, and ceremonial dance performers talk about spirit in experience-near ways, ways that entail immediate bodily engagement. In their respective areas of work they attend to key moments in the life cycle, to subtle changes in health, and to fluid states of awareness. For them, bodily processes make sense as refractions of a spiritual nature. But since they each deal with different bodily processes, getting close to their knowledge of spirit required me to listen to how they each expressed their understanding of the body.

To learn from these specialists, I first had to meet them, and to meet them I initially relied on family and friends for introductions. When family and friends connected me with someone, our first interactions usually went more smoothly than if I had sought the person out myself. But other considerations were also at work. My being male, unmarried, and foreign sometimes affected how I was received. Looking more Ladino than gringo probably added to my ambiguity and, together with other factors, likely affected how much access to them Comalapans would grant me. Nowhere was this more the case than with midwives.

The Kaqchikel Maya midwives I met were very sharing and generous with their time, and two of them went the extra mile to help me. But for all their help in teaching me, basic barriers stood between us. After all, I was a male, and a single one at that, asking about things that are usually reserved for married women. I knew certain pursuits would be off-limits, such as witnessing prenatal massages and births, so I did not ask to attend these. To help me learn more about midwifery, then, and to help me locate more midwives than the four or five I already knew, I enlisted the help of four assistants. The assistants were female, literate, bilingual, and included married and unmarried women as well as Catholics and Protestants. With their help I explored the work of thirteen midwives, as well as a soul therapist who was also a midwife. When I spoke with midwives, usually while sitting in their patios, I kept our conversations within the limits of propriety. Some midwives were surprisingly open, though, and volunteered information I would not have asked about. These conversations first alerted me to the unseen processes that midwives witness and that initiate Kaqchikel spiritual experience. Their deep attention to the maternal body signaled that spirit is instantiated and articulated through a bodily medium. As I will discuss in chapter 6, spirit comes into being through the fetal body and is made perceptible through the maternal body.

The work of soul therapists also signaled this. Many Comalapans seek help for soul debilities like fright sickness, and oyonela' "callers" are the first ones sought. Most, although not all, oyonela' are women. But because most soul therapy unfolds through private oyonïk rituals, my concerns about access centered not so much on gendered knowledge as on closeness to family life. Luckily, with help from people I knew, I was able to attend many oyonïk, allowing me to study their structure and performative qualities. Conversations with oyonela' showed these specialists to be no less knowledgeable about the inner life of the soul than midwives. To reach more oyonela' than the nine I interviewed, I again enlisted assistants, six this time, to find additional ones. They interviewed eleven more oyonela' in 1995–1996, including one I had first met in 1992, bringing the total number to nineteen. As I will discuss in part 3, these nineteen oyonela' spoke about the soul's temperament and mobility, and how this is revealed through the body's experiential pathways. They also firmly connected human spiritual life to the living contours of the land, something that the town's ceremonial dancers took a step further.

Comalapa's ceremonial dancers, the moros, did more than promote local color and dance. They actively worked the crossroads between human spirit and the spirit-owners, beings that preside over different features of the landscape. Through a demanding process, the moros directly engaged the spirit-owners and were in turn intersected by them in very physical ways.

Unlike with midwifery and soul therapy, men dominate moros life, and this allowed me very close access to the group. The mixed public-private nature of the dance activities also helped me stay close to the moros and interview them without assistants. Over time, I conversed with over a dozen dancers, as well as with several dance organizers. I worked with the group during their busiest months, November, December, and January, and I often helped them with my vehicle. Having a pickup truck, in fact, made a huge difference in my relationships with them. I often transported people or equipment for them, and in this way I did some of the "heavy lifting" expected of all participants. To ritually close the season I also drove a group of moros and their costumes to the town where they had rented the costumes. Shared work like this prompted many moros to confide in me about what the dancing did to them. In part 4 I will explore the physical changes the moros go through during their shifting spiritual states and the living landscape in which these occur.

Part Two

THE MIDWIFE AND
SPIRITUAL GESTATION

CHAPTER FOUR

The Midwife at Work

COMALAPANS RELY ON MIDWIVES, KNOWN locally as comadronas or *k'exelona'*, to bring their babies into the world. When a Maya woman realizes she is pregnant, she almost always seeks a midwife's care. Only in very difficult pregnancy cases would most Maya women even consider enlisting a physician as a primary caregiver. To understand why Maya women and their families entrust their pregnancies to midwives, one needs to see the Maya midwife in her larger role as someone who reassures, who provides physiological services, and who facilitates spiritual knowledge. Midwives are seen as "gifted" individuals with an authority to practice. They know not only how bodies develop within bodies but also how soul is enacted within fetuses and children. By handling women's and children's bodies at critical moments, the midwife gains unique insights into the relationship between Maya soul and body, and then stewards this knowledge for others.

The midwife acquires spiritual knowledge at different times in her life, but she learns first and most compellingly during her own pregnancies. Her midwives and other women with children become her teachers and guides. Later, after she becomes a mother, someone may ask her to care for a pregnant woman. If she overcomes her trepidation and agrees to this, she commits to accepting yet more of the spiritual, and to accepting the awakening skills of her hands. But a woman usually does not become fully validated as a midwife until after some momentous or even traumatic things happen to her. These may take the form of dreams, apparitions, or sicknesses, and their intensity reminds her of how spiritually charged her new role will be, if she accepts it.[1] When she does accept it, she continues in her very physical work, only now with a deeper appreciation of what she must do for those who knock on her door.

83

SUMMONING THE MIDWIFE

The Maya midwife's work precedes the birth by several months and usually extends well past it. From the moment a woman finds she is pregnant, her family selects a midwife for her. If the extended family has recently interacted with a certain midwife, they may choose her again. Or, the mother or mother-in-law of the pregnant woman may opt for another midwife friend or neighbor, perhaps someone from her prayer group. If the pregnant woman has been pregnant before, she might request her previous midwife. If this is her first pregnancy, though, the older women select the comadrona.

Once the family decides on a midwife, they pay her a visit. This usually occurs in the second or third month of the pregnancy. The pregnant woman's mother, mother-in-law, or husband, or a combination of these, walk over to her house. When they arrive, the midwife greets them and usually invites them inside, where they then offer her pastries and a chocolate drink. Some midwives prefer something stronger, and they may be given bootleg liquor or beer. In recent decades money can also be offered. Following some conversation, the delegates apologize for disturbing the midwife. They then explain that their relative is with child and that they want to humbly request her services.

Few midwives summarily turn down such a request, although most will claim that they know little about childbirth or that they are too busy. A midwife knows, however, that her good reputation grows from helping those who need her. Her vocational mandate obligates her to attend all who seek her. On the other hand, if the pregnant woman is at an advanced stage of pregnancy, such as the third trimester, the midwife might refer her to the local health center. The body and fetus of such a woman are already "hardening," according to midwives like Celedonia, making the midwife's main activity, the *sobada*, more difficult.

THE HOME *SOBADA*

The midwife must perform sobadas, or manual palpations, of the expectant mother's abdomen numerous times during the pregnancy. Manual palpation makes up the bulk of the midwife's work and seems her most specialized skill. When midwives discuss their revelatory dreams, in fact, they often recall how a personage who instructed them in midwifery showed them how to perform these specialized abdominal massages. The midwife's knowledge is closely bound to this practice, so together with her divine sanction, it distinguishes a woman as a practicing midwife in Comalapa.

More than a simple massage, the sobada forms part of an encounter (Cosminsky 1977:76–79, 2001:353; Jordan 1993:26–30). The midwife first schedules a visit with the woman whose pregnancy she has agreed to *controlar* (monitor and assist). On the appointed day, she may set out to the woman's home well before sunrise. She may have to walk either a few houses down the street or over several kilometers of dirt road and trails to the woman's house in a nearby village. Since formal midwives are concentrated in Comalapa's town center, where sixteen of the municipality's forty-four midwives lived in 1995 (Centro de Salud 1995), it is often these central midwives who must visit women a several hours' walk from home.

When a chorus of barking dogs signals the midwife's arrival, the pregnant woman or a family member welcomes her and ushers her inside. She is allowed a moment's rest and might be offered some coffee and a pastry. The expectant mother thanks the midwife for making the long walk and describes how her pregnancy has progressed, reporting any problems. As she listens, the midwife might recall a case similar to the one before her, hoping to allay the woman's anxiety. The recollection also gives the midwife a moment to suggest that they take a look at the woman's abdomen, at which point both women move to a more private place in the house.

In the past, prenatal exams usually took place in the *tuj* or *temascal*, a small brick or adobe enclosure entered through a low door. There, warmth could be controlled and privacy ensured. Sweatbaths have long been part of Mesoamerican dwellings (Cresson 1938; Moedano 1961) and remain in widespread use in highland Guatemala (Orellana 1987). Not all Comalapan homes have a tuj, though. The disastrous 1976 earthquake wiped out virtually all standing structures in Comalapa. Along with the destruction of most of the town's houses and walls, more than three thousand people died (Asturias Montenegro and Gatica Trejo 1976:117). In the ensuing years of reconstruction, with the help of the Italian agency FratellItalia, many houses were rebuilt, but many tuj were not. Upholding new safety standards in construction, locals built walls of cinder block instead of adobe, and roofs of galvanized steel instead of ceramic tiles. Many overlooked the reconstruction of their tuj in the process. So what was once the ideal room of the house for carrying out a prenatal palpation is no longer available in all homes.[2]

In the room selected for the sobada, the pregnant woman lies face up on either a stiff bed, a *pop* (reed mat), or a couple of gunnysacks on the floor. The woman loosens the long *pas* (sash) fastened around her waist and allows the midwife to pull her *uq* (wraparound skirt) low upon her hips. The midwife then lifts the woman's *po't* (woven blouse) to expose her belly. She does not have to expose the pubic area, since she is interested mostly in the area above this.

With hands lubricated with cooking oil or another unguent, the midwife kneels, warms her hands, and places them on the woman's abdomen. She prays silently as her hands probe the woman's belly, feeling carefully for everything that should be in place. The midwife listens to the woman, notes her concerns, and offers advice. With a clockwise, then a counterclockwise motion, the midwife pushes her hands deeply into the womb's perimeter. She will feel for the fetus's head if the pregnancy is at the corresponding stage. In the later months of the pregnancy, she becomes more interested in whether the fetus is head-up or head-down. If she finds the fetus in the favorable head-down position, she leaves it be. If the fetus is askew, or inverted, she may apply a more specialized procedure, the external version (Jordan 1984).

The external version is extremely important to Maya midwives from different places. Among Maya midwives of Yucatán, for example, Brigitte Jordan (1993) described how this specialized massage can turn a fetus in a breech (bottom-first) or transverse (side-lying) position into the head-inferior position needed for delivery (Jordan 1993:28). This procedure is also critical to K'iche' midwives of Santa Lucía Utatlán and Chichicastenango (Cosminsky 1982a:239–40; FCCAM 1990:25). Comalapan midwives say that in the early months of pregnancy, a woman's body and the fetus's body are soft and pliable. This makes it possible to probe her abdomen and manipulate the fetus, to try to avert malpresentation. This procedure is, in fact, the raison d'être for the midwives' home visits. In a region where it can take hours before a physician can be alerted to an obstructed birth, and still longer before emergency surgery can be done, midwives must do everything possible to reduce the chances of a problem birth.[3] Since both the child's and mother's lives are at stake (as well as the midwife's reputation), a midwife might decline service to a woman who seeks attention late in her pregnancy. The outcome could be disastrous.

Kaqchikel Maya midwives perform massage and external versions not just to avoid problem births but because they attribute these skills to a divine source. Just as they receive their mandate to practice from a supernatural source, or through divinely inspired motivations, their hands receive the skill to perform massages by means inexplicable to them. Midwives say, "The hands already know," when explaining how they know how to massage. They locate the knowledge about massage in the hands themselves. This is also the case with other local healers like bonesetters who also feel strongly that their hands "know" the body's terrain. The best known bonesetter of Comalapa remarks that "the hand knows well the nature of injuries and of healthy bones." By applying his lubricated hands to an injured person's body, the experienced bonesetter detects irregularities beneath layers of tissue. He can then reduce the fracture or dislocation (Paul 1976; Icú Perén 1990; Hinojosa 2004b). Unlike with Maya midwives, though, most Maya bonesetters view their craft as pragmatic, not divine.

Manual massage sets both midwives and bonesetters diametrically apart from the physician's comparatively topical care. What a midwife's hands "know" cannot be taught in medical schools or clinics. When a midwife speaks of her hands' "knowledge," she hearkens to an embodied knowledge discordant with the biomedical profession (Cosminsky 2001:355, 370), a profession that many midwives say relies too heavily on instruments and drugs. As Celedonia aptly puts it, "We have the *don* of the hand, . . . whereas the physicians, all they have are instruments." A don is a divinely conferred gift or talent. With her body's don, the midwife can coexperience the pregnancy of the woman she massages and adjust the birth outcome through methods criticized by biomedicine. Guided by her hands (not guiding her hands), the midwife engages the expectant mother's and the unborn child's bodies, empathizing closely with each.

The midwife must enact this connection with the pregnant woman and perform external versions from early on, some six or seven months before term. Later, warns Celedonia, "the children don't allow themselves to be turned." Near term both mother's and child's bodies undergo a parallel "hardening," interfering with palpation, as mentioned above.[4] Some Maya women require more frequent visits and massages than others as gestation progresses. In the final two months, Celedonia might visit her clients every week or two. Some poorer women do not want her coming by too often, she says, because they cannot offer periodic gifts to her. On the other hand, some women want Celedonia to visit them up to every three days.

Midwives handle several, often over a dozen, pregnancies at any one time. This keeps them hurrying around the municipality, going from town center to the outlying villages, giving sobadas. As a result, midwives often have a hard time caring for their own households. When doing a sobada in some village, the midwife knows that she might have to rush off to another patient's house, or hurry back home to cook her family's lunch. There might even be clients waiting for her at home. But busy or not, she gives each woman the time she needs. To do otherwise would be unprofessional and a breach of sacred trust.

When the midwife thinks one of her clients will give birth soon, she tells the woman's family where they can find her in the next few days. The frantic knock on the midwife's door can come at any hour, so she must be ready to leave at a moment's notice. But midwives like Celedonia know that first-time mothers can have labor pains lasting three or more days. The midwife takes this into consideration when deciding whether the delivery is imminent. If she decides it is, she sets out.

THE BIRTH

At the expectant mother's home, the midwife does the final palpations and inverts the fetus, if necessary. The fetus often corrects its position in the final weeks before term, but the comadrona's hands must verify this. Together with whichever womenfolk have arrived, the midwife assuages the birthing woman's fears and waits out the contractions. The midwife Clemencia says that first-time mothers usually labor for twelve hours, while second- and third-time mothers might only take eight hours. When *ruya'* (its water) finally flows, all prepare for the child's arrival.

The woman then either lies on her back in the supine position or kneels. In the past, almost all women knelt during delivery. Today, because of contact with biomedicine, more Maya women deliver in the supine position, often at the insistence of their Maya midwife (Hinojosa 2004c). Gabriela is one such midwife. Alluding to a practice common throughout the Maya area, Gabriela recalls births in which "jun kolo' nitzeqe' ri yawa'," "the pregnant/sick one hangs from a rope," wherein the parturient would kneel and clutch a rope.[5] She used to have her clients kneel while birthing. Now she calls this position "kneeling and tied" and fears that kneeling creates excessive downward pressure upon the womb, causing it to "fall out." Even worse, she says, the force of kneeling can cause the womb, the child, and the blood to descend with so much force that they can "get stuck" inside the woman.

In whatever position women choose, however, most births proceed routinely. Celedonia explains that delivery begins with "slow" pains. These become increasingly stronger, occurring every minute or two. When the child emerges, the umbilical cord is tied firmly in two places and cut between them. Celedonia waits fifteen to forty-five minutes for the placenta. She then helps clean the infant and tidies up the birthing area. The following week, Celedonia, like most midwives, administers warming reconstituent baths and massages to the new mother, preferably in the tuj.

Although most pregnancies run a predictable course and conclude normally, problems do occur, and the midwife's hands are expected to detect and forestall these. For instance, Clemencia's hands can detect a serious condition like placenta previa, wherein the placenta embeds itself between the fetus and the mouth of the uterus. This condition requires medical attention. Clemencia's knowing hands also guide her in detecting a breech birth. She says that she can deal with these births but stresses that she can *best* handle these if the parturient is not a first-time mother *and* if the child is emerging bottom-first (i.e., without leg obstructions). Whether or not Clemencia would agree to handle a breech birth is unclear, especially if the birth were taking place within reach of a physician.

If Gabriela detects a breech presentation during birth, she also relies on her manual knowledge to deal with it. She is certain that her hands can help her deliver a child emerging "sitting down," or bottom-first. To help such a child, she says, she introduces her hand into the birth canal and locates the child's head, while palpating the womb from outside. Then, she "lifts" the child's head inside the birth canal, places two fingers in the child's mouth, and pulls the head while inverting the rest of the body.

Even "normal" births are considered potentially dangerous. Midwives say that the placenta sometimes adheres too strongly to the womb and threatens to pull it out of the body. This can happen when a birth attendant tries to remove a delayed placenta by pulling on the umbilical cord. An inverted uterus brings grave danger of infection and bleeding. In the past, midwives used special massages to reinsert the uterus, but today, only two midwives say they can correct a "fallen womb." When this happens, Gabriela first gives the woman her newborn to suckle so that "the womb will shrink [and] the hemorrhaging calm." Postpartum nipple stimulation provokes contraction of the uterus by producing oxytocin (Klein 1995:378). Gabriela then gently massages the "fallen womb" back into place. The midwife Eva once faced a similar situation. One of her patients fell off a ladder at term and went into labor. The woman's uterus, she says, began emerging as the child presented. Eva had to "hold the collar" of the uterus while the child emerged, and later massaged the uterus back into the body.

Midwives often speak of "fallen womb" and "fallen stomach" interchangeably, suggesting a close relationship between these organs. In fact, when Gabriela explains how a womb can fall, she draws a picture of a fallen womb that shows the stomach resting on the womb. For her, these organs are interconnected, and when one descends, both descend, to the point that the "collapsed womb" protrudes from the woman's body. Her anatomical conception differs greatly from that shown in the obstetrics manual she likes to leaf through (see figure 4.1).

The organs are physically connected and are therefore therapeutically connected. When the stomach or womb "collapses," the therapy has to return the entire set of organs to its place. Gabriela does not completely conflate the stomach with the womb, but she, like many other midwives, knows that the two organs share the consequences of a mishandled placenta, as I explain later.[6]

When midwives think that a pregnant woman's stomach or womb might descend or displace itself, they fasten a supportive belt around the woman's lower abdomen. An abdominal binding is especially needed, says Celedonia, if the woman experiences periodic early contractions or hemorrhaging. To apply the binding, Celedonia places a folded cloth low on the front of the woman's abdomen. She then wraps a cloth belt firmly around the lower abdominal region and lower back. A midwife sometimes has a

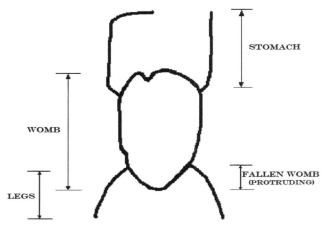

FIGURE 4.1

Gabriela the midwife's drawing of the collapsed stomach and womb.
The two organs are thought to move together and thus need joint treatment.

woman wear this band throughout her pregnancy. Since a fallen womb can cause miscarriage, midwives also apply the bindings to prevent this and to improve the chances of a full-term pregnancy. The binding is done to "support the baby," as Celedonia puts it, by providing padding and support low on the uterus. Having the pregnant woman recline and elevate her legs also relieves pressure on the base of the amniotic sac.

Midwives often affix a postpartum abdominal binding on their clients as well. Celedonia places the binding after each of the baths she gives clients the week after their deliveries. She binds them because the uterus "remains swollen" after the delivery and might even "fall out" of the woman. The binding holds the uterus in place while it "dries" and returns to its proper position. Many other Maya in Guatemala and Mexico practice postpartum binding for repositioning shifted organs and bones.[7]

Manual techniques are extremely important to the midwife, but I could not personally witness these techniques. As a man, and as an unmarried one without children, I could not expect to accompany midwives on their rounds and see their techniques firsthand. My learning was limited and, in many ways, I was taking a big chance even trying to learn about midwifery. It was all the more fortunate, then, that I did attend a sobada in 1994 with the midwife Clemencia Juchuña. Since my observation experience is limited to one sobada, I still have to rely on midwives' accounts for a mental picture of their manual methods. But this occasion with Clemencia did help me close the experience gap, if only slightly.

WOMBS AND WATER

In April 1994, sitting in a dark sleeping room in her compound, I watched as Clemencia finished treating a boy for ruwa winäq. When the boy and his mother left, Clemencia sat on a bed and told me to accompany her to see a xib'iril patient who lived nearby. Reluctant to commit to a long visit at someone's house on what had become a very busy day, I reminded myself aloud of other appointments I had. But before I knew it, I was walking down the street with Clemencia. We arrived at a cobbler's storefront, and Clemencia whispered something to me about nurses and health promoters. Before I could ask her what she meant, a man appeared behind the counter. Clemencia spoke with him and he motioned us inside the yard, smiling at me. We climbed a steep path of steps and entered a room with a few beds. On one of the beds sat a woman in the final weeks of her pregnancy.

The man who admitted us was the woman's husband, and he and I sat on beds facing each other and talked. To my right sat Clemencia and the woman on another bed. My host was very interested in my visit and asked about my specialty in medicine. I clarified that I studied the work of midwives and the way that people cared for health in Comalapa. His great interest in my work puzzled me, until I glanced over to my right and saw his wife stretch out into a supine position on her bed. Clemencia was there to do a sobada.

In moments, the woman had fully reclined, loosened her wraparound skirt, and lifted her huipil, exposing a belly large even for a woman in her ninth month. I tried focusing on what Clemencia was doing with her, without breaking off conversation with the woman's husband. Using both hands, Clemencia leaned into the woman's abdomen, pressed her fingers into its periphery, and glided her hands along the abdomen in a counterclockwise direction. She pressed her hands into various other points of the abdomen, feeling out the womb and fetus.

Someone mentioned that the woman was nine months pregnant, but the woman added that never with her previous four children had she grown so large during pregnancy. Clemencia's hands, meanwhile, leaned and pushed into the womb. Then she paused and said, "She has water, you don't feel twins." "Twins?" I asked. Clemencia continued palpating the woman's lower abdomen, between the navel and the pubic arch. She commented that the woman had high blood pressure, which put her at risk of passing out during birth. When she was done massaging a few minutes after she had begun, Clemencia announced with a touch of scorn that the physician this woman had visited had said that the woman would bear twins. Therefore, according to the physician, she would need to deliver by Cesarean section.

Clemencia said that the delivery was scheduled for May 10, adding, "It'll be a gift for Mother's Day." Forgetting Clemencia's position on the matter, I told the pregnant woman that the birth would be a "double gift" for that day. Clemencia repeated that the woman was carrying a single child with a lot of water, causing the woman to merely *look* as though she were carrying twins. Furthermore, the midwife warned, physicians were sometimes wrong when they foresaw twins. Should they decide to perform a Cesarean section on the woman, Clemencia said, they would have to travel to Chimaltenango, the departmental capital. The couple nodded, and we bid farewell to the weary woman with either twins or too much water in her womb.

Fifteen months later, in June 1995, I visited Clemencia and mentioned the home sobada of the year before. She scoffed that the pregnant woman had been told by one Dr. Cun that she would have twins. Clemencia reminded me that she disagreed with him, arguing that the woman's womb had simply contained a lot of water, causing it to distend to the size of a twin pregnancy. The woman and her husband, however, had decided to follow Dr. Cun's advice, break off their relationship with Clemencia, and go to Chimaltenango to bear the "twins." A single child was born.

Still, I wondered how a womb could take on so much water as to fool a physician and even the expectant mother. "Did the mother drink too much water?" I asked. Clemencia shook her head and explained that when pregnant women handle a lot of water by washing their hands, bathing, and washing clothes, they get a lot of water inside them. This distends the womb and makes the belly large enough even to make the mother believe she has twins. As for Dr. Cun and his diagnosis, well, Clemencia had been sending many women to him for additional monitoring, but no more. She reiterated that she had been a comadrona for seventeen years and that nobody could tell her how to do her job. After all, she said, "God gave me this work."

CHILDBIRTH IN GUATEMALA

Midwifery work like Clemencia's is indispensable to most Guatemalans, because well over 60 percent of all births in Guatemala take place in the home (PAHO 1994, vol. 2:224; Goldman and Glei 2003:691). In Comalapa, the percentage of home births actually approaches 99 percent, according to local physicians. Comalapan physicians credit the prenatal attention of midwives for the low incidence of problem births in the municipality. They insist, though, that Maya midwives are still not up to health-establishment standards, pressuring midwives to change some of their practices (Hinojosa 2004c). In this way they join a chorus of voices from the biomedical sector who insist that Maya midwives must be "trained" in proper prenatal and childbirth methods (Berry 2006; Cosminksy 2001; Greenberg 1982; Jordan 1989).

Midwives provide the bulk of pregnancy care in Comalapa, but many local women have had babies delivered by Cesarean section. To account for this, it should be remembered that midwives do refuse care to some women who approach them late in their pregnancies. If these women find that no midwife will accept them, they will most likely resort to a physician. Women with a history of difficult deliveries often have trouble finding midwives who will take them and so must go to physicians for care, increasing their likelihood of receiving a Cesarean. Women receiving this surgery have to be driven by bus or private vehicle to either Chimaltenango (twenty-eight kilometers away) or, more likely, to Guatemala City (eighty-two kilometers away), assuming roads are passable. Cesarean sections are sometimes done in the local, private Hospital K'aslen, when qualified surgeons are available. In Comalapa and probably elsewhere in the highlands, physicians are likely to order invasive procedures as soon as a woman's labor exceeds twenty-four hours or even less.

Comalapan Maya women have far more birthing choices than did women a generation or two ago. But these choices are conditioned by the person attending the pregnancy, whether midwife or physician. My discussions with midwives, mothers, and physicians makes clear, for instance, that pregnant women under the primary care of a midwife undergo Cesarean sections far less often than do women under a physician's care. Given the Maya midwife's concern for inverting the fetus as term approaches, it is understandable how the great majority of home births proceeds without obstructions, and without need for surgery.

On the other hand, women who select a physician as primary caregiver do not expect the active fetal care, palpation, and version that midwives provide. They cannot reasonably expect that their child will be correctly positioned for birth. Under these circumstances, and given the physicians' propensity for invasive techniques, child malpresentations and births considered too "slow" by physicians are often addressed surgically. In the end, Comalapans have come to see physicians as impatient and too eager to operate. Midwives and mothers also describe how physicians basically end their relationships with patients once delivery and a few follow-up visits have been completed. This contrasts with the continuing relationship between midwife and family following the birth, a relationship that includes giving advice about birth organs, as the next chapter describes.

CHAPTER FIVE

Birth Organs and the Stirring of Will

MIDWIVES, MOTHERS, AND FAMILIES SEE childbirth as a moment when a child passes easily through the birth canal thanks to the diligent attention it received earlier. But as demanding as prenatal and delivery care is for Comalapan midwives, their work is not limited to this. Childbirth is also a moment when a woman's future health and a family's reproductive future hang in the balance. Midwives therefore pay close attention to two organs crucial to gestation—the placenta and umbilical cord—in ways showing how human bodily relationships persist despite bodily disconnectedness. Through her understanding of these organs, the midwife purveys bodily knowledge vital to the well-being of pregnant women and their children. The placenta, with its pronounced health and spiritual implications for mother and child, occupies a primary place in her formulations.

THE SINGULAR PLACENTA

Newborn infants must be accompanied by their placentas, which usually emerge within a half hour of birth. If they are not, the midwife massages the uterus deeply, but cautiously. A delayed placenta causes fear and worry, but the condition is usually allayed through gentle massage. When the delay extends well beyond an hour or two, a physician is usually sought. If the physician decides to accept the patient, for there are some who do not accept emergency childbirth cases, he usually performs a specialized massage to extract the afterbirth.[1] He will probably also administer oxytocin to induce uterine contraction.

When the placenta emerges, the midwife examines it carefully. She checks to see that none of it has detached and remained in the uterus, where it can cause bleeding (Klein 1995:200). When a Maya birth takes place in a hospital, the attending personnel usually consign the placenta to the garbage pile. But in Comalapan homes, where most community births take place, another destiny awaits this singular organ.

Midwives and families insist that the placenta be disposed of by either burial or burning. In practice, though, few placentas are simply buried. This may be, as Clemencia suggests, because the ground is much too "cold" for the afterbirth, especially during the rainy season. The importance of a "hot" outcome for the placenta is evident in the more common practice of placenta burning. To prepare the placenta for burning, Celedonia places leaves of lavender (*Lavandula officinalis* Chaix., Sp. *alhucema*), parsley (*Petroselinium crispum*, Sp. *perejil*), and cumin (*Cuminum cyminum*, Sp. *comino*), plants considered humorally "hot," on the organ, then wraps it in newspaper or old rags. She then burns the bundle in the tuj. If no sweatbath is available, a fire is built on the earth to burn the bundle, or it is burned in the family hearth. Gabriela prefers burning the organ in the hearth because "the heat of the mother is there." Indeed, the hearth is called *ru te' q'aq'*, "mother of the fire." Celedonia, meanwhile, considers the fire more important than the location.

These women prefer burning the placenta to prevent any suffering in the mother. One midwife says that a neglected placenta will cause facial blemishes in the mother. In most cases, though, midwives say the burning is done "so that the woman won't have any stomach pains." Midwives say that the mother's womb or stomach will remain permanently swollen and inflamed if they do not burn the placenta. The incinerated placenta conveys "heat" to the womb from which it comes and with which it is considered affective. The fire dispels any "coldness" from the placenta that produces swelling of the womb. As Celedonia puts it, "Since it was fire that burned the placenta, the womb shrivels up rapidly."

Midwives often speak of women whose wombs swelled because they did not burn their placentas. Celedonia says of women whose placentas were carelessly disposed of in hospitals, "The women's stomachs look like they're very . . . [making an obese gesture], they look as if they were expecting." The midwife Tomasa appends another level of importance to placenta burning. After applying "hot" herbs to the placenta, she arranges the ash in which the placenta is to be burned in a circle, carefully places the placenta in this hollow "mouth up," and then burns it. Tomasa replicates and burns this ashen womb so that the mother will be spared stomach pains and so that she can continue bearing children.

A younger midwife, Eva, is not so sure about placenta burning, though. She scoffs at mothers who ask her to place herbs on the placenta, telling them that the placenta must need a "condiment." Other midwives who abjure placenta burning justify their reasoning within a native framework. For instance, Herlinda recognizes that burning the placenta will avert stomach pains in the mother, but she warns that this might also cause the child's teeth to decay as he grows older.

For Herlinda, a relationship exists both between the mother and the placenta and between the child and the placenta. In each case, the womb is the reference point: the placenta is bound to the womb, just as the child is enclosed by it. The fate of each dyadic component continues affecting the complementary component. But the placenta usually connects more strongly to the mother. This enduring tie, recognized by many Maya peoples, reveals a concern that if the placenta is not hidden or burned, it can be used in witchcraft against the child.[2] Placenta traditions of different groups reveal that the detached maternal nexus, whether the placenta or umbilicus, retains its ties with the child, so these organs must be ritually protected.

So strong is the kinship between placenta and child, in fact, that some Maya call the placenta "the second child," following ever on the heels of the newborn. This term is used among the K'iche' of Santa Lucía Utatlán (Cosminsky 1982a:243). Among Yucatecs, the placenta is likewise known as the "companion" of the child, and its treatment reportedly influences the newborn's health (Jordan 1989:931). For the child's safety and well-being, his or her father must hide and bury this "companion" in an appropriate place.

Piedad, a Kaqchikel woman, also refers to the placenta as a second body or child. She calls the placenta *ruka'n*, "its second," alluding to its sequential appearance at every birth. Eighty-three-year-old Piedad is one of the oldest persons I spoke with in Comalapa. Her age, together with her status as an oyonel (soul therapist), make her insights into children and childbirth especially revealing. However, Piedad's Kaqchikel phrase for placenta, "ruka'n," contrasts with the Kaqchikel phrase most often heard locally.

Most Comalapans call the placenta "ruk'u'x ak'wal" or "ruk'u'x ti ri ne'y," the k'u'x or "heart" of the child. The word "k'u'x" can mean either "heart," "center," or even "soul," in colonial and modern Kaqchikel, incorporating something of each of these concepts in any given use. For instance, *niq'axon pa nuk'u'x* indicates that "my heart is in pain" or, figuratively, "my soul aches." Meanwhile, *ruk'u'x tinamït* refers to "the center of town," namely the plaza. But used as "ruk'u'x kaj, ruk'u'x ulew," it refers not only literally to the "heart/center of the sky, heart/center of the earth" but also to the divinity invoked by this in the *Pop Wuj* (Tedlock 1985:75). The word "k'u'x" is thus a broadly encompassing concept, one that in its totality connotes a life source, a divine fountainhead, or even an animistic center (López Austin 1988), as I explained in chapter 3. This is vividly the case with the human placenta.

Celedonia explains of the ruk'u'x ti ri ne'y, "It is that which gave life to the child, it gave suckle to the child from the inside, that's why they call it the k'u'x, that's why they say it's the child's heart, also." For her and other midwives, the placenta-as-k'u'x engenders the child, nurses it, and provides its life-sustaining heartbeat. In Chiapas, this in-utero world reveals not only the animating role of the placenta but the special state of the fetus. When Pedro Pitarch (2010:167) says that the Tzeltal Maya fetus "feeds on its mother's blood," he sees this as an appropriate feeding relationship, both because the placenta mediates fetal ensoulment by external spiritual forces (lab) and because the fetus itself is in a heightened spiritual state, requiring what other sacred beings consume: blood. Because of these capacities for engendering, feeding, and ensouling, placentas have been treated almost reverently throughout the Maya area, receiving very elaborate care.[3] They cannot be taken lightly.

THE UMBILICUS AND ITS BLOOD

In Comalapa, the umbilical cord is also ritually charged. Because it remains part of the child's body for several days following birth, it must be observed and handled carefully. At birth, a standard measure for cutting the cord, once it has stopped pulsing, is two finger widths or two inches from the baby's navel. The midwife Tomasa, however, differentiates between a girl's cord and a boy's cord, advising that a girl's cord must be measured three inches, whereas a boy's cord must be measured four inches. This is because a man has authority over a woman, she says. Her use of the numbers "three" and "four" is consistent with female and male numerical associations found in the Maya area.[4] Most local midwives, though, consider two finger widths the right measurement standard for both sexes.

Before the midwife cuts the umbilical cord, however, she must first perform an important service for the mother and her family. At the moment of birth, midwives are often asked to examine the umbilical cord and check the drops of blood in it. Celedonia says that if a woman asks her, "Tatz'eta' ri ruk'u'x jampe ak'wala' e k'o chiri'," "Look at the placenta/cord for how many children are there," she has to count the drops of blood. These drops, or *frijolitos* (little beans), are considered children yet to be born. If there are no drops in the cord, then the present child is thought to be the mother's last. If there are many drops, the woman can expect many more pregnancies. The midwife Tomasa says that the drops also reveal whether the woman will have any miscarriages, although she does not say how.

FIGURE 5.1
A midwife examines the umbilical cord to count the number of blood drops,
taken to indicate future children and to identify a future twin birth.
Drawing by Servando G. Hinojosa.

Some midwives say that blood drops are differently colored according to the sex of the future child. A red drop is thus a boy and a white one a girl. Other midwives, like Flora, feel that the drops' color indicates the accompanying newborn's temperature state. For her, yellow and green drops of blood represent abnormal temperature in the child, whereas white drops represent normal temperature.

This kind of attention to the umbilical cord is not unique to Kaqchikel Maya.[5] Comalapan midwives and mothers are vigilant about the cord because they want to avoid a future twin pregnancy. As much care as a single-child pregnancy requires in the highlands, a twin pregnancy can be much more risky. Twin pregnancies are simply not desired. A mother's fears can be allayed, though, if her cord is treated carefully.[6]

In Comalapa, the midwife averts the future birth of twins by first checking to see if any of the drops in the cord are joined in pairs. She considers these twins, and she prevents them from reaching full incorporation by cutting the cord between them, separating the two. Since the drops were in contact with the womb, the source of babies, the drops are manipulated to change the future activity of the womb, in an expression of contiguous magic. One midwife likewise says that mothers often ask her to *aplastar* (crush) the blood twins and other "children" in the cord to forestall their development.

Interestingly, most local midwives who talk about this practice say that it stems from "old beliefs" and claim that they themselves do not subscribe to it. Midwives sometimes discuss it only in the third person, prefacing their knowledge with *dicen*, "they say," distancing themselves from their source of information. They nevertheless provide very detailed information on this native contraception method, making one wonder just how closely it reflects their own thinking.

Some midwives take their criticism of the method yet further. While Celedonia reads and intervenes in the cord's coding, she is unconvinced about "cutting" the blood twins. She sees this as local "ignorance" because the cord, and the placenta attached to it, are burned. If it were to reenter the woman's body, she reasons, "perhaps it would produce some effect," but it stays outside. Gabriela likewise points out that if the umbilical cord is cut outside the woman, it cannot reenter and become children. Both of these midwives may doubt the cutting procedure because of their exposure to

Western empirical training, but this training has not affected their credence in placenta burning, which, by the above reasoning, would be equally futile.

Eva disparages the cord-cutting procedure along similar lines, sneering at how women ask her to crush drops that look like twins and to count the rest of the male and female children. She tries to understand this from a local point of view and concludes that women think the drops of blood are the "ova of the ovulation of the woman" and that these will mature into fetuses. The fallacy of the cutting method lies, again, in how the cord does not reenter the woman and so cannot affect her reproductive organs. Women who believe in drop counting and cutting tend to be older, she says. Many younger women sometimes ask her whether the method is reliable.

Celedonia reveals another aspect of the cord, arguing that its blood drops are the child's food, not future children. She knows the blood is food because if the cord has no blood at the moment of birth, the child immediately looks for the breast. "They say that [the child] is hungry," she explains, because "the child eats through the navel." When the cord connecting to the navel is "clean," the child has finished eating through the cord and is born eager to nurse.

The midwife Mercedes agrees with this and cautions that the cord bleeds the most when it is tied and cut before the child has finished "eating" through it. When food is flowing through the cord, it stands the greatest chance of bleeding and causing the child's death. Mercedes says that midwives should wait five minutes after the birth before cutting the cord to let the child finish eating. This advice concords with Brigitte Jordan on how the cord should not be cut too soon following birth, as often happens in obstetric practice. Jordan (1993:86) points out that premature cutting can, in fact, deprive the child of about 25 percent of his or her needed blood supply.

When the umbilical drops are seen as food or as blood for the child, midwives often view the cord as a conduit for the child's chuq'a' (strength or energy). Thus, midwives call the umbilical blood the child's chuq'a', which is spilled and lost if the cord bleeds. A soul therapist named Antonia says of a bleeding umbilical cord, "The chuq'a' of the baby is being lost." Indeed, as Kevin Groark (1997:52) reports of Tzotzil and Tzeltal Maya, any loss of this highly charged substance, including through childbirth, is viewed with alarm.

This signals the primary reason midwives take such interest in examining, counting, and separating the drops of blood: through these, midwives and mothers can directly gauge the procreative life-force within mothers, embodied by the multicolored, clustered drops. The cord's exposure marks the critical moment when the final life-sustaining energy is exchanged between placenta and child. As the pathway for this generative chuq'a', the cord is closely tied to the child's future development, particularly to his or her gendering.

GENDERING THE ENGENDERED

Comalapans treat the umbilicus, the portion of the cord still attached to the child's navel after the cord is cut, in line with this gendering need. When the umbilicus dries and falls off in the days following the birth, they attend to it ritually according to the child's sex. A girl's umbilicus is usually wrapped in a cloth, placed in a small pouch, and hung in the kitchen where the stove's smoke can hit it. This ensures that she will work well in the kitchen. One midwife says that some women place the girl's umbilicus right behind the comal (griddle) so that the girl will make good tortillas. Another midwife places the girl's umbilicus in the tuj, alluding to the tuj's future importance to the girl.

In a boy's case, his father takes the umbilicus to the forest and places it in the forking branches of a young tree so the boy will fear neither working in the hills nor climbing trees. Selecting a young tree for this ensures that, as the tree grows, so will the boy. The boy's umbilicus is sometimes hung among tools like the hoe and gourd so that "he can be a cultivator," according to Eva. Meanwhile, another midwife says that the boy's placenta should be buried in the tuj so he will know how to start a fire. These procedures mirror other practices found in the Maya highlands and lowlands that connect the umbilical cord with the sexual division of labor (García et al. 1999:15; Villa Rojas 1980). In this way, some Tzotzil midwives of Chiapas cut a girl's umbilical cord over a grinding stone so she will know how to grind maize, and they cut a boy's umbilical cord over an ax blade so he will know how to fell trees.[7] Grinding stones and axes become the media through which adult females are shaped and adult males are hewn.

For Comalapan midwives, umbilicus treatment is most important in how it commits the family to enacting a gendered identity in the child; midwives only occasionally say that they treat the umbilicus for physical reasons. Unlike with placenta ritual, which is thought to provide clear health benefits to the mother, umbilicus ritual is valued for its deferred but lifelong benefits. It sets the child upon a gendered path and awakens her to the kind of person, with the kind of consciousness, her body will enable her to be. This bodily grounded awakening is not unconditional, however. In a very vivid way, umbilicus handling maps out spaces of social possibility for women and men, even as it perpetuates "the circumscription of women's mobility, opportunities, and access to resources by emphasizing that a man's domain is outside the home and a woman's domain is within it" (Carey 2006:41). That the expansion of women's and men's social roles should coincide with a decline of traditional umbilical rituals, then, should come as no surprise. Neither should it be surprising when umbilical rituals eventually come to reflect the new, technology-heavy areas of work that many young Comalapans, of both sexes, today seek out.[8] The midwife Eva offers a telling preview when she recounts, "Some say, they want to commend the cord to the physician, so that he [the child] will become a physician."

Umbilical ritual may set the stage for gendering, but Comalapans also use more conventional means for teaching children to become women and men. From early on, children are encouraged to engage in lighthearted versions of certain adult activities. Girls of about age three sit by their mothers at the backstrap loom and create imaginary *lienzos* (woven panels) at their miniature looms, using tiny weaving implements. At other times, girls pretend to grind maize on miniature *metates* and *manos* (grinding stones). They might even make mud tortillas, patting them together with hands still too inexperienced to handle dough. Mothers who can afford dolls often strap them to their small daughters' backs with a piece of cloth in imitation of how women carry their infants. As the girls grow older they carry their own infant siblings in this way and tend to them while their mother works at the stove, market, or clothes-washing *pila*. At some point, girls are expected to learn the craft of tortilla making and pat their tiny maize cakes alongside their mothers. Girls are gradually allowed to handle thread and try their hand at weaving simple pieces. In these ways, as the girl's physical dexterity grows, her sense of the adult role she will realize also grows.

A parallel operation occurs with boys, but their shift to practical work takes place somewhat later than with girls. In play, boys initially spend much time with girls in the home but gradually get steered away from activities like kitchen and laundry work. Boys might be expected to help carry market purchases for their mothers but are not expected to help prepare meals. Through the ubiquitous kicking of soccer balls or other objects, boys are more likely than girls to be allowed outside the house compound and to interact with neighbor children.[9] Unlike girls, boys begin handling the instruments of their adult role, farming implements, only after they leave the house on trips to the fields with their fathers and other men. Compulsory grade-school attendance now divides the energies of town-center boys between schooling and the family fields. Even so, the trappings of traditional male roles appear among boys. They sometimes carry their schoolbags with a strap across the forehead, as with a tumpline, and they take their machetes to school on certain days for gardening projects.[10]

Although socializing play and work is ritualistic, aside from umbilical ritual Comalapan Kaqchikel Maya seem to have few gendering rituals, compared with Maya elsewhere. Among Tzotzils of Zinacantan, Chiapas, for instance, the midwife carries the infant and sets gender identity into motion by placing gender-specific objects in the infant's hands. A boy is given a digging stick, a hoe, a billhook, an ax, and pitch pine, whereas a girl is given a grinding stone and parts of a backstrap loom (Vogt 1969:181).[11] Ritual allusions to children's future roles are also visible among Yucatecs in Yucatán, where girls and boys who have reached three and four months of age, respectively, are ceremonially placed astride a godparent's hip in the *hetzméek* (hold in arms) ritual. The godparents then instruct the child in the ways of adulthood and place objects in his or her hands such as machetes, axes, or cooking equipment, invoking the child's later adult duties (Redfield and Villa Rojas 1971:188–89; Thompson 1990:166).

Sexed implements help transform the Maya child into the gendered adult he or she must become, in ways reminiscent of how Aztec used sexed implements at baptism and used gendered costumes at other points in the life cycle for this purpose (Joyce 2000). But some Maya people also use sexed implements when an infant's life hangs in the balance through fate of birth. Lois Paul and Benjamin Paul (1975:709) report that among the

Tz'utujiil of San Pedro la Laguna, babies born with the umbilical cord around the neck are considered vulnerable to the effects of meteors and falling stars. The ritual remedy requires either a small spindle and loom sticks for a girl or a machete and tumpline for a boy. Comalapan midwives do consider cosmic bodies, when eclipsed, to be dangerous to fetuses, but they do not apply gendered remedies when dealing with these.[12]

In the hands of midwives, parents, and godparents, Maya children's gendered identities are initiated and guided. But an individual's gendered self begins before birth and can even be changed. Comalapan midwives assert that, just as with the number of future children, the sex and gender of children are mutable. This is clear, they say, in how fetuses can move between wombs and how children can move between genders. Unborn children are allegedly able to change sex by "switching" from one womb to another. Gabriela says that this can occur, for example, if a pregnant woman wants to give birth to a boy, but actually has a girl in her womb. If this woman were to encounter another pregnant woman carrying a boy, the boy fetus would switch to the first woman, leaving the second woman with the girl. This is described as *nikijäl ki' ri ak'wala'*, "the children switch among themselves," and can occur in the sixth or seventh month.[13] To prevent this switching, Gabriela has the pregnant woman attach a safety pin, coin, or some other steel object to the front of her huipil, a procedure known to many women in the Kaqchikel area (Roquel Calí 1995:15).

Although the midwife Celedonia is unfamiliar with these switches, she knows of other momentous instances called *cuando cambia la suerte*, when the fate changes. She explains that when her sister-in-law was pregnant, this woman strongly desired a girl, but a boy was born. Over time, the boy developed unexpected characteristics, becoming *efeminado* (effeminate). Celedonia says that "he would prepare food, he would wear an apron, he would sweep," prompting people to comment, "Perhaps he's effeminate . . . his time changed, his fate changed." The boy eventually took up "acceptable" male behaviors and traits, but Celedonia was left thinking that women should not wish too strongly for a child of either sex. The child's character can be affected by the will, inadvertent or otherwise, of the mother.

Gabriela and Celedonia deal with gender concerns in a preventative way. In contrast, women of other Maya groups take more active approaches to matters of sex and gender. Tz'utujiil midwives, for example, are said to be able to "divine the sex of the child before its birth" and even to change its sex (Douglas 1969:145). Pregnant Tzotzil and Tzeltal women are said to be able to change a newborn child's sex by simply lifting it (Guiteras Holmes 1961b:163). This sexual mutability continues in the K'iche' baby, allowing the infant to change from male to female every three or four days, and to alter behavior and gender identity every three or four years. Some K'iche's also report that if a woman conceives during the full moon, her child will become either twins or transsexual (Tedlock 1992:184).

While Comalapan midwives do not negotiate such elaborate gendering schedules, they are still respected for their knowledge of what precedes and follows birth.[14] This includes alerting pregnant mothers to how the unborn expresses will.

WILLFUL BEINGS

Will is often articulated in terms of *antojos* (cravings). Women with child are advised to satisfy their cravings, especially food cravings, even if they are costly and inconvenient. Celedonia warns women that if they do not, they risk "provoked abortions," miscarriages. Kaqchikel midwives suspect, as do K'iche' midwives (Cosminsky 1977:80), that unsatisfied antojos cause many miscarriages. Celedonia says that when a woman miscarries, her child emerges with his mouth open and his tongue partially sticking out. This is because, she says, "everything that one wants to eat, it is the child that actually wants it." Whenever she sees a miscarried fetus, Celedonia knows that he suffered because his will was ignored. The fetus carries its hunger to its tiny grave. Q'eqchi's recognize that fetal hunger can be so strong that it gets inscribed upon the child's body, making its skin resemble a craved food (Fittin 1993:137), something also documented among the sixteenth-century Nahuas (López Austin 1988, vol. 1:299).

Fetal will can also manifest in fetal restlessness. Restless and potentially problematic babies are recognized by how, at birth, their umbilical cords encircle their necks. The child's agitation in the womb causes the entanglement. Such babies are considered very *listos* (clever and troublesome). This condition distresses the mother both because of the immediate danger and because of the child's likely later temperament. In Chiapas, interestingly, fetal will might even make a Tzotzil fetus "flee" from his mother's womb in search of another womb.[15]

A child's willful hunger can affect his mother's body long after he is born. A woman who has recently given birth might be off on an errand, away from her infant, and suddenly find milk dripping from her breasts, says Celedonia. The breasts are responding to the child's will back home. Although this suggests an enduring relationship between the child's visceral wants and his mother's breasts, it is not considered a serious matter, unlike the relationships implicit in placenta and umbilicus treatment. This is because no one nursing moment is likely to be critical in the child's life, whereas the timely treatment of the birth organs might be.

Fetal will is matched in its frequency, but exceeded in intensity, by what pregnant women harbor. Pregnant women, like the children within them, are very willful beings. These women have great *deseo* (desire) for children, and feel *envidia* (envy) toward other women with children. The mere glance of a pregnant woman can give a child ruwa winäq. Ruwa winäq, the eye of the person, resembles what is elsewhere called "evil eye." The illness name reveals how it is caused by someone's powerful gaze.

Pregnant women can cause ruwa winäq because of the "strength" of their "hot" blood. Their heat can overwhelm more delicate persons, especially children (Cosminsky 1976:166), and they exercise this ability without knowing it. Ruwa winäq does not depend on conscious will to be transmitted; unconscious will suffices. Mothers thus shield their young children whenever a pregnant woman approaches on the street. Red garments and rue in the child's shirt also protect the child. Parents of children diagnosed with ruwa winäq try to recall whether a pregnant woman has recently looked at their child. The woman suspected can be asked to touch the stricken child, and she is expected to comply. In more serious cases, however, midwives or other specialists such as oyonela' are summoned for the cure.

Oyonela' are also sought when xib'iril strikes. Pregnant women are especially advised to avoid this ailment. Sometimes called susto (fright), this illness exists in various forms in Latin America (Gillin 1948; Rubel 1964). In Comalapa, xib'iril can jolt part of a person's soul from his body, causing it to wander, lost, either where the fright happened or in a place the victim likes. The oyonïk rituals, in turn, try to summon the soul back to the person.

If a pregnant woman does get xib'iril, however, she might lose not only her own soul but her unborn child's as well. Celedonia says that if a pregnant woman encounters a wandering "spirit" in the night, the baby inside her might die. Recalling a lynching that occurred on March 26, 1996, in Comalapa, she warns that the hill where this happened, Tz'an Juyu', is now unsafe for people in general and for pregnant women in particular. Since the victim died a "forced death," she says, he might return as a spirit, frightening anyone there. Celedonia explains that a woman took her pregnant daughter-in-law to the lynching site where they saw the cadaver. That night the woman went into labor; her baby died shortly after the birth (see also Nash 1970:131).

Pregnancy and childbirth practices provide a lens into unseen forces acting upon and through bodies. These forces are at work between mother and fetus, placenta and mother, umbilicus and child, mother and child, and even between fetuses. Midwives and mothers pay close attention to specific bodily operations during pregnancy. And as mothers awaken to a larger sense of consciousness enabled through these bodily operations, the stage is set for understanding that consciousness itself is initiated and makes itself known through physical signs. The Comalapa Maya midwife assembles the elusive fragments of reproductive experience and discerns the presence of spirit.

CHAPTER SIX

Knowledge about the Soul and the Child's Fate

FEW PEOPLE KNOW AS MUCH as the midwife when it comes to pregnancy, placentas, umbilical cords, and the gendered dimensions of reproduction. This alone makes her important to Comalapans. But her knowledge also extends to how "spirit" first animates the body, and in this sense she is an invaluable interpreter of bodily signs. She also attends to what birth signs mean for a baby's future and tries to identify the newborn's vocation. With these faculties, the midwife enlarges her already broad range of duties, engaging the physical aspects of reproduction and bringing out the meanings unseen to others.

As I described earlier, Comalapans use the terms "alma," "espíritu," "wanima," "xamanil," and "corazón" when talking about human "soul." Although these terms do not all reference the same thing, they individually convey a dimension or quality of human animistic states that together assemble the local understanding of soul. Comalapan midwives use these terms variably when referring to soul. I too have found it useful to move flexibly between them and use them as operationally equivalent concepts at times. Whatever the term used, this chapter explores how midwives engage an understanding of soul in their work. It underscores the instantiation of spirit and its vocational messages as revealed through the expressive physicality of mother and child.

Even though she outwardly directs herself to women's and children's health, the midwife is very preoccupied with the private life of human spirit. Midwives often allude to matters of spirit with which they are intimately familiar, including concerns of human growth and development.

Central to these concerns is the question of when and how the child first comes to "life," properly speaking, inside or outside the womb. To know how this "life" comes about, the midwife attends to certain physical features of fetuses. Doing this, she comes to understand spirit by understanding the private life of the body.

In several ways, the midwife is privy to invisible changes in the fetus. Her hands closely track the womb's and fetus's growth. She regularly checks fetal head position, especially as the term date nears, and notes whether the fetus inverts or repositions itself. Some midwives have a physician listen to the fetal heartbeat for an additional check on the child's health. They also follow the fetus's projections of will through its mother's food cravings.

For many midwives, the animating essence is what makes these physical developments possible in the fetus. These midwives further recognize that the fetus must be "ensouled" to truly act upon and through the mother's body. Not all agree with this, though. Some midwives and women argue that the fetus's animating essence does not enter the picture until birth. But their differing views all rest upon physical reasoning.

FEELING THE SOUL'S ARRIVAL

To get a sense of how midwives link the soul to the fetus or newborn, and even to that child's future, I ask several midwives and a soul therapist/midwife about when the soul "arrives" in the child. These fourteen women, ranging in age from thirty-eight to sixty-seven, respond in very different ways. Four midwives say that the soul arrives at conception. Five other midwives explain that the soul arrives at a specific moment in the pregnancy such as at twenty-five days, or in the second, fourth, fifth, or sixth month. Other women like Mercedes, Eva, and Tencha are not sure when the soul arrives. Mercedes says that the soul arrives at conception but explains that conception can encompass the first two or three months of pregnancy. Eva says confidently that "the alma is the breath of life that one has received; from the moment of birth or from the moment of being engendered, you have an alma, you are a human being." The ensoulment views of Tencha, a soul therapist and midwife, are equally difficult. One day she insists that "when they [children] are born, that is when the espíritu reaches them," but on another occasion she reasons, "since the child is being formed [in the womb], as he's growing, he must already have his espíritu." Two midwives understand "soul arrival" to mean a state of grace an adult can achieve through spiritual blessings or the Holy Spirit.

Midwives sometimes discuss the soul's arrival in terms of "feel." For instance, Carolina comments, "I think that at four or five months, you can already feel that [the fetus] has life in the mother's womb." Herlinda specifies that what is "felt" is the heartbeat, something detectable starting at six months, even though she argues that the soul arrives at conception. Clemencia agrees that the detectable prenatal beating heart reveals the soul's presence. Conception leads to ensoulment and then heartbeat, says Celedonia. She knows that the child receives spirit twenty-five days after conception because, at that time, the child "begins to move and begins to grow, [and] begins to require his food in order to grow." God gives the child his espíritu at twenty-five days, she says, allowing the heartbeat to begin, although it is still too faint to feel at this stage. Three months after conception, Celedonia says, the child moves more, and you can feel his heartbeat.

Like these midwives, Gabriela firmly believes that the soul arrives in the fetus long before birth. In fact, physicians verify this for her when they listen to the fetal heart with a stethoscope. She explains, "That's why the doctors place that apparatus [on the mother]; when you can hear the *tin, tin, tin*, it [the child] has its ranima." For Gabriela, the audible heartbeat, accessed through biomedical technology, conclusively signals the presence and strength of soul.

Comalapan midwives consider fetal growth and movement the primary criteria for ensoulment, recalling what Calixta Guiteras Holmes found among Tzotzils of Chiapas: "From the time the foetus has acquired the shape of an infant and starts to move, it has a soul" (1961a:104; see also Vogt 1965:33). The Tzotzil fetus was known to have a soul, she said, because it moved in the womb before daybreak; it moved because it *knew* when daybreak approached (Guiteras Holmes 1961a:162). The arrival of the ch'ulel in the Tzeltal fetus, likewise, is signaled by fetal movement in the womb (Pitarch 2010:38). It is worth noting that among the Mexica of central Mexico, when the deities breathed the *tonalli* into the fetus, bodily changes happened in both fetus and mother. The fetus dropped lower into the uterus, and the mother sensed this as a lightening (Furst 1995:64–66). When fetal growth, movement, and even incipient awareness appear in these cases, they mark ensoulment. In Comalapa, ensoulment takes on additional associations.

THE FIRST BREATH

Midwives and other women who say that the child receives soul at birth emphasize the drama of the first breath. One woman says that the newborn convulses when taking his first breath, and that at "the first breath that the child makes, the alma of the earth comes to him." For her, the newborn's struggling and crying decisively signal the soul's arrival. With his first breath, the child gathers up strength and activates his internal organs, especially his lungs and diaphragm, and flails his arms and legs. The newborn can move like this, bursting with life, because ruxla' has resolutely come into play.

As mentioned earlier, the Kaqchikel word "ruxla'" can be glossed as "its odor," "its breath," or "its emanation." The root "-uxla'" must have a prefix denoting possession, since an odor, a breath, or an emanation must come from something. An unpossessed "uxla'" is not found in normal speech. Comalapans most often use ruxla' to refer to an odor or breath, but its ethereal, even stimulating quality likens it to an animating essence. One personified derivation of -uxla' is very revealing. A Protestant pastor uses the word "Uxlayxel" to refer not to breath or odor but to the Holy Spirit. This usage suggests that ruxla''s larger meanings include an extrasomatic soul or spirit. The invisibility of ruxla' further allies it with the Holy Spirit in some cases. Insofar as the ruxla' entity or potentiality comes from the earth or from God and enters the infant as his first breath, it operates as an animating essence.

Comalapans often liken spirit to inhaled air. Clemencia says, "The espíritu is like air, like when one breathes; if one doesn't breathe he will die." For her, the ensouled life begins with conception, but sustained life comes only with breathing. An elderly Protestant man, in turn, asserts that the originary aire (air) that animated the world was exhaled by God himself. He says that this aire sustains human lives and that "when someone has died, there is no longer aire, there is no longer life there; it is because of aire that one is speaking." Breathing (and the speech extending from it) is a crucial bodily movement, akin to heartbeat and motor activities. The active movement of air through the body thus evokes an image of life. People consider breathing a life-sustaining act and a marker of spirit. Breathing reinforces how bodily movement and growth signal ensoulment.

As an extension of this reasoning, the lack of movement and growth in a child implies weakness of soul. Children's souls are considered to be "weaker" than adults' souls, but some children's "soul strength" falls even below expected levels. The main way to determine this is by observing how a child breathes when he is born and in the following days. Babies who do not breathe at birth are considered *debil* (weak), whereas those who breathe well are considered *fuerte* (strong). Gabriela confirms that children's souls tend toward weakness, stating, "They have them [souls] weak. That is why they don't breathe right away; rather, they breathe slowly." Carolina and other midwives concur and insist that a child of weak soul will have trouble nursing. Carolina further says of a stillborn baby, "It isn't alive since it doesn't have respiration, it doesn't have life." Regardless of any previous ensoulment sparking fetal movement and growth, breathing remains critical for the child's ongoing life. Breathing enables minimally favorable soul strength and indexes it physically.

BODY STRENGTH, SOUL STRENGTH, EMOTION

Midwives hold strong views about the soul strength of children and adults and of women and men. But while midwives and most locals consider children's souls to be much weaker, or frailer, than those of adults, the souls of the elderly are an exception. Their bodies have run their course, and their souls have become weaker than those of other adults. So weak, in fact, that they are likened to children's souls. According to Gabriela, the souls of children are of the same lower strength as those of the elderly. "The ranima," she says, "is the same as the corazón of the child as with an old person." We see this in the similar care given to children and elders.

There is less agreement, though, about whether females or males have stronger souls. Celedonia argues that "the male always has the stronger corazón" and offers a physiological explanation. She says that if you look at a two-month-old aborted fetus, if it is a boy, his body will look well formed;

"his body is complete." However, a three-month-old girl's fetus will simply look like a "ball" with another ball inside it holding a yolk-like substance. Celedonia does not say how she can distinguish between male and female fetuses, but she insists on the stronger male soul. Midwives like Clemencia, though, invoke body temperature to show that the souls of males and females are of equal strength. She says that if men's and women's body temperatures each register thirty-seven degrees Celsius, then their almas are equally strong. Clemencia also associates low blood pressure with low body and soul strength. Interestingly, Kevin Groark (1997:45–46) finds that among Tzeltal and Tzotzil Maya, men are usually said to "possess more intrinsic heat than women," and thus more soul strength. Soul sameness or difference can thus be gauged through qualities of bodily development, heat, and fluid pressure.

Regardless of sex or soul strength, when fetuses are ensouled, their flesh begins to act, move, and grow. Soul, however, is responsible not only for growth and fetal pulse; it is also absolutely essential for engendering will. This fetal will manifests most strongly in pregnancy cravings, as described earlier. Fetal emotion also develops as an outcome of ensoul-ment. Upon receiving its animating essence in utero, the fetus senses emo-tions from his mother and those around her. He develops reactive emotions of his own. For example, if the mother is in a difficult or violent relationship with someone, like the child's father, the fetus feels emotional pains along with his mother. The midwife Clemencia relates that when her teenage daughter was pregnant, this daughter was beaten by her husband. Their baby turned out to be restless and would "jump" while sleeping. The infant was born with the fright sickness it had incurred in the womb.

The will and fear proper to ensouled humans also show in the fetus during an abortion, according to the midwife Mercedes. She likens the fetus to a *muxtuq'*, a tadpole, and describes how it swims away in fear from the "poison" introduced into its watery environment when its mother no longer wants it. Even at this stage, the fetus understands death and fears it. It experiences xib'iril in utero. This potential for fear marks a milestone in the development of the ensouled human, for this potential thereafter marks the human's condition.

Testimonies like these reveal how the expression of emotion is what makes the fetus seem most human and close to what Westerners might call a complete being, with a body, soul, and mind. That a newborn child screams leaves little doubt that he is sensate, that he fears pain and seeks comfort. The mother must therefore keep the child inside her comfortable, well fed, and happy by avoiding stressful situations and the feelings they convey within her. The pregnant mother has to shield her unborn child from her own pains, although much of what pains her inevitably reaches her child.

As restless, grief stricken, or afflicted as a fetus can become, the womb remains its originary place of comfort and sanctuary. Children have to be eased out of this protective envelope where soul first takes physical expression and be introduced into the human world.

FROM WOMB TO WORLD

Since mother and newborn are considered spiritually and emotionally interaffective in the days following birth, Comalapan midwives have them stay in close physical contact for a while, and apart from other people. Midwives from around the Maya region have often prescribed strict periods of confinement for mothers and their newborns to ensure that they have time to recuperate and bond, as well as to shield the children from any ill-intentioned individuals.[1]

Comalapans, though, have no inflexible rule of confinement for mother and child. A postpartum forty-day period of restricted activity used to be enforced, according to Celedonia, but it is no longer strictly observed. When women give birth today they are simply urged to stay indoors and keep themselves and their babies warm, usually for one to two weeks. During the first week, Celedonia gives the mothers a tuj bath every couple of days. The bathing ensures warmth, hygiene, and the flow of breast milk. She and other midwives sometimes affix abdominal binders on the mothers during this time. Midwives also have the mothers eat reconstitutive foods, and avoid "cold" foods and medicines like avocado and Alka-Seltzer.

People still remember the earlier confinement practices, though, and even recall the central role played by women's garments in these. One evening after returning with Aurora from the nearby town of Santa Cruz Balanya', she describes having seen an old woman in Balanya' wearing a *semeta' po't*, a cassock-like woven dress similar to the *ri'j po't* or *sobrehuipil* of Comalapa. She says the semeta' po't is rarely seen these days and that only old women wear it, much like the Comalapan ri'j po't. These garments remind her of the confinement practice.

Aurora says that when she was a girl (she is at least sixty when she tells me this), a mother would remain inside the house with her newborn for four weeks to forty days. The mother could not venture out into the street during this time. At the end of this period, the mother would don a ri'j po't, a garment that even younger women wore in those days. She then carried her baby inside the ri'j po't and walked to church, accompanied by her mother or mother-in-law. Inside the church, at the *ruk'u'x ajaw*, the Holy Sacrament, they would burn incense, light a candle, and formally "present" the child. The child would remain covered by the ri'j po't. The women would then return home with the child covered. The next day, the mother could step outside her house if she needed to. She was also permitted to take the child out of the house, although it was usually left at home since it was still small and might catch cold. When the child reached an age of four to six months, the mother could take it out more.

Aurora recalls how her mother-in-law accompanied her and her oldest child to the church like this, but observes that in Comalapa today, newborn children are carried to the church simply in blankets and wraps by their mothers. They are no longer carried under a ri'j po't, since virtually no woman under age forty wears this garment. Aurora says that some Catholics still present their babies at church, but that local Protestants do not.

This account affords a glimpse of a complex rite of confinement and emergence practiced a generation ago in Comalapa. The womb and home emerge as concentric spheres of protection enclosing the child at its most vulnerable moments, during which time many children succumb to illness. When the child is introduced to the community, a surrogate womb, the ri'j po't, marks a transformation of the child from a spiritually frail being dependent upon his mother's body for warmth and protection to a more spiritually fortified being dependent upon community sanction (the church) and upon products of local culture (the ri'j po't textile). Aurora's recollection confirms that recent Comalapans took the postpartum period very seriously and suggests that many people still practice select elements of the confinement ritual.

Just as the ri'j po't enabled the early enculturation of the Comalapan infant, in the nearby Kaqchikel town of Iximche' clothing also helps make the infant a social being. Carol Hendrickson (1995:101) describes how the newborn is wrapped in an *ombliguero*, a square piece of cloth that binds the infant's umbilicus to his body. The ombliguero is a prelude to the woven *faja*, the Maya belt that "will later contain, constrain, and thereby help socialize the growing child" (Hendrickson 1995:101). Shaping and molding the infant's body, the ombliguero prefigures how the child will later submit to the binding norms of local society, norms that act initially and dramatically upon the child's body. Similarly, the Tz'utujiil newborn in San Pedro la Laguna is bound with his arms at his sides and with his legs extended, so that the child "will grow up with straight, strong limbs" (Paul 1974:285). Pedrano babies are also tied into tiny chairs so their backs will become strong enough for the tasks they will later perform. Such procedures literally impress upon the Maya child's body the new reality of his life amid humans and away from the formative comfort of the womb.[2]

Like Tz'utujiils, Comalapa Kaqchikel Maya are concerned about the postnatal development of children. Comalapans extend this concern to the later lives of children, performing gender-induction practices focused on the umbilicus, as discussed earlier. And since parents also want to know whether their children will have specialized vocations, the midwife is often asked to determine this.

VISCERA AND VOCATIONS

Midwives look for signs that portend a child's vocation. When Celedonia delivers a boy whose head and body are enclosed in a *bolsita* (small bag) of amniotic tissue, for example, then he is predestined to be an *aq'omanel* (physician). A girl with such a tissue is said to be a future midwife. A caul on the infant's head is both a portent and an immediate danger, however, since the caul must be quickly removed from the face. Infants in San Pedro la Laguna are similarly observed for vocational signs.[3] As the first person to see the birth signs, the Comalapa midwife is responsible for telling the parents about their child's likely vocation.

When Comalapan children are born without vocational signs, however, their families can be disappointed. But these families can still set a vocation into motion by enacting contiguous procedures. The midwife Eva laughs when describing how some people want to give their child's umbilicus to a physician so that their child can become a physician, as mentioned earlier. She strongly disagrees with people who try to do this. Yet, for Comalapans who pay witness to the symbolic and empirical logic of umbilical and placental ritual, this method makes complete sense. Enough contiguous procedures are available to encourage families to imprint a vocation upon their child's destiny.

Comalapans worry about their children's lives long before they can even feel the fetuses' heartbeats. To properly "grow" a child, the nature of the human soul, and specifically that of the child's soul, has to be understood. The midwife helps parents demystify the soul's inflections through the fetus's movement, growth, and finally emotions, unfolding over several months. She is there to meet the physical and spiritual needs of the mother, and her presence ensures more than just a successful birth. It helps establish the sacrality proper to family building.

Lois Paul and Benjamin Paul (1975:712) called the Pedrano Tz'utujiil midwife "a psychopomp in reverse, conducting souls into the land of the living." While this is also true for the Comalapan midwife, the conduction is not complete in Comalapa with the birth. The child must still be shepherded into the world of humans, where he or she will face many dangers. Avoiding these dangers depends on knowing the child's vulnerabilities and on knowing whether the child has a revealed vocation. It also depends on initiation rites that bind the child's soul to his or her body.

THE BAPTISMAL ANCHOR

The rite of baptism marks a critical moment for the child and reveals the soul's reliance on human action to secure its relationship with the body. Many Comalapans say that fetuses and young children are vulnerable to sickness partly because, until children are baptized, they are susceptible to "soul trouble." Baptism intersects with local beliefs that children are only preliminarily or tentatively ensouled and that a spiritual procedure can protect their physical health. But Comalapans identify with different denominations, and these influence how people apply and interpret this initiatory rite.

Protestant Comalapans, for example, say that baptism signals a conscious acceptance of Jesus Christ, so it is performed during a person's age of reason, usually in the teenage or later years. They openly disdain the Catholic practice of infant baptism, saying that it conflicts with the teachings of John the Baptist. Local Catholics, on the other hand, say different things about baptism. Many say that through baptism, one becomes a child of God, one enters into a good state with God, one is recognized by God, or some similar pronouncement. Some state simply that, through baptism, "one feels that one is Catholic." For Protestants, then, baptism signifies an acceptance *of* God, whereas for Catholics baptism signifies an acceptance *by* God.

Catholics, however, reveal a more practical side to the rite. They feel that the newborn's soul still lacks complete internal cohesion, or that it is somehow not fully kindled. The midwife Gabriela says of the newborn, "When he isn't baptized he doesn't have a living corazón," and that "[when] baptized, he now has a living corazón." This neonatal soul condition accounts for the susceptibility of newborns and children to soul debilities like xib'iril and ruwa winäq. Children who do not yet have "a living corazón" often experience bouts of irritability, sleeplessness, and illness.

Baptism relieves children from these afflictions, many traditionalist Catholics say. Through the church baptism and home reception, "the *mal* [affliction] leaves them [children]; they sleep, they don't get sick much," Gabriela insists. "Baptism helps them to be left alone," she adds, explaining that it allows caregivers to attend to other duties. When a newborn becomes very sick and seems likely to die, parents are urged to baptize the child immediately. People testify that, following baptism, some children promptly recover, renewing faith in the ritual's curative powers. Indeed, a local physician, Dr. Pérez, reports how the parents of a child dying from diarrheal dehydration went to great expense to quickly baptize their child. They did this instead of seeking early medical care. But the midwife Celedonia laments that sometimes even a priestly baptism is not enough to save a child: "Sometimes, children are about to die . . . but, sometimes, at the moment of baptism, the child dies [anyway]."

This pragmatic view of baptism clearly differs from the dogmatic one. Local Catholics think that baptism can strengthen the child's soul, make it resistant to fright, and protect it from the unwelcome attention of others.

Baptism is thus a prophylactic against debilitating physical conditions and can even reduce symptom severity by therapeutically fortifying the soul. Comalapans express this view of baptism only after first insisting that they perform it for the sake of tradition and holy community.

The Catholic Church's view of this sacrament as an expiatory ritual for "original sin" does not seem very relevant to traditionalist Comalapans. The notion of original sin perplexes some people, such as the soul therapist Tencha, who says of a stillborn (unbaptized) child's soul, "Perhaps it goes with God . . . it doesn't have sin, I don't believe. How can children sin in the womb?" Catholics sometimes mention sin in the context of baptism, but usually in reference to the parents' negligence should their child die unbaptized. Infant baptism is a healthful and pragmatic ritual in the popular Catholic view; for a parent to deny this to her child is tantamount to denying life-saving medical treatment. Celedonia expresses that "if a person baptizes his children, his conscience is clean." He has done everything possible to improve the physical state of his child by consolidating the child's soul strength.

This is not to imply that Protestants, who do not baptize their children at a very young age, do not view their children's spiritual and physical state as vulnerable to disturbance and illness. In fact, Comalapan Protestants do perform ritual measures for children, revealing that they, too, consider children vulnerable in their early years. But since Protestant groups do not address this vulnerability in a uniform way in early life, their understandings of the early soul are harder to identify.

Among professed Catholics in Comalapa, though, the desire to strengthen and consolidate the newborn's soul is apparent, and congruent with how other Maya try to "fix" the infant's inner soul to his body to reduce his spiritual weakness.[4] By applying a readily available sacramental procedure, baptism, Catholic Comalapans redress their children's weak spiritual state and deflect the physical problems that can come with it. Early care of the soul through baptism and other means is vital to the sustained health of Comalapan souls and bodies.

Midwives reveal key features of the soul through their work. Chief among these is that the animating essence is detectable via bodily signs from an early point in human life, and that the womb is the first place where it can be detected. Important processes of animation occur in the womb, implicating the placenta, the umbilical cord, and, ultimately, the fetus. As fetal ensoulment takes place, fetal sentience develops and manifests itself to both mother and midwife. The midwife is in a unique position to witness and experience these changes, and to interpret their inflections.

Blood is central to understanding soul. Umbilical blood drops are the embodiment of future children, and blood, especially umbilical blood, is seen as the medium and manifestation of human life-energy. This quality of blood is foregrounded when the midwife glimpses the mother's future fertility in the umbilical cord. Life-energy is also expressed in how vigorously the child takes his first breaths, since breathing is his first visible movement. The placenta, meanwhile, binds to the mother's physical health just as the umbilicus binds to the child's social health, and different practices reaffirm this. Other birth organs and postpartum procedures speak to the vocational aspect of soul by presaging certain dispositions in the child. Of immediate importance to the young child, though, is strengthening his soul and body through baptism. The Maya midwife attends to these and other aspects of childbearing, engaging a world in which spiritual agency takes decisive form through human bodies.

Part Three

THE SOUL THERAPIST AND
SECURING OF SPIRIT

CHAPTER SEVEN

Soul Therapists and Their Beginnings

MANY COMALAPANS TURN TO SOUL therapists when they suffer from spiritual maladies. These specialists, the oyonela', are best known for calling out to the lost soul portions of Comalapans afflicted with xib'iril (fright sickness) in rituals known as oyonïk (callings). By applying their knowledge of spirit, blood, and body through oyonïk, these specialists try to restore Comalapans to wholeness. This chapter will explore how oyonela' enter this vocation, and how dreams often supply them with the knowledge and authority they need to help the suffering. It will then discuss how these specialists rely on their signature calling ritual to address whatever fractioning a person's soul has experienced.

A person first begins restoring souls and bodies to health because she is either compelled by an urgent situation to perform oyonïk or because she is divinely mandated to do so. Established oyonela' emphasize one or the other of these paths of entry into their work, but any one person's story can include elements of both. When novice curers treat people successfully, others hear of their abilities and seek them out. As more people use them, their public legitimacy grows. Gradually, they become known as oyonela'. But to hear it from oyonela', the whole experience feels quite abrupt.

Oyonela' Lola and David entered their roles under conditions of surprise and urgency. In Lola's case, one day she found her son suffering from xib'iril. Not knowing whom to turn to, she was urged by neighbors to do a calling ritual for the boy. She did so at a nearby river, an auspicious place for oyonïk, and the boy recovered. From then on, people came asking her to treat other cases of xib'iril. Stranger circumstances brought curing responsibilities upon David. He recounts that a brother-in-law once accused him, two of his brothers, three of his sisters, and three of their children of plotting to kill David's father. The brother-in-law even persuaded the police to raid the family dwellings and arrest these nine people. A young girl of the family witnessed the arrests and became frightened. During his incarceration, David's mother notified him that the girl had become sick, probably with xib'iril. When David and the others were freed from jail a month later, he performed three calling ceremonies for the girl. She recovered, and other people soon came asking him to treat their xib'iril.

Oyonela' often experience revelatory moments before beginning their healing practices. A divine mandate can signal that a person must accept a vocation or a task, and that to ignore the mandate can bring severe consequences upon her and her family. The mandates might not be clear at first, though. The oyonel Mela, for example, had a couple of dreams that initially puzzled her. Prior to the 1976 earthquake, she dreamed of an angel who approached her, retreated from her, and then finally knelt before her. Then she dreamed of an old man who appeared at her kitchen door. She asked him what he wanted, but he simply peered three times through the door. Some time later, Mela began performing oyonïk, with good results. She eventually considered these dreams the prelude to her curing career.

Linda also received arcane messages in a dream series. In one dream, with the Virgin Mary at her side, she stood facing a large pool of water across which a plank was set. The Virgin told Linda to help individuals cross from one side of the water to the other. When Linda asked how she was to help the almas (souls) do this, the Virgin simply replied, "It is a task I'm giving you." When Linda awoke, she told her father of the strange dream. He told her that the Virgin had given her a vocation. But there was more.

Linda later dreamed that she was running from her house to a curing ceremony, carrying a basket containing roses and three candles. When she arrived where the patient lay gravely ill in bed, she noticed another woman standing in the room. Linda was about to start the curing session when the woman told her, "Not yet. I have something to do first." Linda replied, "But they summoned me," and then realized that the woman was the Virgin Mary. She watched the Virgin anoint the patient's head with oil. The patient then sat up, and Linda performed her part of the curing. Shortly after dreaming this, Linda was asked to treat a Comalapan woman who lived in the town of Iximche'. Other people had tried, without success, to heal the woman, but Linda went there and successfully treated her. Ever since then, Linda asks the Virgin for help when she heals. The Virgin still provides the anointing while Linda provides the roses and candles.

Moments of divine revelation do not always precede a curer's work, however. Many Comalapan curers receive spiritual messages well after they have begun practicing. Angélica is one such oyonel. For six months, she had been dreaming that she was on home visits to treat several young girls. Then, in one dream, she entered a house and noticed a man standing inside. When she realized that the man was Christ, he told her not to worry, that all she asked of him would be granted. Angélica was enjoined in dreams like this to have faith, and that the people she treated also have faith so that their petitions would be granted. As with other oyonela', she did not understand her dreams at first. Eventually, though, they brought clarity to her work while reaffirming her established purpose.

In some revelatory dreams, a helpful presence not only visits the dreamer but teaches the dreamer to cure. Curers who are visited like this usually say, "I learned from my dreams," without detailing the visionary scenarios that taught them. Comalapans hold this means of instruction in very high esteem. Maya of other places also awaken to their vocations through dreams. For example, a Momostenango K'iche' destined to become a calendrical specialist might dream of stylized images of shrines, divining tools, and body lightning, the means by which blood communicates through the daykeeper's body (Tedlock 1981:317). In San Juan Chamula, meanwhile, different kinds of Tzotzil curers and ritual musicians may be visited by saints in their dreams who bestow special skills and knowledge upon the dreamers (Groark 2009:714).

Comalapan oyonela', whether selected through urgent situations or dreams, mainly deal with diagnosing and treating xib'iril and ruwa winäq, which I discussed in chapter 1. Other maladies take up less of their time. Of these two syndromes, though, xib'iril creates the most worry and receives the most specialized care through a very recognizable ritual.

THE CALLING CEREMONY

Sooner or later, the long-term visitor to Comalapa learns of the healing ceremonies called oyonïk or *llamadas*. Observant visitors might see some of their local hosts slip away at dusk with a basket of roses concealed beneath a shawl. Or, they may find a certain older woman appearing, evening after evening, on the family doorstep, who is then whisked away to a bedroom or a corner of the living room. These subtle windows into local life, if they do not escape notice entirely, can alert the newcomer to local concerns about completeness. They might even alert her to how Comalapans enact this state of completeness in a world in which souls are too easily pulled apart.

For Comalapans, oyonïk are important but unremarkable. They are therapeutic and restorative measures for cases of xib'iril, unique only in that they require a bit of unordinary planning, a few special items, and an oyonel. That oyonela' seem plentiful in Comalapa testifies to the frequent need and special place for them in local life. When a family finds itself needing an oyonïk, it is not usually hard to arrange. They can even choose where to hold the oyonïk and how many to have, although certain preferences prevail.

People stage oyonïk to reintegrate or reincorporate a fractioned part of the soul. This being the case, most people prefer holding oyonïk in the xib'iril sufferer's home, since it is the place most familiar and comfortable to her. Oyonela' like Herlinda and Julia thus treat clients in the clients' homes. At other times, xib'iril sufferers have the ritual done in an oyonel's home. People from Comalapa's satellite villages who enter the town center on market days favor this option. They take advantage of their town forays to visit oyonela' they have heard about, and on such days, oyonela' like Tencha and Lencha get inundated with work. But these oyonela' also get visited by many nearby neighbors throughout the week, and I have seen a steady stream of clients entering their homes almost daily.

Oyonïk are usually performed in series. The recommended number varies among oyonela', but the number is typically a multiple of three. Most oyonela' agree that each client needs three oyonïk, but others argue that serious xib'iril cases can require up to nine oyonïk. Lencha is unusual in that she advocates five oyonïk for her clients. Village dwellers can comply with the three-oyonïk requirement by visiting town center–based oyonela' on the three market days: Tuesday, Friday, and Sunday. Town-center dwellers, on the other hand, have the option of visiting with their oyonela' on three consecutive days, ideally in the evenings.

According to oyonela' and other Comalapans, the last oyonïk of a series should be extra special. It should take on a celebratory tone, and, if possible, it should take place where the fright actually occurred. This is why food items like hearty soups, pastries, coffee, and chocolate are offered to the assembled during the last oyonïk of a series. Smaller versions of this food distribution often follow each oyonïk, with the oyonel receiving the first portion. Fewer oyonïk series, though, are completed with a visit to the spot in the hills where the xib'iril sufferer reportedly lost part of his soul. Families who do venture out for the final oyonïk usually bring food to offer in sacrifice and to consume in thanks for the healing.

Like Maya of other towns, Comalapa Kaqchikels consider rivers auspicious places to perform calling ceremonies (Gillin 1948:392; Instituto Indigenista Nacional 1978:550–51; Tetzagüíc Guajan 1997:411), even for cases of fright that do not occur by a river. Some Comalapans claim that rivers carry away ills, while others say that rivers return strength and health to a sufferer. Expressing the latter idea, the oyonel David recommends conducting oyonïk by a river because "water is life, it is for this reason." By way of the river, he says, "the strength of the blood that has been lost returns."

David's confidence in the restorative power of water concords with the widespread inclusion of water in oyonïk. In every oyonïk I have witnessed in and around Comalapa, water is a central element. Typically, the water is placed in a plastic bowl called a *palangana*. The palangana is set on the ground before an altar, and red and white rose petals are sprinkled in and around it. During the ceremony, the oyonel leans over and looks carefully into the water, taps the palangana with a stick, and calls out the name of the afflicted, beckoning him to return home. Gazing at the water, the oyonel focuses on the likely whereabouts of the client's stray soul portion and calls it by name. In this way, most oyonela' utilize water as a visionary portal to track the soul's behavior.

Water is central to oyonïk because, as a vital element of life, it is ideal for summoning the life-force, ruchuq'a', of a xib'iril sufferer. With the "return" of a person's health and happiness through the oyonïk, his blood is also restored to its bodily abode. The oyonel Victor emphatically recognizes this return of soul and blood, stating, "That is why I tell my susto patients, 'cheer up!'—so that the blood will return. . . . The blood is the color of the roses."

Victor here reveals how red roses enable the soul/blood/health recovery process: the redness of the roses invokes the redness of the blood, especially when the roses are placed in water, whether in rivers or palanganas. Red blood is hot, healthy blood. The imbuing of clear water with redness enacts a powerful simulacrum of blood restoration (Hinojosa 2006). But why use white rose petals if redness is sought? The answer might lie in how, while red rose petals can be used without added white rose petals, white rose petals are used only together with red rose petals. This suggests that redness must feature strongly in the flower element of oyonïk. Accordingly, Claudia Madsen (1965:106–7) found that fright curers in Tepepán, Mexico, favor red flowers. There, red flowers, and especially geraniums, are highly valued in fright-sickness curing and are placed in a bowl of water into which the curer shouts the patient's name three times to retrieve the lost soul (see Soustelle 1962:194). In Comalapa, roses are important in this way, but in some oyonïk roses also physically jolt the body back into health, as I explain below.

All of the oyonïk I observed from 1992 to 1996 incorporated water and roses. Other elements like candles, tobacco, meat, chocolate, incense, and liquor, however, are used variably by different oyonela'. Herlinda is one oyonela' who completely excludes candles, incense, and liquor from her oyonïk. She says it is because these items are too expensive, but her evangélico church peers also pressure her to not use them, as they do not align with her church's devotional program. In oyonïk conducted by Catholic oyonela', meanwhile, candles and incense are usually as ubiquitous as water and roses, although different oyonela' prefer to use either wax (*cera*), paraffin (*parafina*), or tallow (*sebo*) candles. Many Catholic oyonela' include liquor, especially *kuxa*, in their oyonïk. It is either drunk, massaged onto the abdomen, or offered in oblations upon the ground. Tobacco and meat are most visible in oyonïk conducted in the countryside when a *día de campo* is held. Chocolate is used in many oyonïk and is often served with pastries following home-based ceremonies.

Ritual elements can be revealed in dreams to oyonela'. When this happens, oyonela' pay close attention, because the elements dreamed may have multiple significance. In the oyonel Linda's case, she was brought a woman who had developed xib'iril after hearing gunshots. The woman's family suspected that witchcraft was involved, but Linda advised them not to think so, warning that the mal, the malevolent agency, might then send more illness. Linda then dreamed of a voice telling her to use seven candles to cure the woman. It seemed a literal message at first, but she eventually understood that the seven candles represented the seven oyonïk she was to perform. After performing the seven revealed oyonïk, Linda "escorted" the woman's soul fragment from the street back to her.

FIGURE 7.1
An *oyonel* kneeling during an *oyonïk* ritual. Note the water,
rose petals, censer, liquor, candles, and stick. Photo by author.

Comalapans point out how important ritual elements like candles and tobacco are for an oyonïk to be successful. Oyonela' watch that the candles burn evenly and completely, without excessive wax spillage. Other people point out that the cigarettes lit and offered during oyonïk must consume themselves completely, as a sign that all ceremonial participants are sincere of purpose. When candles burn irregularly or when tobacco extinguishes itself prematurely, it is said that someone in the ceremony is *de dos corazones*, of two hearts. This condition of insincerity or ulterior purpose can undermine the oyonïk and even endanger those involved.

Participants in calling ceremonies know, then, that for ritual items to be properly offered, officiators and others have to be sincere of purpose. But even though great care goes into selecting and presenting the things to be sacrificed to the rajawala' earth lords, there is more to oyonïk than this. Specific incidents led me to understand just how much natural features like rivers and hills, and man-made objects like statuary and cloth, play important roles in soul therapy as well.

CHAPTER EIGHT

Elusive Spirits and Surrogate Bodies

ONE OF THE BIGGEST DECISIONS an oyonel must make leading up to a calling ritual is determining where to stage it. Most oyonïk are performed in the home, but they can be done to more powerful effect if they take place in the countryside, where the rajawala' reside and where many cases of xib'iril originate. If a client does not know where in the countryside to perform the ritual, the client's dreams can provide the answer. Since people suffering from soul fright often report dreaming of the location where a part of their soul is lingering, dream information can be very helpful. This underscores the role of place in healing, especially in how the animistic terrain around Comalapa must be directly engaged in the soul recovery process.

The outcomes of oyonïk also depend on the kind of ritual tools the oyonel will use, or even make. In one setting or other, most oyonela' use commercially made products like plastic bowls and candles. Other items, like plaster statues and pictures of saints, are more specialized, and not all oyonela' use them. But some oyonela' take their toolkit a step further: they fashion effigies of their clients to use when their clients cannot personally attend a healing session. The use of these different kinds of items signals how Kaqchikels have drawn extensively from Spanish culture to build their own ritual inventory, appropriating and adapting as needed. It also reveals the creative ways that Kaqchikels encourage the pathways of soul.

This chapter will use vignettes to discuss how one oyonel applies her knowledge of soul and body in a specific sacred locale, and how another oyonel sees her ritual tools as alive. These episodes brought home to me, in unexpected ways, how the land plays a vital role in soul therapy and how oyonela' nurture very close ties with their *sacra*. Both of these experiences

made deep, formative impressions on me. Lastly, in this chapter I will discuss the k'al k'u'x, and how this crafted embodiment of a human makes
soul therapy possible in a world in which people's responsibilities take
them far outside the protective embrace of their homes.

AT THE RIVER'S EDGE

It is 10:15 in the morning and I am walking to Alejandro's house in
Comalapa's San Antonio barrio. He is not expecting me, as I arrived in
Guatemala only a few days ago, near the start of the 1995 rainy season, and
in Comalapa just yesterday. His adopted son, Jesús, receives me at the door
and leads me upstairs to the small, cold room where Alejandro and his
apprentice, Julián, paint oil paintings in the local primitivist style. They
seem happy to see me and even happier when I give the two men some
fine-tipped paintbrushes I brought from the United States and give to Jesús
some magic markers and acrylic paints.

Knowing my interest in spiritual healing, Alejandro tells me that he is
about to go to a calling ceremony for his brother-in-law, out on the road to
Panabajal. He asks, "Do you want to go?" "Absolutely," I tell him. He says
that the oyonïk will take place at 11:00 a.m., so we need to start out on the
road by 10:30 a.m. As we leave his tall, four-story house, I ask to stop by my
house so I can pick up my camera and a machete. Collecting these things,
we begin our westward walk on the road going past the health center.

Our progress is blocked by enormous sections of road turned into mire
by the rains of the past few days. Alejandro finds a path through the maize
fields, and we take it. After avoiding the road's trouble spots by cutting
through the fields, we emerge onto the original road and soon pass Las
Delicias to our left. The road skirts a series of fields and climbs up the
winding slopes of a large hill. I watch Alejandro's steady gait. One might
guess from his slight limp that he once sustained an injury, but it is less
obvious that he barely escaped paralysis following a spinal injury from a
1988 car accident. The accident left him in traction for three months.

We descend the hill and arrive at the Pixkaya' River, crossing it at a
bridge just downriver from an abandoned mill. Turning right onto a
marked path, we take a riverside trail that leads us to two log bridges. At
a grassy clearing on the other bank, we find about fifteen people waiting for

Alejandro, including Telésfora (his wife), her parents, her sister, her brother, the oyonel, and others. Several large pots bubble over fires, revealing this to be a día de campo, an outing at which food is prepared. Food, I reflect, and not a moment too soon.

Telésfora greets me and thanks me for coming to the oyonïk of her brother, Raúl. She points out a ground altar, built on a broad mat of green pine needles. Its back wall is a white gunnysack placed against three upright sticks, against which leans a framed chromolithograph of the *santa familia* featuring Christ, Mary, and Joseph. Bundles of multicolored flowers and ferns flank the image. Scattered in front of the picture are white and red rose petals, in front of which sit two baskets, one holding yellow and tallow candles and white and red rose petals, the other a bundle of *copal*. I notice a few pastries and one really elaborate bread, partially wrapped in a red cloth. A label-less beer bottle stands beside a half-full bottle of Coke. A smoking censer completes the tableau.

Raúl tells me that a fright befell him years ago, although he is not sure exactly when. When I ask him how he knows this, he says that for years he had been feeling that something was not right with him. He was feeling weak most days and did not have much of an appetite. And even though each day brought more fatigue, he could not sleep well. The lethargy began interfering with his work and created tensions at home. When his family saw how withdrawn he was becoming, and when he felt himself slipping deeper and deeper into despair, he knew that the fright had finally "appeared." It had been slow in reaching full expression, but it inevitably did. That is when his family asked the oyonel Alicia to begin performing oyonïk for him. Those oyonïk have led him here, to what Telésfora and Alejandro explain is his ninth and final calling ritual. The other eight callings were done at his house back in town.

After a rich and very satisfying meal of beef and vegetable caldo, and more than a few drinks of kuxa, everyone gathers around the altar. It is 11:35 a.m. The oyonel Alicia kneels directly in front of it, facing the santa familia. The family that seeks her help kneels to her right. Raúl, flanked by his parents, casts his eyes low. The oyonïk begins.

Following Alicia's lead, all in attendance cross themselves. She begins her prayer in Kaqchikel, reciting a litany of saints, angels, and archangels. Taking eight yellow candles from the basket, she turns to Raúl, marks a cross upon him with the candles, and calls out, "Katan pe, akuchi at k'o wi,' achike yab'ison," "Come hither, where are you? Why are you saddened?" Alicia recites this invocation, blows twice toward Raúl, repeats the invocation, and blows twice again. Facing the altar, Alicia then collects five tallow candles and rose petals and prays. Again she makes a cross on Raúl and rubs his chest, back, and sides with the bundle. She holds the bundle to his lips, and he kisses it. The rose petals are then sprinkled onto the pine needles before the altar.

As the oyonel prepares to return the candles to the altar, someone offers her a machete. The blade cuts through the conjoined candle wicks. Alicia inserts the eight yellow candles into the ground in a row before the altar, then inserts the five tallow candles in a parallel row before them. She places the bread between herself and the tallow candles. She then lights the yellow candles from right to left and follows suit with the tallow candles from left to right.

Alicia then takes more bread out of the cloth and places it in a plate. Over this and the candles she swings the censer, praying some ten Hail Marys and an Our Father. When this round of prayer is over, she places the Coke bottle beside the bread and continues praying, invoking a litany of saints and the "ángel de la guardia, ángel Rafael, Miguel arcángel," "the guardian angel, angel Raphael, archangel Michael." The attendees all cross themselves and stand.

Alicia looks around and locates two *varejones* (switches). Raúl's parents take hold of each of his arms. We all begin a slow walk down a path leading to the river. At the water's edge, Raúl takes a handful of red and white rose petals, crosses himself, rubs the petals over himself, leans forward, and throws the petals upstream. Brandishing the varejón, the oyonel immediately strikes the water carrying the petals past, calling out again to Raúl. He repeats the procedure three times, as does she. Alicia then takes a handful of petals from a basket, dips them in the river, and throws them at the people standing behind her. She repeats this.

When the river bank phase is complete, Raúl's parents again take him by the arms and escort him back up the path. As we walk, everyone calls out, "Raúl, jo', ak'uchi at k'o wakamin," "Raúl, come along, where are you now?" They lead him to the edge of a square stone pool into which a brook runs. Normally, water drains from the pool to the river, but today its outlet has been plugged with plastic sheeting to allow the pool to fill. Alejandro says that it is a natural pool but that it took some additional digging to bring it to its present form.

Alicia perches herself at the pool edge and prays. Raúl again takes a handful of rose petals, crosses and rubs himself with them, and throws them into the pool. Alicia reaches down and strikes the floating petals, calling out, "Katan pe, achike carro, achike calvario, achike ixoq, kayaketej," "Come hither, what bus (are you in), which sacred hill (are you on), what woman (are you with), awaken, get up." She blows on him three times and then strikes him three times with the varejón; she also strikes the rock they are standing on. Alicia takes a handful of rose petals and throws them at Raúl and then at everyone else. Raúl is again flanked by his parents, who walk him back to the altar, gripping his arms. All follow and call out again for Raúl to return.

When the family arrives at the altar, everyone kneels, and the oyonel leads the group in a Credo. Again, she offers other prayers, including an Our Father and an Ave María. Alicia then pours beer before the burning tallow candles and around the plate of bread. When she has poured Coke around the bread, all cross themselves and rise to greet and thank each other.

One of Raúl's sisters, Mayra, begins a supplemental part of the ceremony. Most of the party remains kneeling around the altar. Mayra reads from a Catholic missal, reading aloud a story about a woman involved with three miracles. The account seems to deal with a woman who brought forth a spring of water that restored the sight of a blind man. "With this they believed her to be the Virgin, and they constructed a temple there for her, and there have been many miracles ever since," she says. She then leads the group in an Our Father, a spontaneous prayer, a Hail Mary, another prayer, five more Hail Marys, another prayer, and a Credo. Following this, Mayra recites a series of supplications, including "Ave María, ruega por nosotros, sagrada familia, ruega por nosotros," "Mary, pray for us, Holy Family, pray for us." Everyone rises to again thank everyone else.

I watch Alicia walk to one of the kitchen fires and pour a roll of copal into it. After visiting a while with the rest of us by the altar, she produces a pack of Casino cigarettes, lights three at the fire, and leaves them on the ground close to the fire. Alejandro tells me that they are for the dueño, the spirit-owner of this place. This is also why the beer was poured out, he adds.

Raúl's father now pours a cup of kuxa for the oyonel. She drinks it. He then pours one for himself, drains the cup, and proceeds to offer a cup to everyone. He places one in my hand, so I drink. Someone is passing out cigarettes, and soon someone is lighting one for me. For several minutes everyone mills about, and I occasionally point out items on the altar for someone to explain to me. They eagerly answer my questions.

After a short time, everyone returns to the altar. Alicia is holding a basket containing eggs, rue, and some other herbs. She takes an egg, clutching a handful of herbs in the process, and rubs Raúl with the bundle. She replaces the egg in the basket and repeats the procedure with the other egg. Telésfora is now standing behind Raúl, holding a palangana of water. When she finishes sweeping Raúl, the oyonel breaks the egg into the palangana. Then she takes the first egg from the basket, breaks it, and drops it into the palangana, shell and all. Nodding at the results, she seems confirmed in her suspicions. She tells Telésfora to take the palangana to the river and throw its contents in, which she does. It is now 12:30 p.m., nearly an hour since the oyonïk began.

When the rites come to an end, people stand around and chat. Alejandro mentions that the place where we are standing is called Chuwatz'an, "place of the salt," so named for the salty sparkle visible in the ground. He adds that the environs of the square pool is known as Chi Kisiwan Aq, "gorge of the pigs," because there were once many pigs kept in this valley. Another man says that the pool is also called Chi Valerio, because a man named Valerio used to own this hillside. Someone gives me another drink.

Raúl says that evangélicos, Protestant Comalapans, come to this pool to get baptized. They enter clothes and all, Alejandro confirms. Suddenly curious about how both Catholics and Protestants use this place, albeit for different purposes, I ask Alejandro whether evangélicos also suffer from xib'iril. They do, he says, but they do not know how to cure it.

Everyone is starting to look nervous about the dark clouds moving in from the east, and people quickly gather up their belongings. Pots and bowls disappear into gunny sacks, and the fires belch smoky good-byes as river water is poured onto them. Over by the bed of pine needles that once bore the altar, the santa familia is carefully placed in a sack and handed to me to carry. Someone hands me a large plastic vessel of sweetened coffee, and I struggle with its wet lip as I try covering my knapsack and the image under my small rain poncho. By the time the drizzle intensifies into a light rain, we are all walking downstream along the river. The rain is falling steadily now and harder, making the trail slippery. My cap is heavy with rainwater. With a bulky object in each hand, I wonder if I will be able to recover my balance if I suddenly slip.

We are now on the main road. As we ascend a steep grade, rivulets of water rush down to meet our feet, and we have to step carefully around them. I feel sorry for the ladies wearing sandals, but my own shoes are trapping cold water and mud with every step. When I look up from the road I see my companions plodding steadily on the slope above me, but to my right lies an unexpected sight. I have been unaware of the height to which we have climbed until now, and the open valley beside us stretches into a sudden depth with the opposite hillside fading into the misty reaches of the rain-soaked air. The rain's angle guides my eye along an oblique trajectory down to the river far below. I feel wary about the edge of the road, but also drawn to it. I tighten my grip on the santa familia sack. It is not hard to understand that things happen here in the hills. If only I were not lugging this amphora of coffee and rainwater.

Ritual objects like the ones used in this outing can, ironically, become a liability to the oyonel. If an oyonel is very successful at soul restoration, other people may become jealous of her and her sacra. One outcome of these jealousies is the kind of theft suffered by the oyonel Lencha.

AN EMPTINESS IN MY *CORAZÓN*

Walking the muddy streets to Lencha's house today, I am thinking about the many calling rituals I have seen her perform over the years. Since I became a regular visitor at her house, she has taught me a lot, although it usually takes me months to sort out the minutiae of her words. Lately, however, she has not been home much. This is strange because she is the one Comalapan oyonel I know who comes closest to being a full-time ritualist. At virtually any hour of the daytime, at least a couple of people can be found waiting quietly for her in her patio. These are usually women with infants in their laps and other children in tow. Local people know her house to have an open door, so they stream in steadily from morning onward, more so on market days. But today is different, and something is wrong.

I enter Lencha's patio and find her walking out of her small altar room accompanied by an old woman, completely distraught. Unsure what is the matter, I hand her the bag of pastries I bought for her. She tells me that something bad has happened. "They've stolen my holy images," she says, and begins weeping. Lencha points behind her to the altar in the small dark room where she performs oyonïk. I glimpse a sudden bareness of the room, and when I return my gaze to her, her face buried in her apron. She says that it happened the other day, Wednesday, after I left her house. I think back two days when I came for a visit but left when I found her extremely busy attending people. It was then that someone came in and took the images, she says, and that is why she did not work yesterday. Lencha struggles to say, "And my parents have already died, now I have nothing," and cries.

When I ask her what was stolen, she says that "they" took some standing images and the Christs she had hanging on the wall; they just cut them off. She says of the main image, "Who knows what forefather it came from?" Lencha says that an aunt had once asked her for that image, but she would not give it to her. She explains how the Virgin Mary told her in a dream that, should anyone ask her for the image, not to give it to them. So, Lencha was never going to give them away or sell them, even if someone asked for them. I ask if they took anything else, and she says no, that she is not going to allege that they took this or that, only that they took the images. She recalls that there were clothes hanging on the line at the time since the rain had kept the clothes from drying, but that no clothes were stolen, only the images. "Who knows how they managed to get in?"

Unsure of what to do next, I comment that we should feel sorry for the persons who stole the images, because they will pay a heavy price for this. She composes herself for a moment and agrees. I add that even though they took the images, the images will not do them any good, because their espíritu stayed here, nodding to the altar room. Again, she agrees and says that, yes, we should feel sorry for those responsible. I remind her that she has cured many people in the little room, and that people will always come for her, because she has healed them in the name of God. She says, "Yes . . . who knows how many thousands were cured?" She places her face in her cupped hands. When she recovers her voice she says, "Thank you for the consolation," repeating this a few times, and adding, "Pardon me for not being able to attend to you." I tell her not to worry about me.

Lencha resumes talking about the images, saying that some people are critical of them: "There are people who say that they don't move, that they don't have ears with which to hear, that they don't have eyes with which to see, but yes, they do move on the inside." She tells me again about how the images have cured many people, lamenting, "I love those images, I adore them, I love them . . ." I repeat that she has cured many in God's name, that many sick people have entered her little room and have come out well, and that people will continue to look for her and trust in her. Nodding, she clarifies, "I do not cure; it is God who cures."

She seems a little more composed now. Trying to make the situation a little easier for her (and for me), I say that, in the end, we will all turn to dust, like the images, but perhaps our espíritu will live on, just like the espíritu of the images lives on in the altar room. "Yes," she distractedly agrees, "our espíritu, only God knows what it does, we ourselves don't even notice what it does." I reflect that he will judge everybody based on their actions. I add that we should be glad we are alive, that we have our family, that she has her daughter, a roof over her head, and food. She thanks me again for consoling her, but her eyes well up in tears again. Lencha says that she does not have anyone to turn to to get the images back, that she has no way of pressing for them, even if she knew who took them. Little by little she will feel better, I tell her; we undergo trials sometimes, but we will prevail. Weeping, she says, "I have an emptiness in my corazón; it doesn't give joy; it doesn't give happiness." Placing my hand on her shoulder, I tell her I will come back again to see her, to check on how she is doing. She thanks me one last time for the consolation and the visit, and I walk out the gate.

Since Lencha lives alone with her adopted daughter in this house, the images have been welcome company to her. But the emptiness of the altar room now tells her that a loved one has moved out of her life, disappeared, with the unexpected swiftness of death. I noticed on her altar today that she still has several images, like the Sacred Heart of Jesus, dressed in white and red, and a couple of other images. But she was closest to one of the images that was stolen, and its loss wounds her deeply. I remember how, when I first met her in 1992, she carefully pointed out her images to me in the little room that always seemed occupied. She had stressed that the images were but representations, and that some had belonged to her grandparents from before the time she was born. They were the centerpiece of her vocation as an oyonel, much as they were the central fixture of her altar.

This meeting reminds me of the real pain in people's lives and makes me wonder when I should switch off the anthropologist and just be a friend. Today really makes me think about how the things I call oyonïk "elements" fool me. I have assumed them to be physical allies with spiritual attributes, when for the people who know them, they are spiritual allies with physical attributes.

SHOCK AND THE RITUAL SURROGATE

The element of shock is spiritually driven, but physically delivered. At some point in almost every oyonïk I have seen, the oyonel takes a switch, usually from the quince tree (*Cydonia oblonga* Miller, Sp. *membrillo*), and strikes the palangana of water, the floor around the client, or the client himself. This stimulates the client's corporality and stirs what is akin to the bodily memory of the lost soul portion. By provoking bodily sensations and emotions, physical shock, like oral prayer, alerts the lost soul portion to its proper place, to its seat in the body. The oyonel Lencha creates this shock by using a membrillo switch and rose petals. She taps the palangana with the switch, as others do. Then she reaches into the palangana, retrieves a dripping handful of the petals, and douses her patients three times with them while invoking "[exhale] Dios padre, [exhale] Dios hijo, [exhale] Dios espíritu santo." The sudden gasp and shudder the clients make when the cold water hits them leaves little doubt as to its awakening effect.

Ritual shock is actually found throughout and beyond the Maya region. In most places, it involves spraying a liquid, usually liquor, upon those seeking healing. John Gillin (1948:394) thus described how a magical-fright patient is sprayed with an alcoholic liquid from the mouth of a Poqomam healer, similar to what Michael Logan (1979:158) reported among Kaqchikel healers. Many other accounts like these show how a sudden stimulation of the body is said to help reverse spiritual fragmentation that, at other times, shock can cause.

In Comalapa, the idiom of shock takes an additional turn with the ritual surrogate. Normally, the xib'iril sufferer attends each of the oyonïk held for him. Some persons, however, because they work out of town or travel a lot, cannot attend each of their oyonïk. In these cases, the oyonel can fashion an object that will permit the client to be mimetically present at the oyonïk. Taking a piece of clothing that the client has worn but not washed, the oyonel affixes it either to an armature of crossed membrillo sticks or onto a small broom. Then, when the time comes to strike or douse the client during the ritual, the oyonel strikes the surrogate, ideally as a family member of the afflicted holds it. Comalapans call this effigy the k'al k'u'x.

The term "k'al k'u'x" contains the word "k'al" and a word discussed above, "k'u'x." K'al implies a wrapped or rolled condition. K'u'x, meanwhile, connotes an animating essence in several domains of local life. Ritualists who make a k'al k'u'x for a person fashion it "as though it were a photo that they make of one, as though it were the form that they make of one, as though it were in the style of one," as the midwife Gabriela puts it. Only a person's unwashed clothes can be used to make this spiritually grounded effigy because, as another woman indicates, "those clothes still have the *aliento* [breath, odor] of his body."

The breath or odor of the afflicted person makes the k'al k'u'x a viable interlocutor of the afflicted at the oyonïk. The clothing is imbued with a detectable emanation of the person's body called ruxla', again, "its breath" or "its odor," allied in different contexts with soul. The ruxla' instantiates the soul in the k'al k'u'x, permitting ritual treatment of the physical k'al k'u'x to affect the soul directly. Other Maya also recognize this principle. Calixta Guiteras Holmes (1961a:298) found that, among the Tzotzil, "[t]hat which has been in contact with the body is impregnated with the ch'ulel," the ch'ulel being a person's inner soul. Ralph Roys (1976[1931]:xxii) also reported a clothing-based ritual surrogate used by Yucatec Maya in an account reminiscent of Comalapa: "If the patient is unable to visit the *ahmen* [curer], absent treatment may be given. A member of the family brings one of the patient's garments, and the doctor performs a ceremony over this, which is called *peɔ-nok*." In line with these cases, the Kaqchikel k'al k'u'x employs the soul's capacity for clothing impregnation to produce an ensouled surrogate bundle, making the sufferer mimetically present in his physical and spiritual near-totality at the healing sessions. In the present day, this means that if a Comalapan person must be in their Guatemala City home the night an oyonïk is scheduled, the ritual can go forward in Comalapa. The oyonel simply asks in advance that the xib'iril sufferer kneel and pray at the exact moment that the calling will take place in Comalapa (Hinojosa 2011:89). So even though many Comalapans now spend much of their working lives outside their hometown, they still have options for dealing with xib'iril. And they do need them, because if anything, the long highway commutes and life in busy cities, where personal violence has been on the uptick since the early 2000s, have threatened their soul-body integrity more than ever. This has meant a steady workload for oyonela' in Comalapa and a continued reliance on their basic tools.

It is worth repeating that oyonela' consider membrillo sticks extremely valuable for performing oyonïk and for crafting k'al k'u'x. An older healer

FIGURE 8.1
A kneeling woman holding a cross-shaped *k'al k'u'x*.
Drawing by Servando G. Hinojosa.

named Fermín explains that "they attribute a *secreto* to [the tree], against illnesses, against spirits. Perhaps as when Moses converted his staff into a serpent. . . . It's a very special privilege, but only for good works." A secreto is magical potentiality or formula. Some families even keep a membrillo stick in the home to wave at unruly children. The ideal stick for this is one that has been placed among the ritual offerings left for the annual *visita del Niño*, when a Christ child is brought to the home after Christmas and set atop an array of flowers and seed. This blessing imbues the membrillo switch with the holy authority to cure fright and chastise children. Aurora remembers that, when she was young, parents used to take the newly blessed membrillo, have their older children kneel, and swat them, saying, "That he not wander in the streets, that he not leave this house." Parents tell me that children today are keenly aware when a membrillo stick has been thus "blessed." Children often hide this rod of discipline from their parents.

Oyonela' try to couple k'al k'u'x rituals, as well as regular oyonïk, with prayers called *evangelios* whenever possible. Following Sunday mass, interested attendees are invited to the altar to receive a special blessing by the priest, and xib'iril sufferers are especially urged by their families to receive this. Xib'iril sufferers are encouraged to bring ritual godparents when they receive the evangelio. Interestingly, although the pastor of the town's main Protestant temple disavows a spiritual basis for susto, he says that church members offer special prayers for fellow members who feel afflicted with susto. Temple members pay home visits to their sick peers to offer support and counsel.

As in these cases, xib'iril sufferers benefit from the attention of family and friends. Oyonela' like Lencha and Julia routinely call out to stray soul portions in the name of the sufferer's family, begging them to return home. The midwife Gabriela says that her own family greatly comforted her when she developed xib'iril at age twelve. She had fallen into a water trough, so her mother arranged an oyonïk. In addition, she says, "they did many things, they made a lunch, made a dinner, and it was all the corazón of my mother who met that expense." Local soul reintegration processes are thus consistent with what Richard Adams and Arthur Rubel (1967:350) argued about Mesoamerica in general: "[T]he cure for regaining a patient's lost soul requires reassuring him that he is necessary to the community and his family."

If Comalapans rely on their earthly families to help them overcome xib'iril, it only makes them more careful to include the otherworldly counterparts of these families in their treatments. Oyonela', particularly Catholic ones, invoke the santa familia as well as a collective of saints and "virgins" in their litanies. Some locals also include the three archangels, San Miguel, San Rafael, and San Gabriel, in their soul recovery. Comalapans reach out to these beings recognized by the church, but also call upon some that are not. They learn about the spirits inhabiting the countryside in fireside accounts of their childhood. As Comalapans grow up, curiosity often merges with fear as they travel, work, and live among those spiritual beings with whom they share ruwäch ulew, "the face of the earth." Spirit-owners have long been tied to changing spiritual and bodily states in humans, something that ceremonial dancers know all too well, as I will discuss next.

Part Four

MAYA DANCERS AND RENEWAL OF SPIRIT

CHAPTER NINE

Performing Soul,
Performing Community

ANYONE BEHOLDING THE PARQUE IN front of Comalapa's two San Juan Churches will notice how bare it is. No prominent crosses or gazebos adorn the grassless, dusty spread. An open basketball court sits on one end, close to a large fountain, but the rest of it is usually occupied only by idling intercity buses and parked pickup trucks ready for hire. The wide-open space comes in handy for market days and for the June feast, but it is December right now and the crowds are here because the town dance season has begun.

For most Comalapans, this is the stage where they see the *baile de toritos*, "the dance of the little bulls," performed every year. This is where they get to watch masked dancers line up, announce themselves, and confront each other in a swirl of velvet and mirrors. If the onlookers stick around long enough on a given day and stay close to the ropes enclosing the dance space, they might even get to see the dance's bloody finale up close. But few people spend the whole day there. Most tire and drift away within an hour of arriving, ceding their places to other people drawn to the dancers' marimba. The going is even harder for the performers. Layered in their thick costumes and heavy wooden masks, they step and sway for hours, watching each other through tiny eyeholes and feeling the sun dig deeper into their backs. After a few hours of this, a growing trickle of dancers ducks out of the arena to take a breather. They lift their masks just enough to get a drink of water, or a taste of something stronger if they have it. Refastening their masks, they step back into the arena where they will stay until fatigue sweeps over them again, or until the dance's spiritual patrons demand nourishment. At moments like these, the dancers are keenly aware that whatever they give their bodies, or withhold from it, will be felt by agents upon whom the community depends.

Like many towns of Mesoamerica, Comalapa features dancing in its annual festivities. The dance season begins on Church holy days of early December, kicking off on the day of Virgen de Concepción (December 8). This is followed by dances on the days of Virgen de Guadalupe (Saturday and Sunday including or after December 12), Christmas Day (December 25), New Year's Day (January 1), and the Day of the Three Kings (Epiphany) (January 6). Dancers showcase many Christian figures in their performances, all the more so in the dance season that squarely encompasses Christmas. But although the dance activities keep a Christian veneer, the meanings behind the dance go far beyond Christian characters and Western modes of experience. When Comalapans first see the baile de toritos in December, dancers have already set events in motion closing the distance between townspeople and rajawala' of the countryside. Dancers and dance organizers work hard to achieve this, and together they reconfigure spirit-body relationships for the duration of the season.

Dancers prepare their bodies to dance and to placate the spiritual owners of the costumes. This sometimes takes place in the countryside and sometimes in the individual dancer's home. Dancers do this so they can have a strong and favorable relationship with their nonhuman counterparts. As the physical and spiritual boundaries of dancer and costume rajawal intersect, creating heavy burdens for the dancers, dancers' bodies experience conditions of spiritual grounding unknown to most Comalapans outside the dance group. Comalapa dancing lets us glimpse locally produced and sustained worlds of meaning, facilitated partly through symbols of European origin. This chapter explores how dancers activate and articulate these worlds of meaning. It examines how, as dancers spiritually embody their costumes and masks and, in turn, become embodied by the spiritual owners of these, the dancers reaffirm ties with the guardians of the natural realms.

THE SEASON'S PREPARATIONS

Comalapans start preparing for the dance season in July or August of each year, once the excitement of the June titular feast settles down. Five to seven men who have danced or organized the dance in the past form a "folkloric committee," so named because it tries to appeal to a general civic interest in the dance. This steering committee needs to build on this appeal because it has to raise money for the upcoming dances. Members of the group say, though, that most people can only give moral support to them, and not money. Still, members try to get contributions from all quarters and collect a workable sum by the time the dancers get organized a few months later.

Preparations reach a pitch in November as the twenty-four dancers are chosen. Dancers and dance organizers say that many men, both older and younger, used to want to dance, allowing the group to even have dancer alternates. But interest in the dance has declined in recent years, especially among older dancers. The net effect is that, while younger men now dominate the dance ranks, they often cannot make quorum. The group faces this problem early in the 1995–1996 season. At don Andrés Caná's house, where the dancers decide to meet, only around fifteen to eighteen dancers report for duty. Organizers urge them to get their friends involved. But even though the group is still short, and new dancers continue to arrive, the dancers begin rehearsing.

For four consecutive Sundays before the first public performance, the dancers, choreographers, and marimba players meet to practice the entire eight- to ten-hour baile de toritos in don Andrés's courtyard. During these morning-to-evening sessions, four older men play toritos dance songs on the marimba owned cooperatively by the dancers. One or two choreographers coach each dancer to ensure that he moves according to his personage's style. Since most of the dancers have danced before, these men and boys move quickly into the dance rhythm and help the new dancers learn their steps.

During the rehearsals, the dancers practice in their everyday clothes, with few props. They will not receive their costumes and masks until the day before the inaugural dance. The Sunday gatherings appear very unstructured, with dancers drifting in and out, resting while others dance, and just disappearing. But this is offset by the fact that the dancers have witnessed the dances most of their lives and partly know what the performed dance will require of them. They have a strong idea of the big-dance picture into which their pieces will fit.

The group pauses only at mealtimes and during talks by the folkloric committee. Mothers and wives of some of the dancers prepare the meals, helped by the head prayer maker. They usually make lunches of vegetable and meat soup served with tamalitos, or chicken with rice, and soft drinks. Before noon, some women serve dancers soft drinks in cups that they rinse out and use for the next person. On some mornings, a man will likewise serve dancers some kuxa, or its legal counterpart, Venado. The parents of the one female dancer give generously of these liquors. But while the father only gives soft drinks to his fifteen-year-old daughter, Antonia Calí, his gifts of liquor to the other dancers earn him a reputation as a welcome dance supporter.

On the fourth and last Sunday of rehearsal, the folkloric committee comes to the house in the late morning to inspect the dancers for the first time. Some members have come on past Sundays, but today the seven-member group pays its official visit. The choreographers are dealing with some dancing and script-recitation problems and tell the dancers that this is their last chance to rehearse and ask questions. The group then gathers around the marimba as the head choreographer, Gabriel Miza, who is also the head of the dancers, introduces himself and asks each of the dancers to do the same. Each dancer, beginning with the chief character, the *patrón*, proclaims his name and how happy he is to be part of the group.

The head of the committee, Martín Chacach, then thanks Antonia Calí's parents for letting her join the group and urges the dancers to build new and lasting friendships with each other. He assures the dancers that the committee will do everything it can to get them funding. The next committee member, Orlando Cun, thanks the marimba players for their time and effort. Member Edgar Juchuña then thanks the choreographers, who are putting the finishing touches on the dance today. Finally, Manolo Calí, Antonia's father, states his pleasure in seeing his daughter dance with the group, something, he says, she does of her own initiative.

To close the salutations, Manolo serves Coke, 7UP, and Pepsi to the marimba players and the committee. Once the dancers get their drinks, bottles of kuxa appear, and Manolo offers some to everyone. Their message delivered, the committee members leave. Cigarettes and fruit drinks are passed out, and dancers are soon drifting out of the compound for their lunch break.

The dance season will begin in only four days, and on the day before it does, the group must build a rustic chapel, the *champa*, where the costumes will be ritually received, prayed over, and fed. The organizers remind the dancers to bring their assigned building materials to the chapel site west of the town, called Las Delicias, on the morning of December 7. Each dancer is to bring two long wooden boards and two yards of plastic sheeting. Some dancers must bring rope, wire, tables, and specific religious images. An organizer is told to get two or three horses for carrying the costume bundles to the champa, and a large flatbed truck is hired to carry borrowed wooden beams and galvanized steel panels to Las Delicias.

But there are a couple of problems. The marimba players are charging more than last year. Not all of the dancers can afford to rent their costumes. The group still lacks dancers. The committee, though, promises to help defray the musicians' fees and costume rental fees for some dancers. As for getting twenty-four dancers, there is still time, even after the public dances have begun, because all twenty-four costumes and masks will be rented as a package, as they must be, and the organizers expect last-minute participants. They believe that everything will work out.

Things take time with the dancers. From my earliest moments with them, I see that neither schedules nor experience can be rushed. Luckily, my presence among them had an auspicious prelude.

AN OFF-SEASON BLESSING

I first see Comalapa's ceremonial dancers in June 1995. This year, the folkloric committee wants to host a dance during the June 24 feast, not just in December, so they must raise the money to rent twenty-four costumes, pay four marimba players, and hire a visiting ritualist. I learn that a *kotz'i'j*, literally "flower" but here meaning "sacrifice-prayer," will be offered for the dancers and costumes in the home of one don Andrés Caná, a longtime supporter of the dancers. On the morning of the kotz'i'j, two friends and I arrive at don Andrés's house.

Although we come expecting the ritual to begin at 9:00 a.m., we are asked to wait. Everyone is served kuxa, and the group grows to about forty adults and children. The prime mover in the folkloric committee, Martín Chacach, arrives around 11:00 a.m., and the kotz'i'j begins. Rigoberta Sisimit from neighboring San José Poaquil officiates.

Rigoberta calls everyone to the center of the patio. She places a new earthen comal atop three cinder blocks, simulating a hearth. Rigoberta's sister later says that the comal is placed on the blocks so that this spot does not become a permanent sacred spot, requiring respect. The comal can be removed, letting the patio be used without worrying about a *mesa*, or altar, being there. The comal can later be used for other mesas.

Many of us still hold a cup of kuxa in our hands. Rigoberta takes some kuxa and pours oblations around the mesa: east, west, north, south. She then hands each adult a copal incense bundle. Everyone next takes a white taper from a basket being passed around. Meanwhile, Rigoberta makes a circle of white sugar around the edges of the comal. Martín makes a smaller circle inside of it, with dots, apparently making a Maya day sign. Rigoberta then selects four couples and stands them in the four directions, facing the mesa. They are not to move. She asks that everyone, in turn, place their copal upon the lines of sugar. Then she places candles of different colors in the mesa's four quadrants: a bundle of white candles in the east, yellow candles in the west, black candles in the north, and red candles in the south. She places a blue candle and a green candle in the center, forming the central axis. Each of the four couples holds a thick candle of a color corresponding to their quadrant. Rigoberta and her assistants then open up many tiny copal bundles and put them aside. She lastly places tallow candles and *ocote* (pitch pine torches) all around the top of the mesa and lights them and the two center candles.

As she prays in Kaqchikel, all of us kneel, white candle in hand, facing south. She crosses herself with some candles and then prays aloud for five minutes. We repeat this, facing north, west, and east (the reverse order of candle placement). After each directional prayer, we kiss the ground. We rise. Rigoberta prays a while longer and then talks about the ceremony and the candle colors. Everyone places their white candle on the blazing mesa. Rigoberta then takes the colored candles from the directional couples and places them on the mesa.

A few men place some boxes on the south side of the mesa. They contain the group's costumes, including ten pale-faced masks and two toritos masks. Ten men and two boys remove their rented costumes and hold them in their arms, remarking on their excellent quality. They come from a *morería*, a costume rental warehouse, in Chichicastenango. The morería reportedly wants to impress the Comalapans with good costumes because Comalapa does not normally rent costumes in June; it wants the town's future business. Rigoberta takes a bundle of *ruda* (rue) and *chilca* leaves, sweeps it through the fire's smoke, and swats each of the men and their costumes while praying. This action would become more significant later in the season. She hands the bundle to a woman who then swats and blesses her family members, after which she passes it to another person. A man offers everyone two candles from a basket of white and yellow candles. Rigoberta then dances counterclockwise three times around the mesa with the men following, each cradling his costume, to the sound of three recorded marimba songs.

We all kneel to offer our silent petitions, facing the mesa. We are then asked to put our additional candles in the fire. A couple of people throw the candles in, prompting Rigoberta to insist that the candles be placed, not thrown. She prays, crosses herself, and then asks everyone to give each other a greeting. We are then invited inside the adjoining Caná house for tamales and glasses of homemade *horchata*.

During the meal, the dancers lay out their costumes and place candles and *pöm* (incense) at the foot of each one. The dancers then perform the toritos dance before the welcomed and well-fed costumes. The men tell me that this kotz'i'j normally takes place at Las Delicias, west of Comalapa, but that due to rain, they decided to hold the ritual in town. Some dancers add mirrors and other accessories to their costumes because they really want to sparkle tomorrow in the San Juan Day parade.

Only later do I discover how fundamental this ritual attention is to the dance experience. Through his prayers, deprivations, marathon dancing, and some alcohol, the dancer will invite stirrings that originate outside his usual boundaries. For the appointed period, he will open his consciousness to that of his entrusted costume.

Being at the Caná house lets me see the surfaces of this process, and lets many of the regular season dancers and organizers see me. Several dancers that I later work with remember me from this visit. This ceremony, though short, sparks my interest in what transpires between the dancer, the costume, and spirit during the regular season.

BUILDING THE *CHAMPA*

The day before the December dance season begins, I drive west from Comalapa and arrive at Las Delicias at 9:00 a.m. Several dancers are erecting the champa, the long shed that will be their chapel. Four wooden posts hold it up, and galvanized steel panels roof it over and wall off the east end of the structure, where the altar will be. The main dance organizer, Gabriel Miza, asks me to take a dancer, Eliseo Mux, to collect some religious images in town. I drive him and another dancer into town where they disembark and disappear down a narrow street by the market where dance organizer Raúl Martínez lives.

An explosion rips the sky. Someone has fired a rocket from the street my companions have entered. The dancers reappear carrying two chromolithographs. One of the images is large, the other small, both of Nuestra Señora de Concepción (Our Lady of the Immaculate Conception), also known as Virgen de Concepción, whose day is tomorrow. The dancers tell me that the rocket was fired because texela', members of the local religious sisterhood, were arriving at the house where they got the images. It turns out that Raúl's mother, the midwife Gabriela, is being inducted today as the texel representing Virgen de Concepción.

Over at Manolo Calí's house, in the Tz'an Juyu' barrio, I pick up a metal table for the images. Manolo is atop a horse that will be picking up the costumes at Las Delicias. People are loading his large truck with all kinds of food and cooking equipment for today's lunch at the champa site. In addition to his duties as the health center's night watchman, Manolo works as a *transportista*, a buyer and mover of goods. This makes him fairly affluent, and he is enjoying the chance to be a dance patron.

The dancers need more plastic sheeting for the champa's rear wall and altar, so at Tienda Tepeyac we buy ten yards of a white, rose-flowered sheeting. Back at Las Delicias, I help put it up. Dancers are hanging cut cypress branches from ropes stretched at waist height along the sides of the champa. With the strewing of pine needles upon the champa's earth floor, the entire structure takes on a verdant ambiance matched only by the forested ravine to the south and west. Early today, Julia Simón, this year's prayer maker, held a ceremony at the bottom of this ravine. In the company of her son Arturo, her husband Chema, and several other people, she sacrificed three chickens for a successful dance season. Both Arturo and Chema are dancing this year. At least one dancer tells me that Julia is a *sacerdote maya* (Maya priest). She does not, however, use the Maya ritual calendar of 260 days found elsewhere in the highlands.

Over time, Julia's role in the dance troupe will become clearer to me, but at first, she confuses me a bit. I do not know her place in the scheme of things. Julia, like Rigoberta months before, catches me off guard because, before I became involved with Comalapa's dancers, I knew little of the spiritual underpinnings of highland Maya dance. Ritualists like Julia play a pivotal role in dance complexes such as this, but because their involvement is more private, happening away from the glitter and clamor of the public dances, they often go unseen and underdocumented. Documenting this in Comalapa will not be easy, though. Keeping a steady focus on someone like Julia will take initiative and a lot of patience.

Back at Las Delicias, Chema insists that I take him to Julia's house to get a large kettle. I drive him to Cantón 8, first taking Elías Calí, Manolo's brother, to the park to buy some film. We get the kettle at Chema's and drive to Aurora Apén's house, where I told Elías I would wait for him. He never shows, so I take Aurora, her son Chuti' Hunahpu', two granddaughters, and a stove of live coals and drive back to Las Delicias. There we find that the retinue has left for Chuwa Burro already, so I drop off most of my passengers and drive on.

ARRIVING THROUGH CHUWA BURRO

Comalapans know Chuwa Burro, literally "before the burro," as the first ritual stop of the dance costumes as they approach the town from the west. A bifurcated road, overshadowed by a promontory inscribed with a burro, marks the spot where the costumes will get their initial blessing. They must be properly welcomed with copal and kuxa. Eager to see the costume reception, we continue down the winding road, keeping our eyes open for the welcoming party.

About halfway there, I pass a group of walkers, so I let a newly reappeared Elías, his new wife, and some other women get aboard my truck. At around 11:30 a.m., I arrive at Chuwa Burro, but Elías insists that Chuwa Burro is further on. So, I drive up out of the gorge, certain that Chuwa Burro is now behind and below us, and wait to see what Elías wants to show me. But as I drive through a rolling plain toward Panabajal village, I realize that he is simply lost. Just as I am about to question Elías, and possibly embarrass him, someone calls out from the back of the truck to say that I have passed our destination. Whatever face Elías saves I lose before

the women in the back of my pickup, who see me as both driver and navi-
gator. Elías shrugs.

I stop, slowly turn the truck around, and return to Chuwa Burro. The
walkers have arrived and now wait for the minivan bearing the costumes.
Dancers Salvador Roquel, Miguel Cúmez, and Carlos Cun were dispatched
early this morning to the morería at San Cristóbal Totonicapán, three hours
away, and are expected back around noon. Miguel expects four horses from
Manolo Calí for the welcome, so when Manolo appears with one horse, he is
asked about the other three. Manolo says that Miguel asked for only one
horse. Organizers restate that they need at least three horses to carry the costumes and are unhappy that Miguel did not follow instructions. They decide
to load whatever they can onto one horse and carry the rest by hand, not by
truck. Manolo stands proudly by his horse. It has some colored foil stars
taped to it.

The horse crisis abated, the welcoming party seeks the roadside shade
for what it hopes will be a short wait. Then, with grand gestures, Julia
explains an important aspect of the Chuwa Burro reception. She recounts
that when the costumes arrive, are piled up high, and kuxa is poured over
them, the costumes drink the kuxa. When something is given to the costumes, the rajawala' of the costumes consume it.

For the next couple of days, the concept of spirit-ownership will be
abundantly played out. Comalapans place great emphasis on the spirit-
owner of the costumes and masks. Some say that a single rajawal tzyaq,
"lord of the costumes," reigns collectively over the twenty-four rented costumes, while others claim that each costume and its mask has its own
rajawal. In keeping with a pervasive Maya idea of simultaneous multiple
and unitary divinity, most people do not bother distinguishing between
collective and single spiritual lordship. The dance group must recognize
both types of lordship at different moments in the season. The activities at
Chuwa Burro and Las Delicias, marking the initial phase of costume veneration, recognize collective lordship.

While the group waits at Chuwa Burro, some people point out the burros inscribed on the two gorge faces above us, each above a road going in
different directions. An older man tells us how the place got its name. There
was a wealthy man, a Señor Matzer, who lived in Panabajal, who owned
many *caballerías* of land and grew many things. He wanted to improve the

road between Panabajal and Comalapa, so he asked the Panabajal villagers to help him hire laborers and equipment. But no villagers wanted to help. Señor Matzer got fed up with all of them and built the road himself, hiring the machinery and the men. He named part of the road Chuwa Burro, because the people of Panabajal were burros for not having helped him.[1]

Since the costumes have not arrived by 12:45 p.m., some dancers ask me to go look for the minivan; perhaps it has had engine trouble. With a few men in my truck, I drive up out of the gorge. I pull over at a store in Panabajal and see a blue minivan whizz past me in my rearview mirror, heading to Chuwa Burro. I pursue the minivan, pass it, descend into Chuwa Burro, and tell everyone that they are coming. The minivan appears around 1:30 p.m.

The welcoming party runs to the back of the minivan when it makes a partial stop, and women rush forth brandishing censers. Dancers lift the hatch and unload the costume bundles as fireworks explode. People splash and pour kuxa on the bundles. Baskets of red and white rose petals appear and are quickly emptied onto the new arrivals. The minivan pulls forward slightly and everyone surrounds the bundles.

Julia leads a prayer. We encircle the costumes, with Julia facing them from the east, the direction of the town. In Kaqchikel she thanks "rajawal ulew, rajawal mundo," "the lord of the earth, the lord of the world," for safely bringing the costumes and the drivers. Julia leads the group in Our Fathers, Hail Marys, Glorias, and Ave Marías, and they offer more kuxa and flowers to the bundles. The men load some bundles onto the horse and distribute the rest among themselves to carry to Las Delicias. Antonia Calí picks up a bundle, but Julia quickly tells a man to carry her bundle, insisting that the women are not to carry anything.

AN EARTHLY DOORWAY

During the welcome, I notice a stratigraphic mark in the earth where the hill has been cut away to make the road. Numerous people call this the *mancha* (stain) and consider Chuwa Burro the best place to view it. Many say that the mancha marks the remains of a great cataclysmic flood. One man explains that in the time of Noah, a flood came. As the waters dried up, everything turned to sand, the trees fell, and a "vapor" turned them into sand and charcoal. But unlike in Noah's case, the earth did not immediately rejuvenate in

Comalapa. It stayed scarred for a long time, rendered barren with carbon-ized trees. But life eventually returned.

Another man, versed in the *Pop Wuj*, says that the flood was preceded by a rain of *trementina*, "pine resin" (Kaq. *q'ol*), which burned the first cre-ated men made of wood (Kaq. *ajamche' tz'ite'*). Then came the *q'eq'al job'*, "black rain," so named because the clouds turned black. This deluge buried the burned logs and wooden people in the sandy earth. He says that the carbonized logs remained because "where things don't decay is in sand."[2]

The mancha thus marks a previous Creation, preserved as a strati-graphic band in the sandy wall of earth above where the costumes and masks first touch Comalapan soil. When dancers bring the costumes down into Chuwa Burro, down past the mancha level, they not only traverse the heart of the mountain and enter the rajawal's domain. They also pass tem-porally through to the earlier Creation when, Comalapans say, Maya of another order of being walked the earth. Perhaps these are the same Maya, men of wood, present in the dance.

At Chuwa Burro, the community first enters the spatial and temporal domain of the rajawal, initiating contact with the rajawal on its own ground. As the place most closely bound to the mancha of a previous Creation, and as the reported doorway to the costume rajawal's corral, Chuwa Burro must first receive the costumes. Once the rajawal is greeted there, the dancers can entreat it into both the town and their own bodies. From this moment onward, the dancers no longer live just for themselves but for the costume rajawala'. The dancers become safekeepers of the costumes and stewards of the visiting spirit-owners, opening their bodies to the agency of the rajawala'. The rajawala', meanwhile, depend upon the sacrifices of the dancers, for as one man puts it, "Blood must be shed, so that the moro [rajawal of the dance] doesn't die."

CHAPTER TEN

The Las Delicias Becoming

JULIA THE PRAYER MAKER LEADS the costume bundles and their spirit-owners east toward the town center. At a bridge on the Pixkaya' River, we stop while she douses the bundles, the men carrying them, and the horse with an aromatic liquid. Julia then pours some onto the bridge and throws rose petals into the river. Two female relatives of Manolo Calí ask me for a lift, as does the dancer Antonia Calí, jokingly. The group resumes its march.

We arrive at Las Delicias, a bit later than expected, and all the bundles are placed before the flower-adorned altar inside the champa. Everyone kneels, and Julia prays for ten minutes in Kaqchikel, recognizing "rajawal ulew, rajawal mundo, rajawal tzyaq," "the lord of the earth, the lord of the world, the lord of the costumes." Many people have arrived since this morning. As plumes of incense thicken the air, folkloric committee member Edgar Juchuña nods toward Julia and whispers to me, "That lady is a real ajitz." K'iche'an Maya often use the term "ajitz" to reference ritual specialists thought to practice dark magic. "She divines things that happen, and she can even do some harm to a person," he adds.

Evidently, many people share Edgar's opinion of Julia. Several Comalapans have told me that she is not to be toyed with. She is said to be able to find lost objects, to divine future occurrences, and to cause unfavorable events in people's lives. People inside and outside of the dance group often associate her with witchcraft, giving critics of the dance more reason to denounce the dancing as paganism. But most people within the moros, like Edgar, simply keep a respectful distance from Julia while recognizing the unique personal conviction she brings to the dance. In past years, prayer makers have taken less structured roles in their ceremonies. Julia seems determined to set a new standard for the spiritual standard bearer of the dancers, and nobody openly questions her authority to do so.

Dancers take their seats all along the inner sides of the champa, and their costumes are placed at their feet. Higher-ranked dancers are seated closest to the altar. Facing the altar, to the left sits the patrón and to the right is doña Rosa, his wife. Seated by the patrón is the next-highest dancer, the mayordomo, and next to doña Rosa sits the mayordomo's subordinate, the caporal. The rank-and-file vaqueros follow, trailed by the *toritos* and *pastorcitos*. Costumes *sin dueños*, "without owners" (i.e., yet without a dancer to adopt them), are placed directly before the altar.

After Julia's prayer, the costumes and masks eat. The dancers' families put plates of tamalitos with *recado* (broth) and beef, plates of pastries, cups of kuxa, Coke, coffee, and a yellow votive candle at the foot of each costume. They also sprinkle kuxa and blanket the costumes in rose petals. The families then give the dancers food to eat while they sit with their costumes. Julia kneels before her son's costume and offers tobacco to its rajawal, in the form of a burning cigarette. This is the first meal shared between the costumes and the dancers, and it further cements the costume spirits' entry into Comalapa, partnered to the dancers' bodies.[1]

Different families have set up fires and have been cooking meals under the Las Delicias pines. I eat with my family. Back at the champa, Julia asks Mario Cun to carry his portable stereo as she dances before each costume, starting with the patrón's. The recorded song, in Tz'utujiil Maya, is on an album produced by the traditional music museum in La Antigua. Julia lifts each mask and cradles it, swaying toward and away from the costume like the *nabeysil* of Santiago Atitlán, a sacred bundle specialist.[2] Mario follows nervously behind her with his stereo. Julia has been drinking for several hours and is having trouble keeping her balance.

By late afternoon, the crowd thins out and the dancers cluster around their costumes inside the champa to make repairs to the fabric. Many dancers sew small round mirrors to the fabric and hats, adding more sparkle. Some comment that these costumes are not as bright and flashy as those rented last San Juan Day, because the present group can only afford medium-quality costumes. They therefore add mirrors, metallic fringes, and other details to upgrade the fabric. They will continue at this all night and through to tomorrow morning.

FIGURE 10.1

Moros dancers in the *champa* at Las Delicias during the costume vigil.
Drawing by Servando G. Hinojosa.

FIGURE 10.2

Julia offering tobacco to the lord of the costume at Las Delicias.
Drawing by Servando G. Hinojosa.

FIGURE 10.3
Julia, the chief prayer maker of the *moros* dancers, dances with the main dance character's mask in the champa at Las Delicias. Photo by author.

Although I want to stay longer at the champa, the persons I brought here now clamor to go home. Many people, in fact, want me to drive them home. Gabriel Miza, the main organizer, wants me to pick up the marimba players. Julia wants me to ask Mario to leave his stereo so that she can continue playing music. Mario does not think it is a good idea. Julia presses her case to me, not to Mario. So before Julia loses her temper, and before more people learn I am leaving, I load up Gabriel, Aurora, her granddaughters, two other girls, and Mario and his stereo and set out.

I drop off my family and go look for the musicians, near Manolo Calí's house. Mario, Gabriel, and I cannot find them, so we instead buy batteries for Gabriel's portable stereo in place of a marimba. Next to the parque, Ladino children dressed as Indians perform a *feos* (ugly ones) dance, with music blasting from a pickup. We head back to Las Delicias.

When I arrive at the champa, Eliseo Mux, the patrón, staggers toward me and hands me a drink of kuxa. Up until this moment, I have not written any field notes on today's activities. But with the increasing effects of the kuxa, I realize that my memory might fail me if I postpone writing any longer. I sit on a bench and begin scratching out my notes. A woman with a child on her lap peers at my writing and asks why I am here. After explaining my interest in costumbre, I ask her if the dancers always drink. She replies, "That's what they say, that if he [the patrón] doesn't get drunk, the mask will turn pale, they say."

This statement, together with many others in later months, points evocatively to a physical and spiritual interdependency between the dancer and his costume, especially his mask. From their first contact at Chuwa Burro, dancers must start "feeding" the costumes, to nourish them, to welcome them, and to rid them of any bad influences they might bring. Dancers especially want to give their masks liquor, for their very lives may depend on it. As Edgar Juchuña emphasizes, "This is an indispensable requirement so that nothing befalls the man, the participant." The masks must be nourished with drink and food, or they might demand much more from the dancers. As night falls, the champa becomes central to this feeding.

With a sputter, an electric generator starts up, and two dangling light bulbs come to life in the champa. This lets the dancers continue mending their costumes as darkness envelops the forested ravine to the south and the milpa to the north. Manolo tells me he has some whiskey and with a grin produces a bottle of Johnny Walker Red. He holds it under a light bulb where I can inspect it, then pours me a glass. Middle-aged Valerio Chex suddenly approaches me and launches into a discourse about how expensive the dance is and how he needs money for his son Maynor's participation. He has the impression that I am a wealthy patron of the arts.[3] I try to disabuse him of this notion, but he simply pours me some kuxa from an army canteen. I have been drinking intermittently all day but have not yet felt the full effects of the kuxa. But within a few minutes of drinking Valerio's gift, I feel unsteady, and the champa begins a slow spin. Seeing its effect on me, he smiles and offers me more. I remind myself out loud that I must drive into town later tonight. The night feels very cold, despite the kuxa.

The patrón has now dressed himself, and he rehearses his lines with great elocution and emotion. Mario is back. A few minutes later a stately Martín Chacach enters with his wife and family. Meanwhile, Julia's son, Arturo, cannot find his cape, and many people are scolding him. He sobs quietly. He later finds the cape, but Julia has become so incensed at this "theft" that she refuses to stay the night at the champa, as is her duty. I greet Martín, and he offers me a cigarette. Many more people have arrived.

It is time to bring out the kuxa I bought this morning from a clandestine seller. I get the liter jug from my truck, find a cup, and go around pouring a drink into the masks' mouths. The dancers look surprised, but pleased. A couple of men ask for a shot. I chat with Martín's wife and another woman with her. At his insistence I give these two ladies kuxa and pour the last of it into a glass on the altar. Then I drink some Coke with Mario. Martín's youngest daughter chats with me, cheerfully throwing in some English words. When the Chacach family leaves in their gray Isuzu, my weariness takes over, and I go sit with Antonia Calí's family. One of Antonia's cousins asks me for a ride home, but I tell her that I am in no condition to drive. This prompts some other ladies to seize my notebook and make sexual innuendoes about me and the "doña Rosa" I have written about. Around midnight I feel better and decide to leave, before the highland night air claims my lungs. I drive Manolo and his family home. Everyone is tired, but tomorrow will be an even longer day.

Virgen de Concepción Day, December 8, dawns cold. I arrive at Las Delicias at 7:20 a.m. and help take down the champa. Only a few dancers actually spent the night here, the majority having slept at home. Those who did stay stoked up the fire for the women who arrived by dawn to make them breakfast. The other dancers are arriving, some already in their costumes. The rest get dressed in the brush near the champa or, like Antonia, in the milpa. A new man joined yesterday, and he now dons his *negro* costume. The costumed bodies increase in number, and before long the moros stand ready to step forth with the rajawal.

DANCING IN PRINT AND PRACTICE

Comalapa's dance tradition is deeply infused with spiritual meaning, but not all studies of Guatemalan dance have focused on this aspect of the tradition. Most accounts either take a broad look at local dances (Subcentro Regional de Artesanías y Artes Populares 1992), or give historical-descriptive information about them (Bode 1961; García Escobar 1989; Schultze Jena 1954), at times pairing this with performative and oration analysis (Tedlock 2003).

Other accounts consist largely of dance scripts (Correa 1958; Edmonson 1997; Mace 1970; Paret-Limardo de Vela 1963; Raynaud n.d.), or spotlight the artistry of masks and costumes, and the work of morerías (Frost 1976; García Escobar 1987; Hill 1998; Krystal 2000; Luján Muñoz 1971, 1987; Pieper and Pieper 1988). Documentation of the more external aspects of dance goes back at least as far as Thomas Gage's (1958) seventeenth-century account of Guatemala life.

Some scholars have been mainly concerned with classifying Mesoamerican dances. Gertrude Prokosch Kurath (1967:158), for example, grouped ethnic dances according to their underlying ecological, ecclesiastical, or secular motivations. Meanwhile, Roberta Markman and Peter Markman (1989:163) differentiate Guatemalan from Mexican dances in that "[r]ather than being performed by a dance cult that makes pilgrimages to various fiestas, the Guatemalan dance is village based, being performed in villages by masked community members . . . at the annual festival of the patron saint." Accordingly, ethnographies show that there are nearly as many Guatemalan dance traditions as there are Guatemalan Maya communities.

Those works on Mesoamerican dance that do affirm a magico-religious awareness on the part of dancers consistently point to the active agency of the landscape (Luján Muñoz 1971:143–44; García Escobar 1989:44–48; Ortiz Martínez 1993:111–12). Garrett Cook (1986:141), for instance, describes dance of the conquest characters in Momostenango as manifestations of Dios Mundo, a collective of anthropomorphic original beings animating the landscape. Cook and Thomas Offit (2013) later analyze the deep engagement between this landscape and individual Momosteco deer and monkey dancers. They discuss, for example, how the dancers ritually fell a tall tree to be used as a climbing pole, and then bolster themselves with wild animal spirits in order to climb the tree-pole (2013:74, 77–80, 88). Barbara Bode (1961:232–34) also reported that Maya dance participants gave offerings and prayers at special sites in the hills before and during the dance season, and later in the dance director's home. The prayer maker of the Rabinal Achi dancers likewise makes invocations and burns offerings at five hilltop shrines to the earth lords, as well as to the spirit-owners of the dance characters themselves (Tedlock 2003:256). Maury Hutcheson's (2003:265; 2008) work in Rabinal and Joyabaj reveals that the hilltop ceremonies are necessary for awakening the spiritual essence of the dance masks. These rituals, which sometimes also take place on church doorsteps, ask permission of the Holy Earth to do the bailes, and reach out to the ancestors and the spirits of dead dancers (Hutcheson 2003:167, 396). Harry McArthur (1972) likewise found a cult of veneration of the dead, and especially of dead dancers, to be a central observance in the Maya dances of Aguacatán.

Although Comalapa dancers do not openly profess such a cult of dead dancers, they do dedicate themselves to spiritual entities of the countryside, the rajawala'. This aspect of Kaqchikel dance, though, is poorly documented, with Carlos René García Escobar (1989:44–48) only alluding to it in Mixco. Like Mixco, however, Comalapa puts the baile de toritos at the center of its dance tradition.

Although the baile de toritos takes center stage in Comalapa, locals remember how other dances, like the *baile de mazatí* (dance of the deer) and the *danza del diablo* (dance of the devil) were also performed here. The baile de mazatí is known elsewhere as the *baile del venado*, and probably originated in pre-Columbian dances of the hunt. Local dance organizer Víctor Perén dislikes this dance, though, calling it a *baile mudo*, a "mute dance," lacking wordplay. Of the danza del diablo, the curer Alejandro recalls his grandfather's stories and exclaims, "In that dance, somebody really does die!" Guatemalans typically enact the danza del diablo during the feast of Virgen de Concepción (Ortiz Martínez 1993:44–45). Many other Maya towns perform the baile del venado and danza del diablo (Cook and Offit 2013; Correa 1958; Hutcheson 2003).

The *baile de la conquista* (dance of the conquest) is also absent from Comalapa. This dance commemorates the conquest and conversion of the K'iche' Maya by the Spaniards, but it likely hails from the *baile de los moros y cristianos* (dance of the Moors and Christians) (Bode 1961). In different parts of southern and central Mexico, this dance has portrayed struggles between ethnic groups, religious groups, and even between zoomorphs and humans (as in highland Chiapas) (Bricker 1973:198), addressing along the way enduring issues of (re)conquest stemming from European events (Harris 2000). Comalapa dancers are unsure if their forebears ever did this dance. Together with negative evidence in the literature, this suggests that Comalapans have not danced it for at least a few generations.

That Comalapans enact only one dance, the toritos, is also significant because, until recently, a dance-mask maker worked in Comalapa (Luján Muñoz 1971:140, 1987:46). He would have known about different masks and dances, and dancers would have known him. And since Comalapan dancers have interacted with regional morerías for over a century, they would have had ample time to learn about different costumes and dances.[4] It is unclear how the toritos dance came to inherit the Comalapa dance tradition, but a deeper study of local dance might reveal how political, religious, or even linguistic variables had a hand in this.[5] Comalapans use the term "moro" to refer to all things dance related. But different people attach their own values to the word. For some people, moros simply means the public dance season. Other townsfolk recognize in moros the curious group of local men and boys who go to great expense to entertain them. Polite evangelical Protestants (and some catechist Catholics) smile stiffly and say that moros refers to a folkloric colonial holdover, one prefiguring an enlightened Christianity available to all who accept the Bible and reject the wasteful and misguided practices of the Maya past. Persons from other "progressive" Christian sectors insist that moros recalls all that is bad, and that the deity at the center of moros devotions is certainly not God. Similar to what Hutcheson (2003:263) found in Rabinal, where Maya bailes "stand twice outside of evangelical Christian belief," Comalapa dances likewise face censure because they are allied with the cult of the saints, and their costumbre practices excite the imaginations of those Christians who already see the moros as victims of syncretic error and as perpetrators of witchcraft. The word "moros" remains intriguing to most, anachronistic to others, and demonic to still others.

For the dancers, however, and for most middle-age and older Comalapans, "moros" evokes concerns of balanced human/spirit-owner relationships, as well as of local tradition. This word, some dance participants say, was adopted from the baile de los moros y cristianos, and a few recall that this dance commemorates the Moors' expulsion from fifteenth-century Spain, or a battle between the Moors and some vaguely defined enemies. Comalapans with more formal education, like priests, or with an affinity for history explain that these dances were used as pedagogical tools for the newly subjugated Indians, who were thought to be best evangelized through public drama. Whatever the dance's purpose, the common genealogy of the moros complex and the Morris dances of Europe (Gage 1958:246; Kurath 1967:171) never surfaces as an explanation for the term "moros."

Dancers and their supporting cast identify strongly with the word "moros" and show little concern for how others disparage it. They worry more about how the dancers intersect with the rajawala' through the ground of costume, body, and spirit. By allying the torito dance's patron spirits with the rajawala', the dance renews ties between town-dwelling humans and hill-dwelling rajawala', reminding people of their obligations to the spiritual coinhabitants of the earth. The lived dance incites awareness of Kaqchikel kinship with the spirit world and reveals how the world of spirit manifests through the body.

DAWN OF THE DANCERS

Beneath the imposing pines of Las Delicias, a striking tableau takes shape. Some eighteen people now sparkle in moros fabrics and hats. Most are fully costumed, others hurry around looking for a place to suit up. The fair-skinned wooden masks with their golden beards, curled moustaches, and red cheeks smile with crystalline blue eyes and bob amid more familiar human faces. Family members collect the removed clothes of their relatives. The array of dance costumes slowly comes into view as more moros emerge from the roadside. The shady forest births a cacophony of color and movement, and anyone even suspected of carrying a camera is immediately accosted by dancers—and made to take photos of them. It is easy to see why.

The dancer radiates vitality in his tinseled velvet tunic (*pechera*) and gaily adorned hat. The lead figure, the patrón, and his two lieutenants, the mayordomo and caporal, wear long pants with boots, an even-hemmed, richly appliquéd velvet tunic with shoulder epaulets, mirrored cuffs, white gloves, sash, sheathed sword, and a feathered Napoleonic hat. The two negros at the patrón's side also bear swords. The negros are accessorized like the mayordomo and caporal, but the former's clothes and mask are predominately black. Doña Rosa, the patrón's wife, wears a tricolored dress reaching her ankles, an unevenly hemmed velvet tunic, the ubiquitous cuffs and white gloves, and a fringed round hat topped with plumes. She carries only a staff topped by a ten-by-fourteen-inch chromolithograph of the Virgen de Concepción.

Nearly ten field hands, the vaqueros, make up the rank and file. They wear heavily tinseled knickers, low shoes, tall white stockings, an unevenly hemmed tunic, mirrored cuffs, white gloves, and a short double-cape. Their trifoil hats bear mirrors, small plumes, and in one case, ostrich feathers. Five odd toritos wear what the vaqueros do but sport flamboyant swallow-tailed capes, which they will flail about when charging. Toritos top off their costume with a cylindrical, marching band–style hat locally called the moro hat. Two or three boys gradually enter the group as pastorcitos, little animal-tenders, completing the quorum of twenty-four. Pastorcitos are smaller versions of vaqueros but wear moro hats, not trifoils.

Scenes like this stir up powerful narrative recollections among Comalapans. The confluence of dancers on the edge of a piney gorge outside of town lingers in the memory of those who have taken part in Las Delicias events. And for those who have never witnessed the moros costume reception, vigil, or materialization, oral lore provides a ready inventory of experience and images.

LOCAL *MOROS*, LOCAL NARRATIVE

Las Delicias narratives highlight two aspects of this place: habitation by a spiritual moro and the presence of a morería. The spiritual moro, or costume rajawal, is expressed both as a single spirit-owner and as a group of spirit-owners linked to specific dance costumes and to dwarf-like *moritos*. Like spirit-owners in general, the moro exists in both unitary and multiple forms. A morería, meanwhile, is a business that makes dance costumes and masks and rents them out. Comalapa dancers, however, see morerías not only as physical sources of costumes but as figurative domains of costume spirit-owners. In this way Las Delicias also has a morería, about which seventeen-year-old dancer Fidel Caté says, "Chila' k'o ruk'u'x ri ajmoro, ri ajaw," "There you find the animating-essence of the lord of the moros, the spirit-owner." By situating a morería in the Las Delicias spiritual geography, the dancers localize the being or beings their bodies will host.

Whether emphasizing individual or collective spirit-ownership over the costumes, Las Delicias narratives stress human-rajawal interaction. In these accounts, events unfold in the way that former dancer Paulino López tells me during dance rehearsals:

FIGURE 10.4
A standing *torito* dancer. Drawing by Servando G. Hinojosa.

Many years ago, they say, a man decided to go where there were moros dancers practicing. This man, a *natural* [indigene], liked the dancing very much, he loved the whole tradition, but he didn't have the monetary resources with which to participate in the group. He felt very sad, like when a man loves a woman whom he knows he'll never have, since a man seeks satisfaction. He wasn't able to pay the rent of the costume, but he still wanted to collaborate with the group.

One day, on a seventh of December, the man went to the countryside, taking his ropes with him, and he arrived at a place where a man appeared before him, a man who had your [my] physical characteristics [i.e., fair-skinned, foreign-looking]. The man who had appeared asked the man, "What are you doing around here?" The startled man replied, "I'm collecting firewood." The *canche* [fair-skinned] stranger then asked the man why he looked so sad. The natural sighed and told the strange man about his problem with money, about how he couldn't afford to rent a costume to participate in the moros dance. The natural said that he was really interested in the dance, that all those experiences were wonderful to him. The strange man said he had a *traje* [costume] he would lend the natural. At that moment they both turned around, and as if by magic, the natural suddenly stood before a luxurious house, like those in the United States. They entered, and the natural saw a storeroom filled with those kinds of costumes, dance costumes. The host told the natural to pick one he liked and to put it on. The man chose one, put it on, and suddenly he was back at the place where he'd first seen the strange man, in the vicinity of Las Delicias, alone.

When the natural came back to town, the people were amazed at the sight of him. He was now admitted as a moros dancer. In the public dancing he had the most lustrous, most beautiful and radiant costume there, that nobody could've afforded. But the canche had told him that, when he was through wearing the traje, he would need to return it to the place where he had been at Las Delicias. So the costumes are always left there.

Paulino finishes by noting, "This is the legend that is told of that place," and that now "people invoke memory, highlighting the act that occurred back then." In an account by the midwife Gabriela, whose son, Raúl Martínez, is treasurer of the moros, the details shift slightly:

> Once there was a man who wanted to dance with the moros but didn't have the money to rent a costume. His companions wouldn't let him rent a traje on credit. So, he decided that if he couldn't dance with the moros, he would at least take some pine needles to Las Delicias for the trajes when they were to be brought. He was very sad about not being able to dance, and wept at the "door" of Las Delicias.
>
> Then a man came to him, he was very tall, very pale, like a gringo. The poor man told the stranger what had happened. The stranger told the man, "Don't be sad, because now I'm going to give you a traje." The stranger added, "But look me not in the face, just look down."
>
> All of a sudden they were in the patio of a house. The house was full of moros trajes, clothes of the finest quality. The stranger gave the poor man a traje right then and there and told him that the day the moros come to turn in the trajes at Las Delicias, he too was to come turn in the traje. And this is why the moros always turn in the trajes at Las Delicias.

In both accounts, the poor Maya wants to be a dancer, but cannot. At Las Delicias, the costume rajawal confirms the man's sincerity and tells him that he will get his chance. He then takes the man to the lord's opulent home and morería, where he gives him a costume. The man returns to society with the admonition that he must thereafter bring his costume back to Las Delicias.

Some Comalapans say that the strange man dresses like a moro. He dances and even talks to people, sometimes in Kaqchikel, when they sacrifice an animal to him. In his multiple forms he appears as many vividly adorned moritos, sometimes seen dancing at noon or late at night at Las Delicias. As Antonia says of the gorge, "Over there is where the sacrifice must be made. . . . They say there where there is water, to the side of it, that's where some moritos come out, they come out dancing."

Only a person with *suerte*, a kind of fateful luck, can see the moros. Someone with lots of suerte might even be beckoned by the moros and offered costumes, riches, or other favors. But José Fernández, a nine-year-old pastorcito, warns, "If they call you, you go with them; maybe they'll give you gold. If you don't go, you're going to get sick. And if you don't obey, you sleep, you die." To the chosen person the moros "look just like people, [but] only you see him; the others don't see him," says José.

Prayer maker Marco Curruchich says that the Las Delicias moros can come so close that you can even smell the ruxla' (odor or emanation) of their clothes. Antonia's family hired Marco to sacrifice cocks to the rajawal tzyaq early on December 7. He argues, though, that while many costume-allied spirits converge on Las Delicias, the rajawal tzyaq that presides over all the costumes actually comes from outside the region, from the very morería that rented out the costumes. Oyonel David insists, meanwhile, that the spiritual morería of Las Delicias is far more important than the earthly morería that supplied the physical costumes: "They have to bring the clothes from Toto[nicapán], but the storehouse of those clothes is there at Las Delicias; there it smells like a storehouse of clothes." Our physical ability to smell the moros' clothing at Las Delicias proves, for some, that the rajawal tzyaq dwells there.

Las Delicias narratives often feature enclosures and corrals, especially when the gorge houses the moritos and a morería. At other times a water catchment quality of the gorge stands out. This motif resurfaces in the champa, where the dancing moros undertake a critical costume feeding, refashioning, and nighttime cohabitation before they emerge. The champa's rectangular, valley-like structure, lined with cypress branches upon ground strewn with pine needles, replicates the Las Delicias gorge next to it, vividly marking human engagement with a spiritual corral. The champa used to be made entirely of tree branches. Then, as now, humans and rajawala' convene in its wooded interior to consummate their pact of stewardship. The champa instantiates the spiritual corral in the hills where the rajawal moro awaits his annual invitation to town. The invitation formalized and sealed, the champa comes down early on the day dancing begins. Thereafter, in every public dance, the moros must first build a corral to separate their space from spectator space and to reengage the spiritual pact underlying the dance (see Bode 1961:236). They afterward disband the corral, like at Las Delicias.

As if identifying the rajawal moro closely with the rajawal of animals that protects and corrals forest animals, images of two saints associated with animals adorn the champa altar. The first, San Juan Bautista, is associated with the lamb, and the second, San Antonio del Monte, often appears with farm animals like cows, sheep, pigs, and chickens (see Gage 1958:234). Rajawala' that guard animals reportedly "grab" part of the souls of humans who kill forest animals without compensating the rajawala'. People who merely trip in the forest can also get their soul grabbed and captured by one of these rajawala'. These perils prove to the oyonel Patricia that the rajawal tzyaq has dominion over human souls. She says that if the dancers do not perform costumbre for the rajawal of the costumes, one of the dancers must die. The dancer's soul "will go to that place," Las Delicias, where the rajawal will claim it.

THE ROAD TO TOWN

With the group nearly assembled at Las Delicias, anxiety builds as the dance to town nears. The four marimba players have installed the group's marimba in the bed of a pickup and are ready to escort the moros out of the domain of rajawala' and into townspace proper.

At the signal, the costumed moros start off down the road, and the marimba kicks in. The patrón and doña Rosa take the lead, flanked by the mayordomo and caporal, the three men dancing in a stately toe-heel step. Doña Rosa carries her staff bearing the Virgen de Concepción and sways in a marimba step. The negros keep close to the senior couple and mimic the patrón. Just behind them the jubilant vaqueros spring about flailing their tin rattles. Heading up the rear, the pastorcitos and toritos display their step-step-knee lift dance with their hands on their hips.

Once the dancers begin moving down the road, I put my truck in first gear and trail along behind them. I slow down to let Paulino López put his bicycle in my truck and ride with me. After a few minutes, a little torito reports that he has a headache and asks to be driven, so he climbs into the cab and puts his wooden mask on the dashboard. He is soon fast asleep in the dusty heat.

The *Moros* in Public and Private Space

THE MOROS DANCE ALL THE way to town, growing visibly tired as they approach. But they renew their step when they see the townspeople lining the street to greet them. Many onlookers laugh when they see me. The sight of a gringo driver with a sleeping morito next to him and a torito mask smiling through the windshield stands out even here.

As they dance down Comalapa's main western street, the moros move as a masked group. Only a few people know which dancers are who. For the townspeople watching the group, this is where the moros of the countryside decidedly enter their midst. For the dancers, bearing their heavy costumes and wooden masks for hours in the morning heat, something similar is happening. By the time they reach their corral in front of the old San Juan Church and finish the dance, they will find the moros closer than ever.

Today's dance lasts only seven hours. Moros usually dance for much longer, even up to ten hours, but the dance to town has exhausted them. And five all-day dances remain. The dance *parlamento*, or unwritten moral charter, stipulates that they must stage six public dances. Four of the six dances will take place at the parque, the other two at the Virgen de Guadalupe Chapel on a hill just north of town. Each performance will be enacted largely in the following way.

THE PERFORMANCE

When the four-man marimba begins, the moros spring into action. The drama unfolds in Chi Cacao, far to the west, in the finca (estate) of the patrón, don Benjamín Alvarado. His wife, doña Rosa, carries an image of

179

a Virgin, Christ child, or Nativity, according to the date of the dance.
Today, she honors the Virgen de Concepción.

Two senior finca employees, the mayordomo and the caporal, flank the
patrón and doña Rosa. Beside them stand the two negros, the blackmen,
sworn protectors of the patrón. The marimba at their back, the senior couple commands the head of an alleyway formed by two lines of vaqueros
facing each other. The ten vaqueros, five odd toritos, and two or three pastorcito boys each move to their own rhythms.

The patrón and doña Rosa announce that they will honor the Virgen de
Concepción on this occasion. The patrón brandishes his sword when he
speaks, as do the other characters with swords whenever their turn comes.
Two by two, vaqueros approach the senior couple, praise the Virgin, and
declare their offerings of various fruits. Following a few pairs of vaqueros,
pastorcitos come forward to offer praise. The patrón reflects upon Christ's
death and crucifixion, upon how *judíos* (Jews) pierced his crucified body.
The patrón and his wife clamor for the Virgin's love and protection.

Group dancing and marimba music mark pauses in the dialogue.
Before a finca worker speaks, he first dances in the alleyway and before the
couple. He then stops, draws his sword, and speaks while waving his blade,
handkerchief, or rattle. If the patrón or his wife is up to speak, he or she
dances between the lines, returns to his or her place, speaks, and then
dances in place.

The mayordomo and caporal next dance before the patrón, heaping
praises on the Virgin. Two vaqueros then ask the patrón for some bulls
from his finca so that they can fight them and make merry. The boss
agrees, and asks the mayordomo and caporal to first make a banquet for
him. The vaqueros promise the patrón a feast, and they put a small table at
one end of the alleyway to hold the kuxa and glasses.

Holding the first glass high, the patrón salutes the mayordomo and
caporal, and they respond in kind. He then salutes his wife and the entire
assembly. Mayordomo and caporal then toast all in order of seniority:
patrón, doña Rosa, mayordomo or caporal, negros, and pastorcitos. The
dancers rarely name every class of character, but they keep the order of
salutation. When these men finish, doña Rosa raises her glass to all. Paired
vaqueros then dance to the table, take their glasses, and salute the group.

The toasting over, the patrón orders mayordomo to send the vaqueros off to fetch some *toros mansos* (docile bulls) from the pasture. The mayor-domo relays the order, and the vaqueros set out. They reiterate that the patrón wants easy-to-fight bulls. In Lise Paret-Limardo de Vela's script (1963), the vaqueros, although told to get the bulls, get drunk instead. The patrón asks the mayordomo where the vaqueros and bulls are, and the mayordomo angrily sends the caporal and negros after them. The repen-tant vaqueros first ask pardon of the mayordomo, then of the patrón. He absolves them and sends them out again for the bulls, reminding them to bring a docile bull for doña Rosa to fight.

Today, the vaqueros keep drinking even after the patrón repeats the order to get the bulls. After their drinking, several vaqueros dance to a far corner of the corral and find the toritos milling about. Two vaqueros tie ropes to some bulls' horns, then the other pairs of vaqueros follow suit with the other bulls. The retinue of toritos and vaqueros dances down the alley-way, around the two lines of dancers, and back to the far end of the corral.

The first toro, the flamboyant and irate Jasmín, bursts into the alleyway, declares his enmity to those who have brought him here against his will, and demands to know why he has been mistreated. Doña Rosa proudly declares that she is the most beautiful woman of the whole coast of Chi Cacao and that she will subdue the indignant Jasmín, to which Jasmín responds with death threats and charges. When doña Rosa negotiates the first charge, the marimba begins its bull-charging *son*, or tune. She grace-fully dodges three more charges. The mayordomo deals similarly with the next bull. The caporal, the two negros, the ten vaqueros, and two or three pastorcitos then each face a torito about their own size.

The patrón finally enters the fray. He again calls for a docile bull, at which Jasmín enters and protests his captivity for sport, threatening the man responsible. The patrón responds with a few threats of his own, to which Jasmín responds with a jeer and an angry charge. The patrón evades the first charge, and the marimba launches into its bullfighting son. Some vaqueros place a straw mat in one corner of the corral. Jasmín charges furiously at the elusive patrón. In his final charge, Jasmín does the unthinkable. The patrón tumbles under the weight of the exuberant bull, gored by Jasmín's silver horns.

The patrón lies on the mat, and the mayordomo calls all finca workers to his side. The bulls keep their distance, unless they choose to approach the mortally wounded man. In this tangle of bodies, the patrón dancer's human wife approaches and discretely opens a bundle at his side. Suddenly his bloody, wounded face appears, to the awe of onlookers. A dancer quickly sits on the ground behind the patrón, and the latter sits and leans back against him. Doña Rosa and the finca employees begin an eerie wail.

The patrón, surrounded by all who love him, bids farewell to doña Rosa and to his employees, sometimes bequeathing them properties. He invokes the Virgen de Concepción, takes his last breath, and dies. The dancers lift him on a stretcher and carry him around the inside of the corral. Doña Rosa wails, then the workers each voice their sadness, if they can still remember their lines.

The scene usually unravels as the patrón is dying. Kids stream into the corral, and the ropes collapse. The crowds disperse, and few people stick around to listen. This was not always the case, though, as the 1963 script has a serpent biting a vaquero after the patrón's demise.[1] Senior organizer Víctor Perén admits that today's dance is not Comalapa's "original" one. He says that the *originales* (originary dance scripts) were stolen from the moros, and when they rebuilt them, it resulted in the altered scripts they now use.

At moments like these one might wonder just how much the dance scripts have changed over time, and whether the public even notices. That they have changed is irrefutable. But more importantly, as Maury Hutcheson (2008) argues, the narrative content of the dances should be seen as secondary in importance to the act of *doing* the dances. The baile is about enacting ritual obligations in a way that flexibly and creatively reinstantiates what has been done before in the community. Since the delivery of an unchanged, uninterrupted narrative is not the intent of the dance, it matters little whether the audience members hear an "authentic" story line, or one free of pauses and interruptions. Nor does it matter whether the audience can even hear what the dancers say. The dancers play to each other, Hutcheson (2008) says, not to the assembled public. By advancing the idea that the dances are to be enacted, not presented, Hutcheson (2008:879) locates the dances' enduring strength in their embodied, lived quality, not in their acts of narrative delivery.[2] This might contextualize why, as Garrett Cook and Thomas Offit (2013:82–83) report, deer dancers in Momostenango no longer recite their lines during performances. Although the stated reason for this is that the plaza where the dance is held has become too noisy in recent years, this adaptation might actually be signaling how Maya dancers are trying to keep those aspects of the dance centered on bodily discipline and spiritual transformation, while accepting the attrition of other dance elements like scripts (Cook and Offit 2013:156).

Few people in Comalapa's chaotic parque are thinking about scripts right now, though, as they squeeze in to get a better look at the slain dancer. For all the changes it has seen, the baile de toritos continues to captivate. In few other places, after all, can the public see the striking transformative power of the rajawal tzyaq shown in the patrón's bloody face.

FEEDING AT THE DANCE

Public dances combine choreography with visceral drama, and private ones are no less intense. Comalapans willing to pay several hundred quetzales to host the moros in their patios can get a closeup look at the many visceral elements of the dance not easy to make out in the parque dances. The act of feeding, in particular, stands out. This duty toward the rajawal tzyaq, begun at Chuwa Burro, continues unbroken throughout the season and is essential during private gatherings.

We see this at the first private dance, hosted by Mauricio Corona on Christmas Eve. A negro pours a cup of the party drink, *ponche*, over his gold-moustached ebony mask. A girl filling in for doña Rosa pours some on her mask. Gabriel Miza, meanwhile, splashes kuxa all over the marimba's *teclas* (keys) and *tecomates* (gourds). "It wants its drink," a musician tells me of the marimba. During preseason rehearsals, when another musician had poured kuxa over the moros marimba, he similarly explained, "This thing drinks also. . . . It drinks water." The kuxa is given to the marimba, he added, "so that it sounds well." Here at Mauricio's house, a musician takes the feeding a step further. He pours kuxa into his hands, rubs them together, and then rubs the drink over his arms. A nearby musician says of the kuxa, "It is oil . . . the machine takes oil. We are a machine . . . we are all machines."

The moros take care to feed every participant in the dance. At a rehearsal dance, for example, the patrón pours a cup of kuxa on the dance ground. When Gabriel offers me a cup moments later, I ask him, "Do you sprinkle kuxa on the ground?" He replies immediately, "Se lo damos a *todos*," "We give it to *everybody*." For the moros, the ground participates and requires the feeding given to every mask, costume, dancer, and instrument.[3] When this kind of ritualized feeding is given to apparently non-ritual objects in other Maya settings, it is likewise because those objects are inhabited by spiritual beings. In Didier Boremanse's (2000) intriguing account of how Q'eq'chi' Maya ritually feed sewing machines, for instance, these machines get anointed with blood, food, and cacao precisely because their resident, conscious spirits need sustenance. To deny them their due food can cause mechanical problems, or even invite retaliation, not unlike with the costume spirits in Comalapa.

Mindful of the need to satisfy the dance participants, the Comalapa moro reaffirms his covenant with the dance rajawal with every feeding. At home and in the dances, he pours liquor into the mask's mouth, for he knows that the rajawal tzyaq thrives on it. Satiated, the rajawal tzyaq bestows health and physical endurance upon the moro. When a dancer gets tired, it is because "the dueño of [his] clothing wants his due." The moro must give his mask liquor to turn its pale complexion a hot, healthy red. The tired dancer is also expected to drink, but if he is too young, or prefers not to, he must still feed his mask liquor and cigarettes.

When a dancer feeds his mask, his body immediately benefits. He feels invigorated, and the upsurge of life and strength in his mask makes his own face ruddy. He can resume dancing with the rajawal tzyaq's support. A moros organizer explains that "the aguardiente is sprinkled so that [the mask] acquires more of a natural color, a lively color that represents energy, that represents vigor." In a similar way, some people turn red when they drink, he says. The mask's complexion and the dancer's complexion index their mutual strength, energy, and life. Red denotes chuq'a' that, when properly enkindled, moves between the fluid boundaries of dancer and costume.

Every person dancing or playing in Mauricio's patio today feeds the rajawal tzyaq in his own way, and in so doing heightens his own body's vitality. Dancers must also feed the rajawal in their homes, but this does not come easily for all. Some dancers cannot afford to give their masks much liquor, or their families will not even let them keep their costumes at home. During a pause at Mauricio's home dance, dancer Fidel Caté tells me that his father does not want him to be a moro and so does not let him bring his costume home. For this reason, Fidel entrusts his mayordomo

FIGURE 11.1

A *moros* dancer giving drink to his mask, which is expected to redden with satisfaction.
Drawing by Servando G. Hinojosa.

costume to Antonia Calí, who keeps it on her altar. More importantly, she feeds it regularly while Fidel is away at his Guatemala City job.

This still distresses Fidel. Antonia says that Fidel had a dream two weeks earlier in which a moros mask asked why Fidel was not caring for the mask himself. Fidel described his father's prohibition, but the mask replied, "Thank you for slighting me." Fidel insisted that he really did appreciate him, and the next day Fidel went to Antonia's house to personally give his mask kuxa. Antonia then dreamed that Fidel's costume and hers were dancing. The next morning she gave Fidel's mask a cigarette. Reappearing to her in a dream, Fidel's costume thanked her for taking care of him, adding, "And what's more, I really like your mask." Since the feeding, Antonia says that her mother hears people walking at night in the altar room, where the masks are kept.

JULIA HOSTS A DANCE

A week after the first private dance, the prayer maker Julia Simón decides to host one. Although she and her husband, Chema, are sponsoring it, Chema is not Comalapan, nor does his persona loom as large as Julia's. The December 30 dance is thus seen as Julia's doing, and she makes her usual powerful impression. I take a friend, Reyna Cutzal, and her niece, Brenda, with me to Julia's house. Reyna attends the Protestant church, Iglesia Betlehem, so I am surprised when she asks to come along. Local Catholics say that this large church has hurt local interest in costumbre. I am eager to see how Reyna will react to the moros, and especially to Julia.

We find a couple dozen people gathered in Julia's house, in addition to the marimba and the dancers kicking up dust in the patio. Reyna and Brenda become very amused, especially when people come up to greet me, since by now I am a familiar face at moros events. Before we know it, Reyna is asked for a donation, so I slip her a ten-quetzal bill. Children crowd the rooftops of nearby houses to get a better view of the dancers. I notice that a substitute is dancing as doña Rosa yet again. When Antonia Calí arrives, I ask her if she will be dancing today, to which she replies, "Yes, later." But another girl dances in her stead the whole afternoon.

Chema suddenly appears, in his negro attire. He staggers from guest to guest, occasionally balancing long enough to pour some Pepsi and hand it to a person. If the public Chema goes heavy on the kuxa, the private Chema seems determined to test his limits with it. People often remark on his and Julia's heavy drinking, so no one seems surprised to see him like this. He abruptly stops what he is doing and pours oblations of Pepsi into the two western corners of the roofed-over patio. I do not see him do this in the other corners. Other moros, meanwhile, set up a table where they take turns drinking.

When lunch begins, Chema bids me a long and breathy welcome. A woman appears and puts a hefty bowl of chicken caldo in his gloved hands. He looks at it, looks at me, sees that I have not been served, and hands me the bowl. The woman protests, as do I, but Chema insists. Reyna is given a bowl to share with Brenda. As I eat, I notice there are some choice pieces of chicken in my bowl; I feel really special. Reyna tells me that the bowl was really meant for Chema, which is why the server wanted him to take it.

FIGURE 11.2
Moros dancers sitting at a table during the performance at Julia's house.
Photo by author.

All the same, it is my first full meal since becoming sick from amoebas three days earlier, so I devour it.

Amoebas become my excuse for turning down kuxa. When people offer me some, I clutch my stomach and say it still hurts from the microbes. Some people shake their heads, others assure me that kuxa will cure me.

The dancers, on the other hand, are soaking up the liquor. Julia moves nimbly through the crowd, which has grown since lunch began. She pours drinks into cups, offers them to the dancers, and retrieves the cups for the next persons. Although she carries a bottle labeled "Venado," I cannot tell whether it holds this legal liquor or kuxa. Either way, it is hard to say no to Julia, but I hold my ground when she offers a drink.

The afternoon turns out to be anything but peaceful. An older woman who insists I take her photo becomes angry at me after I tell her I have run out of film. When the toritos begin to dance, Julia breaks a branch off a peach tree, fashions a varejón (switch), and starts swatting all the dancers she can, telling them to pull out the stops. Smaller dancers dodge her flailing arms, but older ones stay put and feel her esprit de corps across their back ends and legs. Reyna says that Julia is chastising the dancers, telling them that if they do not dance well today, something will happen to them tomorrow or the next day. Julia singles out Chema for an especially thorough whipping, but I am not sure he feels it.

This is not the first time I have seen Julia strike the moros. On the first day of Guadalupe celebrations on Guadalupe Hill, Julia and some other women spotted me and insisted that I eat with them. I sat by their cooking fire, and they put a bowl of chicken caldo and a cup of kuxa in my hands. The mayordomo and the caporal were eating across the fire. Julia suddenly took a long string of fireworks and began thrashing the seated moros, hitting them even in the crotch. They chuckled and kept eating. She then gave the fireworks to some boys to light up a short distance away. I finished my meal, thanked everyone in the customary way, and returned to my friends waiting on the hill.

As the dance on Guadalupe came to an end and the patrón was hoisted onto his stretcher, the doleful cries of the moros filled the night. At that moment, some children began laughing and pointing toward the marimba. They said that a woman was dancing. I turned and saw Julia swaying by herself in the corral, in dark silhouette against an illuminated vendor's stand, holding aloft a long string of fireworks. Moving to the marimba's dirge, she would lift and wrap the fireworks around her shoulders as though she were handling a serpent. The light, shadow, and sound effects made the scene even eerier. For a moment I thought I was watching Marie Laveau, the voodoo queen of New Orleans.

Back at Julia's house, the dance reaches its bitter end. Following his death, the patrón comes around and thanks everyone for coming. As he thanks Chema, Julia erupts into tears, not wanting the dance to end. She pulls herself together and beseeches the marimba players to play their instrument one last time. But they have already covered it up and do not want to play beyond their agreed-upon time. Chema demands that they play. He even shouts at them, while others try to calm him down. The musicians pack up the marimba, lift it, and walk out of the house. The party quickly disintegrates, Julia in tears.

RETREATING BODIES

The moros try to close the dance season on January 6, Epiphany. On this day, the spirit-owners begin receding from the townspace and from the dancers, but not before a final dance is performed. Because January 6 falls this year on a Saturday, the moros debate whether to hold the dance the following day, Sunday, when a bigger crowd is in town, or to wait a week longer. Grumbling, they finally select Sunday, January 7, and early that day they erect the corral and start the dance at 10:30 a.m. Within two hours, though, torrential rain hits the parque and sends the moros scrambling for cover. The sporadic afternoon rains force them to call it a day.

They regroup the next Sunday before the old San Juan Church, in a corral festooned with plastic fringe streamers. But only sixteen dancers are in costume. Gabriel says that Candelario Pérez, a vaquero, is not dancing because of a hand injury. Fidel Caté, mayordomo, says that he will dance later today. William Caná is setting up a sound system for the marimba, even as it plays. To my surprise, Gabriel says that they rented this equipment from the Iglesia Betlehem, the largest Protestant congregation in town. He arranged it through some friends in this church. William is not dancing because his wife will be having their third child any day now.

By late afternoon, many people have descended on the parque, and I see many familiar faces. Something is different about the choreography, though. The patrón walks around and embraces each dancer in turn, bidding him farewell with grandiose gestures and stride. To bid good-bye properly to the other dancers and to the spirit-owners of their costumes, the patrón must do so while fully costumed and while embodying his own entrusted rajawal.

When the bullfighting begins, each moro who is about to confront a torito invokes Our Lord of Esquipulas, the Black Christ, whose day is tomorrow, January 15. Then all eyes turn to the patrón. But before confronting torito Jasmín for the last time, the patrón proclaims his gratitude to the moros, to the folkloric committee, and to the public. Jasmín follows suit and then charges at the patrón. In one of his raucous attacks, he even loses a horn, snagging it on the patrón's handkerchief. As the audience erupts in laughter, Jasmín partially lifts his mask, finds the horn, then holds it to his mask while he finishes his charges. At the coup de grace, Jasmín tumbles down along with the patrón, somehow winding up beneath him.

Mayhem ensues. Someone throws fireworks into the corral, while others fire mortars and Roman candles. People crowd into the crumbling corral and laugh hysterically as a dancer hops and leaps in a string of exploding fireworks. Children chase each other into the corral, and the patrón's human wife delivers her fallen husband the secret bundle that will complete his transfiguration. More fireworks overhead. Amid the ruckus, the patrón's voice crackles through the speakers as someone holds the microphone to his bloody face. He offers his final pleas, bids farewell to all, and is lifted upon the stretcher that has borne his weight many times. His trusted negros support his feet. Gabriel's broken, semiamplified voice then fills the parque. He thanks everyone who helped and reads the names of all the dancers, starting with the little toritos and pastorcitos. Antonia Calí then takes the microphone and encourages women to participate as doña Rosa. Gabriel also thanks her father for letting her participate. When the moros see me taking a picture of Gabriel reading out of his notebook, many people ask me for photos. After explaining how useless my cheap camera is at night, I take the photos.

Following the dance, I help transport the sound equipment. Several dancers load three chairs, an amplifier, microphones, two speakers, and a mortar into my truck. A handful of people then climb aboard, with Gabriel up front. We make the delivery, and Gabriel insists on paying me five quetzales (eighty-three cents) to drive everyone to Julia's house. I leave everyone at Julia's and drive back to my house, where I park the truck. From there I walk back to Cantón 8.

Everybody crowds into Julia's altar room. Chema kneels before an enormous image of San Juan Bautista, with the patrón at his side. The women are in the back kneeling on *petates* (reed mats). Some Hail Marys are in progress, interrupted by Our Fathers and outbursts by Chema. In this impromptu rosary-moros-prayer session, Chema calls out to San Juan Bautista, invokes God, and declares that the two negros must protect and guard the dance. He laments that not all the moros have come and names those who have, and then urges the patrón to speak. But before ceding the floor, Chema makes the sign of the cross over his negro mask and has the patrón make this sign over it as well. The patrón offers a few words of prayer, and everyone gets up off their knees and takes a seat.

Arturo's torito costume and mask are propped up on a chair to the left of the altar, looking lifelike, with a candle at the costume's feet. If Chema were not wearing his negro costume, it would be propped right next to it. A little deer doll, dressed as a moro, faces the room from a small stand before the altar. Arturo carried this doll during some dances. Julia staggers over to us and tells me that more people should have come tonight. "Oh, how I love this sacred dance!" she says, weeping and moving out the door. I accept a cigarette and walk to the altar.

The moros' coffer sits on a chair a few feet before the altar, next to a case of liter beer bottles. Chema pours me a glass of beer, containing mainly froth, which I drink down as he watches me with glazed eyes. He pours a lot of frothy glasses for people, sending large amounts of beer to the floor. The floor gets more than we do.

When it is time to count the money, some moros insist there are too few witnesses present. Gabriel says that we must count it and asks me to witness the counting. Everyone agrees, and Gabriel makes the sign of the cross over the coffer and opens it. Different bills are sorted out and counted. The patrón, somewhat sober, thanks me for my help. Chema offers a glass of beer froth to Gabriel, who tells Chema that they will deal with the money first and then drink. Chema takes my hand and says he is giving me a "clean" receptacle to drink from, the bottle itself. Despite everyone's encouragement, I cannot drink the whole liter, so I give it back to Chema.

The counting done, some of us go warm ourselves at the kitchen fire with hot chocolate. Some young men begin to joke about me. They somehow decide that I will drink the chocolate from a big *xarito*, or clay vessel, which provokes immediate laughter and shrieking. But back in the altar room, the patrón has become very upset with Chema. Chema is accusing people of entering his bedroom, where his television is, and has been telling someone to watch for those out to rob him. The patrón tells Chema that none of us are thieves, that we were invited, and that it is time to go. Julia is sobbing. I leave with the other disillusioned, but not really surprised, guests. A woman carries the empty coffer to her house, and Gabriel hurries home with the moros money tucked away in his jacket.

THE COSTUME *ENTREGA*

With the dance season officially over, the moros prepare to return the costumes and masks to the morería. Two days after the last public dance, Manolo Calí hosts the entrega, a prayer meeting and party that will formally separate the dancers from the costume rajawala'.

At Manolo's house, the arriving moros place their costume bundles, containing their masks and costumes, before the altar in the main room. Some moros mill about, others wander outside. The marimba players are out in the street, waiting for their instrument, which never arrives. Other moros appear. William Caná has come to turn in a costume for someone who cannot make it tonight. Miguel Cúmez looks nervous. The morería has sent him two telegrams in the past week telling him to return the overdue costumes, and he does not like this pressure.

Miguel is looking for Gabriel Miza, the moros director. When he cannot find him, he asks William to say a few words later to the assembled moros, since William is on the board of directors. William shakes his head, saying that he is not on the board of directors; he is on the *comité folklórico*. When Miguel protests that the two boards are the same thing, William clarifies that the committee is only responsible for acquiring funds, and having done this, his work is done. Miguel concedes and keeps looking for Gabriel. Manolo begins motioning everyone inside. He is serving kuxa.

Gabriel finally arrives, and everyone gathers at the altar. He announces that each dancer will come forward with his costume, and he asks Miguel Cúmez and Salvador Roquel to help him inspect and sort them. Everyone must remove all personal adornments from their costumes. The first dancer called is the patrón, Eliseo Mux. Eliseo's wife replies that he is out of town working but that she has brought his costume bundle. Each dancer lugs his bundle forward, unwraps it, and pulls out the pechera (tunic), *pantalones* (pants), *capa* (cape), sombrero (hat), *peluca* (wig), *máscara* (mask), and whatever else comes with it such as swords, belts, and manikins. Gabriel inspects the items and puts them in designated piles. Feather sticks go into a sack. Trifoil hats are unfolded and stacked. Napoleonic hats are stacked. The masks are reverently placed at the foot of the altar. Gabriel levies small charges if part of a costume has gotten unsewn or appears damaged, or if any feathers are damaged.

As the moros bring their bundles, I tell Salvador how well he danced as torito Jasmín. He thanks me and says that this is the third time he has danced; he also danced once in a regular season and also during last year's fair. Salvador says that he always dances as torito Jasmín because he enjoys this character the most. He chuckles that the dance used to be even more festive.

Back at the altar, someone hands in a small moros doll, enclosed in the pouch used for donations. Salvador admires the doll's fine moros costume. He confirms that this doll and pouch collect donations by the *sacar de repente* method, in which a dancer singles out a spectator (with a loud rattle) and obligates him to give money. I ask if the doll has the same rajawal as the costume it comes with, and he says it does. Salvador explains that about twenty-five years ago, the doll had a quetzal bill tied to its uplifted hand. The dancer would hold up the doll so it could "ask" for money. Now, the two vaqueros who carry the doll, Pascualillo and Martinejo, tie the money to their hands to successfully sacar de repente. The dancer has assumed the doll's magical function, attaching to himself what was once attached to the doll: the talismanic quetzal bill. Doll and dancers "conjure up" donations. When I tell him that some moros call the doll the brujito (little witch), he simply responds, "Ah, yes." This particular doll came with one of the moros costumes, he says, but the doll was not used. The person adopting the costume used his own, more embellished doll.

That person was Miguel Cúmez. He later tells me that his doll took him two days to make, with material costing around fifty quetzales ($8.33). He also says that the doll has the same rajawal as the costume it accompanies. When he had finished dressing the doll, he explains, he said a prayer over it. "Then, it has its corazón," he says. After this, he could dance with the doll and use it. Only after the brujito is spiritually "primed" can it be used in the dance; its corazón (heart or animating essence) must first be enkindled. Salvador wants to buy the doll, so Miguel might part with it for one hundred quetzales ($16.67). This is the cost of materials, plus two days' labor.

The inspections take a couple of hours at Manolo's house. Four moros did not report to the entrega and will have to be dealt with later. Resolved, all kneel before the altar. Gabriel leads in some standard prayers and pleas to San Juan Bautista. When a censer is waved over the costumes and masks, a striking scene emerges. Two dozen painted wooden faces stare up through the smoke, framed by piles of sparkling fabric. The air is heavy with sadness as the moros bid good-bye to their costumes and separate from their rajawala'. This is probably the last time these stewards will see their masks. Manolo gives each mask a taste of his liquor.

After the good-bye prayer, Gabriel, with Manolo at his side, addresses everyone. He proclaims his love for these activities and for the moros and extends a special thanks to the comité for its monetary help and to Manolo for lending us his house several times. Then, William declares that the comité has done its job well. He proudly reports that during a recent moros dance, a young spectator came up to him as he danced and complimented him. This proves that young people appreciate the dance, he says.

FIGURE 11.3

The dance masks arrayed on the floor of Manolo's house during the *despedida* ceremony. The wife of one of the dancers swings a censer over the masks. Photo by author.

Some men place a metal table with a coffer and ledger before the altar. Raúl Martínez, the moros' accountant, begins to read out all the group's monetary transactions. He lists what they paid for the marimba, portable generators, diesel fuel, and other items. He also covers what donations were collected at each dance. During a break in the accounting, Manolo's family serves a small meal. We eat while Raúl finishes up, the room carrying a culinary silence. Some men ask Raúl to clarify certain details, and for a moment, Raúl, Gabriel, and others raise their voices. They then read out what various people, including myself, gave to the group. I feel embarrassed I did not give more, although I did contribute some money and use of my truck on many occasions.

When the accounting reaches what seems a satisfactory end, the guests get up and talk. I snap pictures of Raúl by himself and with Salvador amid the masks and costumes. One dancer tells me that his silk handkerchief cost him a whopping thirty-five quetzales ($5.83). I approach the masks, admiring the tableau. Some people urge me to put one on, so I do, with some difficulty. Holding my handkerchief in my hand, I do some poorly executed dance kicks, to everyone's delight. Louder laughs follow when I remove the heavy mask. A woman suddenly pinches and holds my nose, shaking my head vigorously, commenting on my nose and the mask's nose. When I regain my airway, I hold the mask next to my face and say, "Junan qatza'n," "Our noses are the same." Bursting into guffaws, they repeat my words and laugh even harder.

Music explodes from a corner of the room. A tape player has kicked in, belting out Selena favorites as well as many other Tex-Mex songs and medleys. Salvador is the first one dancing, but others soon follow his brave example. Before the first song wanes, Salvador is pushing his dance partner against me, urging us to dance. The entire room is then clapping and laughing at the sight of us, of me, actually, trampling the pine needles and giving my squealing dance partner reason to never again show her face in public. Her husband and two children watch us from a distance. Salvador is determined to dance with a certain young girl; she breaks away and hides, but he always finds her.

By now I just want to sit down. Several small children are putting on the moros masks and dancing around. Some wear the masks of toritos and vaqueros, and of doña Rosa. They are uncannily mimicking the steps of each character and enacting certain parts of the dance. One boy has become the patrón and struts about. Meanwhile, a torito understudy charges a small, unsuspecting vaquero and refuses to desist. And since I have accepted many libations tonight, I melt into the escalating jubilation, clutching my stomach at the utterly hysterical sight of the next generation of moritos. The mission of the moros has not been lost on these kids.

But for all the merriment, there is also great pain. A couple of dancers tell me how sad they are to see their masks go. Salvador, overhearing this, tells me that "one grows very close to the costumes." Another dancer confides that "one becomes really sad upon handing over his traje." At that moment, two men approach the altar. These men have shared in the cost of a vaquero costume, and tonight they are bidding farewell to the mask's rajawal. They walk over to the array of masks on the floor, quickly locate their adopted vaquero, and pick it up. One dancer makes the sign of the cross over it and holds it close, whispering to it. He then hands it to his partner. The other man also crosses it, speaks privately to it, and holds it to his chest. He shares more words with it, wipes his eyes, and hugs it again before putting it down. The two then step back, turn around, and quickly walk out of the room.

Shortly after sunrise, the moros organizers collect the costumes of those who missed the previous night's entrega. All that remains is to drive the costumes back to the morería in San Cristóbal Totonicapán. The moros have asked me to this, and to be ready for them at 6:00 a.m.

RETURN TO THE *MORERÍA*

In the early morning I am scraping a thick layer of dust and ice off my truck windshield when Miguel Cúmez walks up. We drive over to Manolo's house to pick up the costume bundles and Gabriel Miza. But Gabriel is not there, and Miguel gets worried. The morería people are breathing down his neck. The two telegrams they sent him have him worried for his financial future. We go pick up Miguel's wife, who will be coming with us. Just as we are collecting her, a shirtless Salvador Roquel drives up in his van. Gabriel is with him.

After a quick stop at the gas station, we pick up Miguel's sister-in-law, who needs to see a ritual specialist in San Cristóbal Totonicapán. We then head west out of town. Gabriel says we must follow the same route back to the morería that the costumes took from the morería to Comalapa. My truck and its complement of four men, two women, and twenty-four glittery personages is soon bumping along toward the village of Panabajal.

We are barely ten minutes into the drive when something happens. My stomach or intestines begin cramping, and the pain is excruciating. I want to stop, but I am hoping the pain will pass. Maybe I am too embarrassed to stop. I just grit my teeth and keep moving. Although I am fixating on my stomach, I still want to ask Gabriel a few things. He has not noticed my sudden sweating and pallor. So as we ascend Chuwa Burro, I mention the place to him.

Without blinking Gabriel says that Chuwa Burro is like the *puerta* (door) that opens to the corral of Las Delicias, which we passed some minutes ago. I almost forget about my pain as his words sink in. This is why the costumes enter through Chuwa Burro on their way to Las Delicias. There is no way to enter the corral but through the door, especially of an animistic enclosure like Las Delicias. This is the first time someone has described the relationship between these two places in this way. I engrave his words into my memory as the door of Chuwa Burro closes behind us.

The truck passes through Panabajal and enters the Inter-American Highway. I exchange one type of driving tension for another, now engaging high-speed, two-lane highway culture. We arrive at San Cristóbal Totonicapán at around 11:00 a.m. and quickly locate the morería. Miguel's relatives go off on their errands. A man rides up on a bicycle and asks, "Are y'all from Comalapa?" Hearing that we are, he turns glum, and walks his bicycle into the morería.

Over the next hour or so the Comalapans defend themselves from the morería workers, who accuse the Comalapans of reneging on their contract and overkeeping the costumes. My companions plead that everything from torrential rains to the presidential runoff elections interfered with carrying out the last dance. Everything thus got delayed by a week, we claim.

The morería manager finally throws up his arms and tells us to present the costumes for inspection. He wants to close the books on this. In a large room with four sewing machines and a lot of costumes, the morería assistants open our bundles and pull out the masks and other parts of each costume. We are told that some pants, a cape, and the pechera of doña Rosa are missing. The manager is fuming. He mutters, "Malísimo, malísimo,"

"Terrible, terrible," as he digs up the price of the missing items, Miguel looking over his shoulder. We were certain the bundles were complete. Miguel
must leave a seventy-five quetzal ($12.50) security deposit and promise to
send the items later. But the manager then discovers that his assistants have
wrongly separated two of the piles. They have found doña Rosa's costume
pieces.

Everyone breathes a sigh of relief. The manager shakes his head, stop-
ping short of an apology, saying that it would be a sin to charge us for
something that we had actually turned in. But when we ask him to sell us
a vaquero mask, he refuses. William Caná had bought a torito mask for
seventy-five quetzales ($12.50) when the moros first rented the costumes,
and other moros wanted to do the same. I am later told that the manager
had sold the mask without authorization, *por debajo del agua*, beneath the
water's surface. Morerías like this one deal with Maya from many places
(Krystal 2000:155), and, as the manager explains, dancers from certain
towns often come to really like a certain mask, even writing their name on
it. Since they later ask for the same mask, the morería must keep it in stock.
So they cannot sell any masks. In the final tally, some sashes are said to be
missing, and we pay a total of ten quetzales ($1.67) in fines.

Our spirits buoy once they shut the ledgers. Gabriel produces a bottle of
Venado liquor and asks the morería staff for some glasses. Drinks are
shared all around. I ask to see the *almacenes* (storerooms) where the masks
and costumes are kept. Perhaps sensing a chance for foreign publicity, I am
cordially invited into two rooms literally filled with dance items. Piles
of folded costumes stuff the shelves lining the walls, and over a hundred
masks of different dance characters hang from the rafters. These costumes
will bind the rajawala' to many dancers' bodies. As I look around, I can
picture the rajawal tzyaq's corral.

On the return trip, we stop at a roadside market. A little later we pull
into El Mirador, where I discover I have a flat tire. I am not happy about it,
but I am very relieved that the tire did not explode on the highway. My
passengers are amazed that I can fix a tire and that I even have a spare tire
waiting. But their interest soon wanes, and they wander off to admire the
view of Lake Atitlán and its volcanoes. When I am done, everyone marvels
at the devices I have on hand: a tire pressure gauge and a portable electric
pump. They board the truck before I have even finished stowing the tools

and dusting myself off. I tell Gabriel that I need a breather, and I walk around in the cold wind of El Mirador eating a snack, grumpier than I want to admit.

Back on the highway, Gabriel and I talk about the moros' future. He wants advice about keeping the tradition alive. I suggest that the moros involve more women in the group as dancers, maybe through shorter dances like during San Juan Day. Without thinking, I venture that moros brujitos dolls can be sold to raise money. Gabriel reflects that the costumes they rented last San Juan Day were really good. They were from Chichicastenango. Veteran moros felt that this year's costumes were not good, he says, and one vaquero left the group because of this. Gabriel wishes that Comalapa had Chichicastenango's competitive dancing spirit. There, some dancers will pay Q1,500 ($250.00) or more per costume (Comalapans pay Q150 [$25.00] per costume). I suggest that he talk to dancers of other towns for fundraising ideas and maybe involve Comalapan artists in mask painting. He asks me to tell the moros about my ideas.

We pull into Comalapa, and I leave my tire to be patched at the Texaco station. When I have left everyone off, Gabriel insists on paying me twenty-five quetzales ($4.17) for my driving services, apologizing about Guatemala's low daily wage. Happy that I finally accept the money, he tells me that he has something for me from Esquipulas, home of the Black Christ, which he will bring to me on Sunday. I thank him and leave him at his street corner, watching him walk away unburdened of dance responsibilities for the first time in months. Back at the gas station, the tire is not yet ready, so I will get it tomorrow. Right now it is too cold to be out.

A BODY OF CHANGE

A little unexpectedly, I now empathize more with what the moros have been doing, enough to say that people like Gabriel Miza never really unshoulder their burden. They simply consider how to shift the weight around in a time when many forces pull young men away from community rituals. It is as though Gabriel wants to make sure that other men and boys (and girls) do not miss out on witnessing the rajawal's transformations up close.

I think Gabriel would agree that at the end of each dance season, the moros feel they have undergone a change. They have seen and felt how the costume spirits affix directly to their bodies and manifest through them. They have become very close to beings that guard the natural bounty and that elude direct observation. They have fulfilled vows. Amid their exhilaration, loss, and trepidation, they stand reminded of how their daily life depends on local rajawala'. In doing so, they embody lessons for personal living and adult responsibility.

However, although many person-centered operations have taken place, so have many community-centered ones. Comalapans love to showcase "their" dance and to tell the toritos story as they want. The December lull in the agricultural cycle also lets people renew and reperform their link to their group forebears, the abuelos. And since there are both human and nonhuman abuelos, the moros connect with these as each requires.

Moros dancing achieves these operations in a short nine weeks. During this time, however, many physical and spiritual transformations play out among the dancers, the costumes, and their patron spirits. At every level of the dance experience, bodies reach beyond their boundaries and become subject to shifting agency. There is also a blurring of agency within dancers akin to shamanic trance, something reported in other communities (Cook and Offit 2013:68, 88; Hutcheson 2003:98). As specialists in the bodily grounding of spirit, the moros accommodate agency and keep alive the drama at the intersection of matter and spirit.

Conclusion

SOME OF THE MOST NOTABLE works of Maya ethnography have
focused on Maya soul. Whether set in highland Chiapas or in highland
Guatemala, these works remind us that Maya have kept many of their soul
ideas, or have creatively adapted them, in the face of centuries of Christian
evangelization. Even if Maya souls today bear some resemblance to "Western" Christian souls, the message in these works is that there is still something different about Maya souls, something fundamentally non-Western.
From these works emerges a Maya soul that resists change and resists the
hegemonic forces sent against it. It is so tenacious that Maya outlooks on
the world hinge upon it. The resulting portrait of soul is compelling and
agrees with our sense of historical vindication, but like all portraits, it is
incomplete.

This study has tried to show that discussions of Maya being and spiritual knowledge must attend to what Maya themselves consider important.
And what Kaqchikel Maya consider important as the ground of spirit and
as a vehicle of knowing is the body. If there is a central message in this
book, it is that to better understand Maya outlooks on spiritual reality, we
should turn toward the body. What is more, we should consult the body
even though research on Maya spirituality favors focusing on phenomena
like ritual specialists and the resurgence of Maya religion on the national
stage. While these things are important and merit study, a focus on them
deemphasizes the body and can suggest that spirit enjoys primacy over
body. It may also be adding to the sense that Maya spiritual knowledge is
predicated on a resilient spirit coupled to a pliable body, when in reality
spirit and body are part of a resilient continuum that deserves another look.

We sometimes think that people are unwilling to change their ideas
about soul, but that they are willing to change their ideas about body. To a

certain extent this may be true. After all, the body is more directly accessible to shifting paradigms of science and more vulnerable to outside manipulation than the soul, shielded behind layers of privacy and obscurity. I would argue, however, taking into account the experience of Comalapa Kaqchikel Maya, that not only do people resist changing their ideas about the body, too, but that the very persistence of their bodily understandings helps to shape and sustain their ideas about soul. When a person describes how humans are animated in the womb, he or she confirms this with embodied information. When soul specialists diagnose soul loss, they look to bodily signs in the sufferer. And when dancers wonder if they are feeding the spirit-owners properly, they consult their own bodily states. The body becomes more than just a diagnostic frame for soul. It becomes a critical vehicle for understanding the presence, completeness, and state of soul.

Since beginning this research in 1991, I have become more convinced that it is incorrect to think about soul and body as fully separate entities. Comalapans show a strong narrative pull toward the idea of soul and body contiguity. The closer we look at their experiences of health, sickness, and connection with the living landscape, in fact, the more we find the boundaries between soul and body becoming increasingly faint. Each entity is revealed more as an inflection of the other than as something autonomous, and this is heavily reflected in local ways of talking about soul and body. This means that we do not yet know enough about soul or body in Comalapa to arrive at a final portrayal of either. It is clear, though, that we will have to look more closely at bodily operations and bodily consciousness to repair gaps in our knowledge, as others have already demonstrated (Eber 1995:136; Stanzione 2003:209; Tedlock 1992:138–46).

At the same time, we need to reassess the role of landscape within the soul-body construct. For Maya, of course, landscape is not a static, inert expanse of green, but a material expression of the immanent spiritual world. The hinterlands hold riches and dangers in their contours, and no Comalapan can avoid dealing with them in some way. But despite the trepidation many feel toward the living landscape, people recognize their kinship and interdependence with it. They reach out to it and it responds to them. As a stage through which human embodiment experiences take place, the landscape not only feeds people but ties them to a local agency that makes itself known through their bodies and anchors their identity there. Q'eq'chi' Maya, as Richard Wilson (1991:52) explains, come to know their geographical surroundings well and identify with the earth lords there. They, like Maya of other places, offer devotions to their local earth lords in return for health and fertility. In doing so, they physically bind their identity to the land. K'iche' Maya likewise develop an embodied engagement with place, as Jean Molesky-Poz reports:

> K'iche' traditionalists attach meaning to place through their own embodied, interactive participation with it. They not only perceive the physical features, tonality, or mood of the landscape, but also feel, recognize, and respect a dimension intuited: the heart or spirit of the place. (2006:113)

When Kaqchikel Maya of Comalapa enter the hills, they carry with them the stories they have heard about the land and their own physical memories of the land. And when they refer to the heart or spirit of a place, they mean it in a very tangible way. They recognize agency in the landscape as acting through their bodies, at times even appearing before their eyes. When it causes partial soul loss, this agency reveals how it can move in and out of a human bodily frame and connect intimately with human soul. If John Watanabe (1989:273) convincingly explains that part of the Mam Maya soul roots people to specific "ancestral locales" and local ways of being, it is because many Maya consider local places essential to referencing who they are, and to supplying a meaningful vocabulary for lived experience.

To explore local understandings of spirit and body in San Juan Comalapa, I have drawn attention to certain domains of belief and behavior, but I do so with a qualifier. While these domains have included people who hold experiences in common, I have artificially designated and bounded the domains. Midwives, soul therapists, and dancers constantly intersect each other in the community, at some times more than others, and might not even see themselves as members of discrete groups. It would be a mistake, then, to assume that each domain exists in an absolute sense and in isolation from other domains in local life, or even in isolation from global processes (Fischer 2001). But by exploring the grounding of spirit in these constructed domains, I have found the body to be the primary vehicle through which Comalapa Kaqchikel Maya affirm and vitalize their cosmology. Even when the Maya body suffers, or perhaps especially when it does, from the suffering can emerge spiritual knowledge. I propose that the Maya body is a multisensory field that actuates spiritual experience and knowledge at the same time that it provides the starting point for daily awareness. The body's consciousness enacts and works congruently with spiritual consciousness, and it does so even as formal religious structures change over time.

A casual visitor to Comalapa would probably notice the many church buildings around town. Especially large buildings dominate the parque, and a dozen smaller ones, some little more than storefronts, lie scattered throughout its neighborhoods. The loudspeakers of some of the smaller, evangelical congregations forcefully remind us of their presence. Unlike in some other highland towns, though, there is no public divinatory cult with altars in the town square or cemetery. The cofradía often accompanies church processions, but men do not gather on the church steps to wave censers. It is easy to come away with the impression that local Maya restrict their spirituality today to institutionalized forms and do not practice their ancestral traditions. The fact that people like to talk about the churches they attend might even convince us that Maya spiritual experience has retreated from local life. But we have to be cautious. Although Comalapa may not bear the visible imprint of Maya spiritualities in its public spaces or conversations, Maya spiritual knowledge is still enacted here. It is enacted in places that churchmen have long baptized, that armies have long targeted, and that health workers have long treated. Maya spiritual knowledge germinates in a bodily ground.

Appendix

Origins of the Community

SAN JUAN COMALAPA HAS EXISTED since at least the sixteenth century, although its Kaqchikel forebears occupied the central highlands from an earlier period. Comalapans speak a variant of the Kaqchikel Maya language belonging to the Western Kaqchikel dialect area, which today encompasses the towns of Sololá, Santa Catarina Palopó, San Antonio Palopó, Patzún, Poaquil, Tecpán Guatemala (Iximche'), Patzicía, and Santa Cruz Balanya' (Richards and Richards 1987:35). This dialect area corresponds to the postclassic Kaqchikel segment that was allied with the K'iche' Maya and that opposed the Eastern (Akahal) Kaqchikel. When the Western Kaqchikel ended their alliance with the K'iche' in the late fifteenth century, they left what was probably their first capital, Chichicastenango, and reestablished themselves at Iximche' (Guillemin 1967:25). They remained at Iximche', outside of present-day Tecpán Guatemala, until the Spaniards arrived in the sixteenth century. From the moment the Kaqchikel settled Iximche' until Pedro de Alvarado arrived in 1524, they engaged in continual battles with their former allies, the K'iche'.

Once Alvarado subdued the K'iche' and destroyed their capital, Gumarkaaj, he and his Tlaxcalan allies entered Iximche' in April 1524 and were well received by the Kaqchikel lords B'eleje' K'at and Kaji' Imox (Maxwell and Hill 2006:260). Alvarado knew that the Kaqchikel and the K'iche' were in a state of conflict, and he further fueled their enmity. But because the Spaniards forced many demands on the Iximche' Kaqchikel, these fled the city in August 1524. The flight was provoked in part by the mysterious apparition of *jun achi' k'axtok* (a demon-man), who incited the Kaqchikel lords to leave (Maxwell and Hill 2006:267). The Kaqchikel took refuge in the surrounding mountainous region and clashed with the Spaniards for the next six years.

During this time, the disaffected Kaqchikel convened under the command of a Kaqchikel lord, Ajpop Sotz'il, and organized an army of "over thirty thousand combatants" (Juarros 1981:364–65). Kaqchikels from the Comalapa vicinity participated in this army. Meanwhile, a seditious band of Alvarado's own troops set fire to Iximiche' in February 1526 (Guillemin 1967:25). Thirteen months later (in March 1527), the Spaniards reorganized and relocated to Chi Xot, present-day Comalapa (Maxwell and Hill 2006:274), but they abandoned this site, probably south of the present town, within a year. With this mention of Comalapa in the *Xajil Chronicle*, considered part of the larger *Annals of the Kaqchikels* (Maxwell and Hill 2006), Comalapa enters the pathway of conquest.

A year after the Spaniards left the Comalapa environs, in January 1528, some of the rebellious Kaqchikel submitted to the tributary demands of the Spaniards (Maxwell and Hill 2006:275–81). The remaining Kaqchikel presented themselves to Alvarado in May 1530, and heavy tributes were immediately imposed upon them. After this period, aside from occasional skirmishes between the Spaniards and individual Kaqchikel resisters, Spanish political domination was virtually complete. In later centuries, the Spaniards and Spanish creoles continued forcing an irreversible course of European acculturation upon the Guatemala natives.

Comalapa the town probably resulted from Spanish attempts to congregate towns in the 1540s (Farber 1978:50; del Busto 1961:29). A royal decree of June 10, 1540, initiated the gathering of Indians into towns "to be indoctrinated and civilized" (Juarros 1981:381; also Recinos and Goetz 1953:136). After Pedro de Alvarado died in July 1541 and the colonial capital (later called Ciudad Vieja) at the foot of the Volcán de Agua was destroyed in September 1541, Dominican, Franciscan, and a few Mercedarian clergy intensified their missionary work in the region. They even created catechisms in Kaqchikel Maya. The Mercedarians, though, left their Indian charges with the Dominicans and went to minister in Huehuetenango (Juarros 1981:379). By 1553, Comalapa was among many other highland towns ministered by Franciscans (del Busto 1961:29).

In later centuries, Comalapa remained isolated compared to neighboring towns like San Martín Jilotepeque, Patzicía, and Chimaltenango, which were situated on principal trade and travel routes (Farber 1978:50).

This is probably why Comalapa is infrequently mentioned by sixteenth- and seventeenth-century Spanish conquerors and chroniclers. Indeed, until the 1990s, only footpaths and unreliable dirt roads connected Comalapa to outside communities.

Some colonial chroniclers provided glimpses of an early, growing Comalapa. For instance, when Francisco Fuentes y Guzmán visited Comalapa in 1690, he noted that the town had around 2,050 inhabitants, a decrease from the previous century (1932–1933:348). From Archbishop Pedro Cortés y Larraz's visit to Comalapa in 1770, though, came the report of approximately 7,000 inhabitants, a significant increase from the previous century (Farber 1978:52). He also described the town's major economic activities as maize, bean, and wheat farming, and chicken raising. Early in the nineteenth century (1808–1818), Domingo Juarros (1981:46) recorded that 7,000–8,000 Indians lived in Comalapa. Although we cannot know how accurately these chroniclers counted the Comalapans living in outlying areas, their figures suggest steady local population growth.

Notes

CHAPTER ONE

1. Many writers have investigated susto in Mesoamerican communities, affording many insights into the spatial and experiential distribution of this illness complex (Adams 1952; Adams and Rubel 1967; Douglas 1969; Eber 1995; Fabrega and Silver 1973; Foster 1948; Gillin 1948; Guiteras Holmes 1961a; Logan 1979; Madsen 1965; Merrill 1988; Oakes 1951; O'Nell 1975; O'Nell and Selby 1968; Parsons 1936; Rubel, O'Nell, and Collado-Ardón 1984; Vogt 1969), as is true also of susto research taking place elsewhere in Latin America (Foster 1976; Gillin 1948; Rubel 1964; Uzzell 1974). Susto research of the past fifty years has gradually moved susto into the arena of psychological and medical debate (Weller et al. 2002).

2. Among the Ch'orti' Maya, pregnant and menstruating women, being ritually unclean, could *cause* many frights (Wisdom 1940:314). This did not appear to be the case in Comalapa, however, where pregnant women more often caused ruwa winäq.

3. Eva described the case of a pregnant woman who lived in Guatemala City. One day, the patient discovered her husband's infidelity, and she fled, out of control, to Comalapa to have her baby with Eva's help. The child emerged, but the placenta did not. Eva notified a physician, who placed an IV in the woman and attempted to retrieve the placenta, but their efforts failed. The woman died, said Eva, because of the shock from the infidelity (see Gillin 1948:389).

4. Among the Yucatecs of Campeche, fear is said to be transmissible from mother to child during pregnancy, or during lactation through the breast milk. For these Maya, anemia, known as "hollow blood," can produce weakness that can lead to conditions like diabetes and lack of mother's milk (García et al. 1999:46, 48).

5. See especially Adams (1952:34), Adams and Rubel (1967:345), Cosminsky (1976:166), and Redfield and Villa Rojas (1971:168–69) in this regard.

6. This condition is also attested to among the Yucatecs of Campeche (García et al. 1999:16).

7. In Momostenango and Santa Lucía Utatlán, the heat principle was also invoked against ruwa winäq by having children wear bracelets made from the bright-red seeds of the coral tree (*Erythrina corallodendron*, K'iche' *tz'ite'*), the same

type of seeds used for K'iche' calendrical divination (Cosminsky 1976:167; Tedlock 1987:1074; see also Merrill 1988:138). In Campeche, Mexico, mothers are likewise advised to put bracelets of nine pieces of red yarn, an *ojo de venado* amulet, or an amulet made from the umbilical cord on their babies (García 1999:238–39).

8. Ruwa winäq healers sometimes attributed their healing knowledge to dreams. These dreams usually connoted that the person was to begin a healing vocation. The midwife Clemencia, however, simply dreamed that she was to use lemons instead of eggs for ruwa winäq treatment. She then imported this therapeutic element into her midwife work. Still, Clemencia did not consider herself qualified to treat xib'iril cases, and so she referred them to oyonela'.

9. For Mexican Maya like the Tzeltal of Tzo'ontahal, Chiapas, for example, pulsing was essential to illness diagnosis because it let the curer listen "to what the blood wants" (Nash 1967:132–33). By "speaking with" and "grabbing" a person's blood, the Tzeltal curer in Oxchuc would get a confession of sins (Nash 1967:138), while a Tzeltal curer in Tenejapa would even employ a home "saint" to assist with his own pulsing (Metzger and Williams 1963:217–19, 222). Many Tzotzil curers in Zinacantan and San Pedro Chenalhó, meanwhile, pulse to get illness diagnoses directly from the blood (Eber 1995:157; Fabrega and Silver 1973:151).

10. Comalapans expressed different opinions about whether soul (alma, wanima) and spirit (espíritu, xamanil) were singular or differentiated entities. Opinions about this fell partially along religious lines, with self-identified Catholics tending to conflate alma and espíritu, and Protestants tending to differentiate them.

   One Protestant man explained the difference between alma and espíritu: "The Word of God says that espíritu and alma are two corazones, it seems"; he then explained how the alma is located on the left side of the chest, while the espíritu is on the right. A Protestant pastor disagreed, though, adhering to another model of differentiation: "Some people say [that the alma] is the corazón, but this isn't so." Referring then to 1 Thess. 5:23, he asserted, "Man is composed of espíritu, alma, and body." He explained that the espíritu, alma, and physical heart reside side by side in the chest and are each party to the holy and baser joys of man. The Protestant tendency to isolate espíritu from alma seems attributable also to the greater scriptural emphasis placed on the independent agency of the Holy Spirit, to which Protestants frequently refer when discussing what espíritu means to them.

11. Significantly, in Santiago Atitlán, Tz'utujiils recognized *rukux*, the physical heart, as the bodily seat of the ranima, the coessence or soul of the living person (Douglas 1969:91–92, 264).

12. In Chamula (Gossen 1989:391), secular and ritual heat are understood through the vehicle of the Tzotzil words *k'ak'al* (day) and *k'in* (fiesta). However, the Kaqchikel correlates of these words, *q'ij* (day) and *nimaq'ij* (fiesta), do not operate in a like manner in Comalapa. Kaqchikel ethnohistorical sources, however, do

reference *q'aq'al* (related to the word "q'aq'," "fire") as indicative of a lord's power and glory (Maxwell and Hill 2006:32, 35), suggesting a relationship with k'ak'al. Comalapans today, at any rate, consider chuq'a', like the permutations of heat in Chamula, critical for maintaining the physical body and the social body.

13. These earth lords are known as *tzuul taq'a* in Q'eq'chi' and preside over natural features of the land, animals, and atmospheric phenomena (Boremanse 2000:15).

14. Both Protestants and Catholics relate that many Protestants either send children to adorn their family graves with flowers, or do this secretly themselves at night "to avoid gossip."

15. Maud Oakes was herself accused of being a *dueña de cerro* (and a witch) during her stay in Todos Santos Cuchumatán (Oakes 1951:51). As a white stranger with unusual medical abilities and a keen interest in *chimanes*, she was accused of carrying away the spirits of those persons who died during her visit from 1945 to 1947.

16. Among Larraínzar Tzotzil, for instance, if a person falls or is attacked by an animal, the gods of the earth in that place could imprison his spirit (Holland 1961:222). Meanwhile, the person's chanul (animal-spirit counterpart) could be locked out of its safe abode in the mountain of the lineage spirits (1961:222). When a Kaqchikel of Magdalena Milpas Altas was frightened in the hills, the dueño del cerro was said to have abducted that person's soul (Adams 1952:30). See also Douglas (1969:97, 106), Eber (1995:46), Fabrega, Metzger, and Williams (1970:614–15), Logan (1979), Oakes (1951:184), and Vogt (1969:370).

17. Eighteenth-century K'iche' Maya, for example, felt that "[o]ffense to supernaturals could result in their causing illness by assaulting or capturing the offender's *natub*. Such beings might relent in return for an apology made on the proper day of the divinatory calendar, accompanied by a gift of food (incense) that only humans could provide" (Hill 1992:144).

    Hill (1992:89) described natub as a divine life-force imparted to each person via the ritual force of a particular sun (day), either of his birthday or of the ritual fixing of this force in him.

18. In the late seventeenth century, Francisco Antonio de Fuentes y Guzmán described in his *Recordación Florida* a tract of land north of Comalapa to which local Indians strictly controlled access. He reported that a local official, the Alcalde Ordinario Corregidor del Valle, suspected that animals were being hidden on the land, and conducted a search. Instead of finding animals, though, the official found a clandestine *oratorio* (prayer place) with a "multitude of idols." He promptly laid them to waste (del Busto 1961:32).

19. Her name is likely connected to the K'iche'an and Q'eqchi' term for gorge, *siwan*, and perhaps also to the Nahuatl *cihuatl*, "woman" (see Correa 1960:73–75).

20. Oliver La Farge (1947:106–7), for example, related a Q'anjob'al narrative of Santa Eulalia in which the ceiba tree was said to have a "saint" that it could entrust to a person. Charles Wisdom (1940:401–2) reported that the Ch'orti' recognized spirit in every type of animal and plant.

21. Six months after the 1995–1996 dance season ended, one of the moros negro dancers died. It was his first season dancing. His wife, the group's prayer maker, died a few years later.

22. Cutzal relates the following story:

> There was a woman, a couple actually, that never lived happily. They were always very restless. They lived in a village, but *la violencia* pushed them to the town center. The man decided that he didn't want to live as always, poor and always lacking, so he decided, "I'm going to Sarima'." So one night at midnight, he arrived at Sarima', and he did a ceremony, and there, his memory changed.
>
> He came upon a gleaming portal, and he heard someone say, "Identify yourself." The man gave his name. The voice asked him, "With whom do you wish to speak?" The man replied, "With the boss." The voice told him that since the man didn't have *licencia* [authorization], the man was going to have to pass several trials before he could speak with the boss.
>
> The man had to cross a river that reached up to his eyes, and he crossed it. Then he had to pass through a place where there were lions, tigers, and other carnivores, and he passed through it. Then he was taken to where there was a lot of money, and he was told that he needed to lift up a trunk full of money. But the trunk was too heavy, and he couldn't lift it. He was then told that whatever he was able to lift up would be what he would be given. So, he did pick up a smaller amount, and this amount was "authorized" to him.
>
> Then the señor, the lord of the place, appeared to the man, but the man became afraid of talking to him. When he worked up the nerve, the man said, "I beg your pardon, but I'm very poor, I don't know, but perhaps you would be willing to make me a loan?" The señor replied, "Well, I can give you money, but we are going to have to evaluate you first. I am going to pass over there through Kantaria [a Comalapan barrio]; you'll recognize me because I'll have two horses with me. Just call out to me when you see me passing by." The man was instructed to take with him things like *chuchitos* [steamed bundles of maize and meat], chocolate, and *guaro* [liquor]. The man was then allowed to leave, but he had first to go through some more trials.
>
> This whole time seemed to last about an hour for the man, but when he returned to his house, he found that he had been gone for three days. He described to his wife the things he had seen: people who looked like children, many animals that didn't harm anything, plants, everything well tended, and even snakes that wouldn't bite. He asked his wife to cook up the things he had been told to bring; then he waited at midnight at Chuwi Krusin Ab'aj [an area west of Kantaria].
>
> They waited, and then the señor appeared, with horses carrying big chests of money. But the man grew afraid of calling out to the señor and so didn't call him. The señor kept going and went on his way. Since this was during the Violence, the man disappeared, but maybe the señor took him.

23. Charles Wagley (1949:56), for example, said that in the Mam town of Santiago Chimaltenango "there are stories of a famous hunter, who either has a pact with the Guardian and daily secures his deer, or who forgets to pray to the Guardian before hunting and is punished." The "Guardian" is called dueño de los cerros, "spirit-owner of the hills." When a Mam ritualist struck a deal with the dueño del cerro in Todos Santos Cuchumatán, he incurred censure upon dying: "[N]o prayers are said over him, for he is a person apart" (Oakes 1951:51). The ritualist cannot be buried like other people; he must be left in a box atop the cemetery ground, separate in death as he was in life (Oakes 1951:51; see also Redfield and Villa Rojas 1971:199; Saler 1970:131; Falla 1971).

24. See also Douglas (1969:107–8) and Vogt (1965:34).

25. When a Kaqchikel of Magdalena Milpas Altas dreamed of a deceased person, it was because he had not paid enough religious homage to him (Adams 1952:31). Among Nebaj Ixils, dreams brought messages directly from the ancestors (Colby and Colby 1981:50), as they did among Zinacantan Tzotzils, for whom "dreams reflect the activities of the ancestral gods" (Fabrega and Silver 1973:149).

26. In this regard also see Eber (1995:155), La Farge (1947:160), Oakes (1951:91), Paul (1975:456–57), Redfield and Villa Rojas (1971: 211), and Tedlock (1981:322).

CHAPTER TWO

1. The *Xajil Chronicle* refers to the town as Chi Xot, "at the comal," from *chij* (Kaq.), "place of" or "place on," and *xot* (Kaq.), "earthen griddle." The name "Comalapa" is a nearly direct translation of this Kaqchikel toponym into Nahuatl (Farber 1978:49), also denoting "river of the comales": "comal" (Nah.) means "earthen griddle," and *apan* (Nah.) means "river." The Nahuatlized form of the town's name, "Comal-apan," is found in early documents (Farber 1978:49). The locale's Maya name may derive from an early manufacture of comales there, or, as some Comalapans today say, from flattened rocks found in local riverbeds. At any rate, while many Comalapans still call their town Chixot, the name "Chiq'a'l," "at the ashes," has also taken hold as a toponym (Maxwell and Hill 2006:274). This name may stem from the term *chi aq'a'al*, "place of charcoal/embers," that became conflated into "Chiq'a'al," from which "Chiq'a'l" may later have been derived. The toponym "Chiq'a'al" refers to a time when Comalapa nearly burned to the ground, according to local narrative.

Other derivations of the town name are possible. According to one source, the "Chicahl" refers to *el lugar de los susceptibles, orgullosos o aristócratas*, "place of the touchy, prideful, and aristocratic ones" (Herbruger and Díaz Barrios 1956:74), suggesting that it was applied by outsiders. Another possible derivation for "Chiq'a'l," or "Chicahl" (Herbruger and Díaz Barrios 1956:74), is "Chi K'a'äl," "place of the easily angered, touchy, mean ones." This derivation is unlikely, though, because Maya distinguish between velars and post-velars. My thanks to Judith Maxwell for bringing this toponym information to my attention.

2. Información Poblacional de Guatemala 2010, 42. Gobierno de Guatemala, Ministerio de Ambiente y Recursos Naturales, Sistemas de Información Ambiental.
http://www.sia.marn.gob.gt/Documentos/InformacionPoblacional.pdf, accessed
February 13, 2014. This source also provides the estimated numbers of persons living in the town center and the surrounding villages.
3. Numerous Maya orthographies have existed since the colonial period, and a few
are in use today. In this book, written Kaqchikel and other Maya words generally
conform to the orthography endorsed by the Academia de Lenguas Maya de
Guatemala. But since many printed sources like ethnographies and maps utilize
other Maya orthographies, I employ their spellings when citing them. I thus
include many Maya words in nonregularized orthography.
4. Over the years only a few persons have been identified to me as diviners or a prayer
makers. I met one diviner who uses water and cards in his work, and another who
uses a handful of candles. Other persons would not reveal their tools.

CHAPTER THREE

1. When discussing soul arrival, midwives usually do not bring up the subject of
conception, unless I ask them about it. This concept is more closely tied to clinical understandings of pregnancy stages.
2. Charles Wisdom (1940:344) related how a Ch'orti' diviner chewed tobacco and
applied the saliva to his right leg, then awaited the muscular twitching indicative
of the leg's resident spirit's responses to his questions. Tzeltal curers pulse the
patient's blood as part of their diagnostic process, primarily to detect spiritual
messages (Nash 1967:132–33; Pitarch 2010:72–73).
3. In Pedro Pitarch's (2010:166) study of Tzeltals, he sees the changing of clothes,
or the envelopment in clothing, as the vehicle for understanding how the
saints "come out of themselves" and make themselves able to communicate
with humans.
4. In some cases, like in San Pedro la Laguna, parents might keep their children's
birth signs a secret until the child herself shows an uncanny propensity toward
a vocation like midwifery (Paul and Paul 1975:711; Paul 1975:459).

CHAPTER FOUR

1. Revelatory elements like dreams, illnesses, and emergency childbirth cases are
common among Maya midwives of other communities, as among midwives in the
Tz'utujiil town of San Pedro la Laguna (Paul and Paul 1975:711). Magical objects,
found by the candidate and considered a source of her knowledge, also form part
of the revelatory experience in San Pedro and in nearby Santiago Atitlán (Paul
1975:459; Douglas 1969:144–45). I did not find a parallel concern for magical objects
in Comalapa, but one local midwife did use ritual objects extensively. The late
Sarita, with forty-five years of midwifery experience, worked with divinatory candles for some thirty-five years. She kept six yellow tapers in a cloth wrapping for
this purpose and was reportedly able to find lost objects and to ascertain the
health of faraway people.

2. The tuj has long had symbolic ties with heat, the womb, and midwives (Groark 1997). According to David Carey (2006:41), in fact, children used to call midwives *watit* (grandmother) "because they were known as *watit tuj* [grandmother of the sweatbath]."

3. That Comalapan midwives were skilled at positioning the fetus for birth was reaffirmed by health center records. The center reported that, of 585 local births in 1995, only 8 were stillborn (Centro de Salud 1995). The *mortinato* (stillborn) category, though, included infants who died during delayed delivery, perhaps due to transverse or breech presentation, as well as miscarried fetuses. Health center personnel visited the municipal birth and death registry every month to update the center's own records. But since the municipal records relied on reports by surviving parents, they lacked necessary detail (e.g., not differentiating among miscarriages, term stillborns, and malpresented infants who died during labor) and did not provide clear causes of stillbirth to health center records. The 1995 records indicated no maternal deaths in that year. It appeared that delivery was achieved in all cases, even if this meant resorting to biomedical personnel for emergency procedures.

   These official records were probably incorrect, though. The Pan American Health Organization (PAHO) reported, for example, a 1990 maternal mortality rate of 9.6 per 10,000 live births in Guatemala (PAHO 1994, vol. 2:223). But this agency also warned that a 1989 Guatemalan study revealed a 50 percent under-registration of maternal deaths at the national level (1994, vol. 2:223), raising questions about the reported absence of Comalapan maternal deaths in 1995. It also raised doubts about the reported number of Comalapan children who were either born dead or who died in their first year of life in any given year. Clearly, if maternal death was concealed in Guatemala, neonatal and infant death must have been concealed far more often.

   Even without factoring in the likely concealment of infant death, Guatemalan infant mortality rates are startling. For Guatemala, from 1988 to 1990, PAHO (1994, vol. 2:223; 1986, vol. 1:394) reported 45.7 child deaths under age one per 1,000 live births, down from 81.1 such deaths in 1983. In 1993, however, the reported national infant mortality rate increased to 59 (Population Reference Bureau 1993). In Comalapa for 1991, the corresponding official figure was 43.03, decreasing to 32.48 in 1995 (Centro de Salud 1991, 1995). Compare these figures with a Cuban infant mortality rate of 10.7 in 1993, or with the United States figure of 8.6 in 1993 (Population Reference Bureau 1993). Guatemala's 2005 infant mortality rate remained high at 32 (World Health Organization 2007:24).

4. A North American obstetrician, in a departure from conventional obstetric thinking, concurred with how version should be performed early in the pregnancy: "[P]rior studies . . . have established, and this study confirms . . . that earlier attempts at version are easier, and consequently safer, because there is less uterine tone and irritability and relatively more amniotic fluid present. Therefore, we preferred to convert these fetuses earlier, rather than later, even though some would have converted spontaneously later" (Ranney 1973:240).

5. Birthing while holding a rope tied to a roof rafter has been reported among Yucatec Maya (Redfield and Villa Rojas 1971:183) and among rural Guatemalans (Cosminsky 1977:84; Solien de González 1963:414). In the Tzotzil area of Chiapas, birthing women were said to grasp either a rope, a chair (Guiteras Holmes 1961a:107), their husband's neck (Eber 1995:108), or the center pole of their hut, before which they squatted (Holland 1961:217).

6. In comparison, Ch'orti' Maya conflated the stomach, womb, and intestines into a single organ and located the fetus and placenta in the stomach (Wisdom 1940:307). Yucatec Maya recognize an organ called the *tipte'* or *cirro* that is closely linked to reproductive functions. It is located in the abdomen, and if it moves out of place, all the organs of the abdomen must be massaged to return it to its place (García et al. 1999:106).

7. Postpartum binding has been reported for other Kaqchikels (Hendrickson 1995:100–101) and for K'iche's (Cosminsky 1982a:245; Greenberg 1982:1604), Mams (Greenberg 1982:1604), Q'anjob'als (La Farge 1947:41), Q'eqchi's (Instituto Indigenista Nacional 1978:102–3), Tz'utujiils (Paul 1975:458–59), Yucatecs (Jordan 1993:43–44; Fuller and Jordan 1981:41; Redfield and Villa Rojas 1971:182; Roys 1976[1931]:xxiii), and other midwives (Cosminsky 1977:89; Goldman and Glei 2003:696; Solien de González 1963:414).

CHAPTER FIVE

1. Physicians often called their specialized removal of the placenta the *maniobra del barrilete*, the "barrilete maneuver." A barrilete is a kite made for All Saints' Day and All Souls' Day, November 1 and 2. On and about these days, dozens of these kites hovered above the town and the cemetery, tethered to children trying to fly them as high as their spool of sewing thread permits. Bringing the kites down was another matter, however, for the thread could not be pulled too abruptly, or it would snap, sending the hexagonal or octagonal kite drifting away to a distant cornfield. There were also power lines and competing kite strings to negotiate. The shredded kite casualties appeared on power lines beginning in late October. Children tugged regularly at the thread to keep the kite aloft without breaking the thread. They quickly learned what happens when the string is not properly tugged.

   Like with the barrilete, physicians would hold the severed umbilical cord protruding from the mother and tug at it gently while applying pressure to the uterus. An indigenous physician, Dr. Serech, said, "You do as with a kite, while a massage is applied to the woman's abdomen." If the placenta still did not emerge, Dr. Serech would inject oxytocin to stimulate further contractions. He argued that midwives sometimes ask the woman to push too hard, for too long, and simply wear her out, leaving her unable to expel the placenta.

2. Sheila Cosminsky (1982a:243), for example, found that the K'iche' of Santa Lucía Utatlán burned their placentas. In Chan Kom, Yucatán, Robert Redfield and Alfonso Villa Rojas (1971:182) also said that the placenta was either burned

or buried, but that it was preferably buried under the hearthstones of a deserted house. There, the "warm" ashes would make the mother experience warmth. Chiapas Tzotzils held that the afterbirth should be burned or buried near the home (Fabrega and Silver 1973:42; Guiteras Holmes 1961b:165; Vogt 1969:181) or in an inside corner of the house (Holland 1961:218). The placenta had to be kept warm and close by. To distance it from hearth and home would deny its ties with the mother and its kinship with the child.

At times, however, Tzotzils and Tzeltals even threw the placenta into a river, to keep the organ away from those intending to harm the child (Guiteras Holmes 1961b:165). The Q'anjob'al felt disgusted by the placenta and cord, referring to them as *suciedad* (filth); they disposed of the placenta and cord either in a river, by burning, or by burial (La Farge 1947:40). As among Tzotzils and Tzeltals, this thwarted witchcraft directed against the child. Witchcraft fears also motivated the Ch'orti' of eastern Guatemala and western Honduras. To protect the child, the Ch'orti' father placed the placenta inside a gourd, wrapped the gourd in a banana leaf, and buried the bundle in a secret place in the house compound (Wisdom 1940:288).

3. Elsewhere in Mesoamerica, the nexus between placenta and child is conveyed still more strongly, as with the Nahuatl of Huautla, Hidalgo. In Huautla, the birthing mother buries the placenta outside her home (Edmonson 1980:100–103). Then, when the child reaches four to six months of age, he is ritually bathed, and a large tamal (steamed maize cake) is prepared. The midwife then lifts her hands in prayer over the opened ritual tamal and also over where the placenta has been buried, saying, "I quench the light, I lift my hands in prayer, we leave this placenta for our departed ones of the earth to pick up" (Edmonson 1980:103). With this gesture, the placenta approximates a very human being, requiring the intervention of deceased humans for its safe conduct to the otherworld.

4. Referring to Yucatán, J. Eric S. Thompson (1990:166) explained this numerical association by pointing out that "four" was a fit number for boys because "four are the 'sides' of every milpa," whereas "three for the girls because as women they will spend their lives stooping over the three stones which form the hearth."

5. In the K'iche' area, as well as on a coastal plantation, Sheila Cosminsky (1982a:243, 1977:86) reports that midwives also see the number of children, their sex, and the intervals between them in the cord. For these midwives, round lumps in the cord signify girls and long ones, boys (Cosminsky 1982b:215). Among the Tz'utujiil of San Pedro la Laguna, the K'iche' of Totonicapán, the Mam of San Marcos, and the Tzotzil of San Pedro Chenalhó, midwives also read future birth signs in the umbilical cord (Paul and Paul 1975:708; Greenberg 1982:1604; Guiteras Holmes 1961a:108–9).

6. In contrast, Kaqchikel of Concepción, Sololá, consider twins a blessing, in part because large families are favored there (Tetzagüíc Guajan 1997:411). In Concepción, twins are welcomed into the family and bring social recognition to the parents.

7. For gendering rituals, see William Holland (1961:218) and Calixta Guiteras Holmes (1961a:108).

8. Significantly, a local Maya midwife reported that the umbilici of Comalapan Ladino boys are simply thrown into a river by the boys' fathers, and not placed in trees. As a result, she says, the Ladino boys and men leave town in search of work and do not return. They are not bodily rooted in the town, as Maya boys are, and so are more likely to emigrate than Maya men.

9. Children also play "funeral": they lift a box upon their shoulders and walk in mock solemnity. One mother (a Protestant) who saw her children do this told me that she considered the "funeral" play a portent of someone's death. On another occasion, witnessing her daughter enclose herself in a wooden box, the same mother scolded the child, saying that such behavior would bring about the girl's death.

10. Variations on traditional gender roles have been introduced recently, like the increasing participation of girls in organized sports, especially basketball. Even more striking is how many girls' basketball teams now outfit all their players, Maya or Ladina, in athletic shorts and even form co-ed teams. This was quite a departure from the dress norms of Maya women, who have routinely lived and slept in long wraparound skirts.

    Another site of change was the moros dance organization. Traditionally an all-male group, a girl has participated as a dancer since about 1991, albeit only in the female character's position. I suspect, though, that the community is still a long way from encouraging girls to play soccer or from allowing them to participate in every position of the dancing moros.

11. Analogous procedures are reported for newborn Tzeltal girls in Yochib, Chiapas (Gerdel 1949:159) and for Tz'utujiil girls in San Pedro la Laguna, Guatemala (Paul 1974:284). Gendering rituals involving male and female tools are also reported among the Huastec Maya (Teenek) of northeastern Mexico (Laughlin 1969:309).

12. In Comalapa, like in other Maya communities, Ch'orti' midwives warned pregnant women of the dangers that solar and lunar eclipses pose to unborn children (Cosminsky 1977:82; Fittin 1993:137; Lang and Elkin 1997:28; Tedlock 1992:184). Local Kaqchikel midwives said that if a pregnant woman were exposed to an eclipse, her child might be born with a physical deformity, such as a cleft palate. Similarly, Ch'orti' cautioned that if a pregnant woman were thus exposed, her child might be born missing a body part (Wisdom 1940:285). Albinism is another effect of eclipse exposure in Comalapa. Locals call albinos *hijos de la luna*, children of the moon, pointing to the source of their skin condition.

    Pregnant women in Comalapa protect themselves from eclipses by sequestering themselves and their small children in their homes, with windows shut. One woman said that the husband should join them indoors because "in that couple, the two of them bear the burden." Pregnant women sometimes wear red garments for protection and cover themselves with blankets during an eclipse. For more protection, mothers-to-be affix a metal pin to their clothing or insert a pair of scissors into their sash. Interestingly, this outlook on eclipses resonates closely with that reported among precolonial Aztec.

Among the Aztec, according to Fray Bernardino de Sahagún (1979 books 4 and 5:189), a pregnant woman who sees a lunar eclipse will give birth to a baby with a cleft lip. To protect from this, she is told to place an obsidian blade in her bosom. Echoes of this procedure surface in Comalapa and throughout contemporary Mesoamerica in the placing of metal objects on the pregnant woman's body (see Ortiz de Montellano 1990:142–43).

13. Calixta Guiteras Holmes (1961b:164) reports something similar among Tzotzil Maya.

14. See also Lois Paul (1974:284). As a child grows older, the midwife could be consulted on his or her development, like the handling of a child's baby teeth or the cutting of a child's hair. When a child loses her baby teeth, say Comalapans, they should be "given to the mice." The teeth are placed in holes where mice move so that the mice will "eat" the teeth. A young girl said that she gave her teeth to the mice so that her permanent teeth would emerge level and straight. If her teeth were not given to the mice, the permanent teeth would emerge crooked. A Kaqchikel Maya from the neighboring town of Iximche' reasoned, "I think that since mice are constantly eating things, they have strong teeth; [this ritual is] so that the person who is eating [will] have strong teeth."

A Comalapan explained that his grandmother would place fallen teeth in the cracks between wall adobe bricks "so that the new tooth would come out well and come out strong." Others said that when a child's teeth fall out, the teeth must first be wrapped in a cloth or piece of cotton and then thrown onto the roof of a house. The roof must be the older, harder, ceramic tile kind, not the newer sheet metal type. The child's maternal grandmother must do this, calling out as she throws the teeth,

> Qoch, qoch, qoch [three repetitions], taya pe ruk'exel ri wey
> qoch, qoch, qoch [three repetitions], xtasipaj xti ri wey
> qoch, qoch, qoch [three repetitions], xtasipaj xti jun chwey.

> Qoch, qoch, qoch [three repetitions], give me the replacement for my tooth
> qoch, qoch, qoch [three repetitions], concede another tooth of mine
> qoch, qoch, qoch [three repetitions], concede one more tooth of mine.

This ensures that the replacement teeth will arrive quickly and in good form. The first ritual invokes the hardness and straightness of rodents' teeth, and the last two invoke the hardness, durability, and orderliness of adobe bricks and ceramic roofing tiles.

Fray Bernardino de Sahagún, interestingly, noted an admonition among Aztec mothers prohibiting their children from licking the surface of the grinding stone. Offending children would be scolded, "Do not lick the grinding stone; your teeth will thus quickly break and fall out" (Sahagún 1979 books 4 and 5:188).

When it comes to cutting a child's hair, it first depends on whether it is a girl or boy. As a general rule, a girl's hair should not be cut. A boy, on the other hand, should get his first haircut only after he has reached a year or so of age. In the Kaqchikel town of Iximche', to cut most of a boy's hair while he is very young is to cut away his *na'oj* (knowledge and reason). If his hair is cut off, it has to be saved, collected in a pouch, and hung on a wall so that his na'oj can be conserved and so that he does not become dumb. Otherwise, it is said of the boy that *xenusäch runa'oj, xenuk'ïs runa'oj,* "he loses his na'oj, he finishes his na'oj."

A Comalapan mother of five observed that a local boy's hair used to not be cut during his first year. People feared that boys whose hair was cut prematurely would *ye'el men,* "become mute." If a child became mute, this could be remedied by feeding bits of tortilla to a parrot, and then feeding the mute child any pieces of tortilla that fell from the parrot's mouth. When a boy's hair was cut after age one, it was placed in a small pouch. If the family had a *güisquil* (*Sechium edule* [Jacq.] Swartz) plant in the patio, they might dig a small hole under the plant, place the pouch in it, and cover the pouch with soil. This was done, the mother observed, "so that the güisquil, growing, grows very large [said with a flowering motion of the arms], so that the hair grows out like this." Girls' hair was not cut because they grew their hair in order to braid it, she said.

One mother did cut her daughter's hair, albeit an older daughter and only in very small amounts. It seemed that her seventeen-year-old daughter's hair was not growing as much as desired. So the mother would cut off a little bit of her daughter's hair and bind it in the fork of a growing güisquil stem. The mother said that her daughter's hair then grew very long, down to her waist, in fact. After a while, though, mother and daughter stopped putting the hair in the güisquil plant, and they began cutting the daughter's hair more often. The daughter's hair never again grew as long as it once had.

15. Among the Tzotzil, a two- to three-month-old fetus might decide to flee from his mother's womb to inhabit another woman's womb (Guiteras Holmes 1961a:104–5). Such a fetus was considered clever and restless because he wanted to be in a womb more suitable to him. In many cases, however, he would return to the womb in which he was conceived.

CHAPTER SIX

1. Yucatecs, for example, recommend seven days for this purpose (Jordan 1993:42). Some Tzotzils extend this period to one month or even forty days (Guiteras Holmes 1961a:110). Q'anjob'als are more concerned with the mother's avoidance of work than with her isolation, so they have the mother "stay quiet" for twenty days after the birth and do only light housework (La Farge 1947:41). Mams, on the other hand, forbid work altogether for the mother for twenty days postpartum (Oakes 1951:42).

The period of seclusion in Yucatán has the additional purpose of helping the mother and child "get to know the significance of the other's touches, movements, sounds, and smells, and learn about each other's cycles of hunger and satiation, wakefulness and sleep, excretory pressure and release" with few outside distractions (Fuller and Jordan 1981:47).

2. As a literal and figurative enclosure, the womb evokes a place of security, where the fetus is animated and prepares for a terrestrial life. Although this view of the womb generally holds true throughout the Maya area, in San Pedro Chenalhó, Chiapas, the protective, enclosing quality of the womb can also become a liability. There, if the mother and fetus die, the fetus's soul remains *trapped* inside the womb (Guiteras Holmes 1961a:102, 162). The child's inner soul (Tzotzil ch'ulel) is confined to the womb until a ritual specialist performs the necessary postmortem Cesarean section to free it. Only then can the soul make its way to the *ch'ulte'* (tree of breasts), where it will nurse and wait to enter the body of another infant. In the Tzotzil vision, it is vitally important for the infant to reach his terrestrial life because, following this life, his ch'ulel can embark on its eternal existence and return to his earthly kindred during *día de todos santos* and *día de santos difuntos* (Gossen 1975:450).

3. Among Tz'utujiils there, amniotic features also distinguish children's future vocations (Paul and Paul 1975:708–9). There, a boy with a little "shoulder bag" has the calling of a shaman, whereas the future midwife is noted by a white "mantle" on a girl's head. Other ritual specialists could also be foretold by the amniotic tissue there, such as the transforming witch, signaled by a child born rolled up as a ball in an unbroken amniotic sac, or the rainmaker, born with a sort of a cap or a cape. There is also the Tz'utujiil sorcerer, who emerges holding worms or flies in his little fist.

4. The Tzotzil child of Zinacantan, Chiapas, for instance, ran a high risk of losing part of his soul before his baptism (Vogt 1969:370). In San Pedro Chenalhó, Chiapas, the ch'ulel of the unbaptized child was not considered a child of God and had to go with the *Pukuh*, a manifestation of evil, after death (Guiteras Holmes 1961a:162). A Tzotzil informant said of the unbaptized soul, "It cannot go away, it only weeps. Its father and mother are going to pray and I think that then God deigns to receive its ch'ulel" (1961a:162).

CHAPTER NINE

1. There were many local narratives about Nemesio Matzer, who lived in the early twentieth century. As a mayor of Comalapa and as an intelligent and forward-thinking man, Matzer made many improvements to the physical infrastructure around Comalapa (Carey 2001:233–36).

2. See Calixta Guiteras Holmes (1961a:156–57) in this regard.

CHAPTER TEN

1. Similarly, Didier Boremanse (2000:14) reports how Q'eq'chi' Maya formalize the entry of spirits into the community, in their case feeding the spirits of sewing machines that were brought into the community by outsiders.

2. Sacred bundle use has been explored among Tz'utujiil Maya by Michael Mendelson (1958:170; 1965:57), Robert Carlsen (1997:80–81), and Allen Christenson (2001:58). Merle Greene Robertson (1972) analyzed ritual bundle use by classic Maya in Yaxchilán.

3. Maury Hutcheson (2003) also reports how, early in his interaction with the dance director of the Rabinal Achi, he was assumed to be someone who wanted to underwrite the dance.

4. Robert Hill (1998) argued that the precursors of morerías in Guatemala were already in place by the late sixteenth and early seventeenth centuries.

5. At the historical and political level, Hutcheson (2003:32, 131) reports how, between the period of the Liberal revolution of 1871 to the fall of President Jorge Ubico in 1944, the church's doctrinal influence over highland Maya life weakened. This allowed cofradías to operate more freely, for many morerías to be established, and for many Spanish-language dance scripts, like the toritos, to be produced, with more nationalistic, rather than evangelical, aims.

CHAPTER ELEVEN

1. In the 1963 script, the mayordomo, now in charge of the finca, orders the caporal to return the bulls to the pasture. The caporal gives this order to the vaqueros, and they set out. Carrying out this order, however, the vaquero named Curcura gets bitten by a serpent. The mayordomo is told, and he orders that the bitten vaquero be collected. Doña Rosa is next informed by the mayordomo; she bemoans the tragedies of the day. The vaqueros produce the captured serpent and dismember it. The bitten vaquero bids good-bye to all, just before he is sent to the hospital on the mayordomo's orders. The mayordomo consoles the vaqueros that Curcura will get well, even as the marimba plays a sad song. In the end, each of the toritos bids farewell to the Virgen de Concepción.

2. The importance of *doing* ritual over understanding it is also reflected as an early priority of Christian evangelizers in Cancuc, Chiapas, a Tzeltal Maya community. According to Pedro Pitarch (2010:141), "The efficacy of the sacrament resides, regardless of whether its meaning is understood or not by those who receive it, in its performance, in its staging."

3. Evon Vogt sheds light on why Comalapans ritually feed all elements of the dance. He reports (1965:34) that for the Tzotzil Maya of Zinacantan, "[v]irtually everything that is important and valuable to Zinacantecos . . . possesses a ch'ulel [inner soul]." Staple foods, hearths, houses, and salt each possess a ch'ulel. Ritual implements such as saint images, crosses, and musical instruments also possess ch'uleletik (pl.) and cannot be treated simply as material objects. Among the Tzotzil of Chamula, the feeding of musical instruments and other ritual objects has a more pragmatic basis. According to Victoria Bricker's (1973:109) informants, if liquor is not fed to gruel pots, musical instruments, and cannons, these objects will explode, squawk, and improperly explode, respectively.

Bibliography

Adams, Richard N.
1952   Un análisis de las creencias y prácticas médicas en un pueblo indígena de
        Guatemala. Guatemala: Instituto Indigenista Nacional, no. 17.
Adams, Richard N., and Arthur J. Rubel
1967   Sickness and Social Relations. *In* Handbook of Middle American Indians,
        vol. 6: Social Anthropology. Robert Wauchope and Manning Nash, eds.
        Pp. 333–56. Austin: University of Texas Press.
Asturias de Barrios, Linda
1985   Comalapa: el traje y su significado. Guatemala: Museo Ixchel del Traje
        Indígena de Guatemala.
1994   Woman's Hand, Man's Hand: Textile Artisan Production in Comalapa,
        Guatemala. PhD dissertation, Department of Anthropology, University at
        Albany, State University of New York.
Asturias Montenegro, Gonzalo, and Ricardo Gatica Trejo
1976   Terremoto 76. Guatemala: Editorial Girblán y Cía.
Benson, Peter, and Edward F. Fischer
2009   Neoliberal Violence: Social Suffering in Guatemala's Postwar Era. *In* Mayas
        in Postwar Guatemala: Harvest of Violence Revisited. Walter E. Little and
        Timothy J. Smith, eds. Pp.151–66. Tuscaloosa: University of Alabama Press.
Berry, Nicole S.
2006   Kaqchikel Midwives, Home Births, and Emergency Obstetric Referrals in
        Guatemala: Contextualizing the Choice to Stay at Home. Social Science
        and Medicine 62:1958–69.
Bode, Barbara
1961   The Dance of the Conquest of Guatemala. New Orleans: Tulane Univer-
        sity, Middle American Research Institute, Pub. 27.
Boremanse, Didier
2000   Sewing Machines and Q'echi' Maya Worldview. Anthropology Today
        16:11–18.
Bourdieu, Pierre
1977   Outline of a Theory of Practice. Richard Nice, trans. Cambridge, UK:
        Cambridge University Press.

Bricker, Victoria Reifler
1973   Ritual Humor in Highland Chiapas. Austin: University of Texas Press.
1981   The Indian Christ, the Indian King: The Historical Substrate of Maya
         Myth and Ritual. Austin: University of Texas Press.
Brinton, Daniel G.
1894   Nagualism: A Study in Native American Folk-lore and History. Philadel-
         phia: MacCalla and Company.
Bunzel, Ruth
1952   Chichicastenango: A Guatemalan Village. American Ethnological Soci-
         ety, no. 22. Locust Valley, NY: J. J. Agustin.
Carey, David, Jr.
2001   Our Elders Teach Us (Xkib'ij Kan Qate' Qatata'): Maya-Kaqchikel
         Historical Perspectives. Tuscaloosa: University of Alabama Press.
2006   Engendering Mayan History: Kaqchikel Women as Agents and Conduits
         of the Past, 1875–1970. New York: Routledge.
2011   The Historical Maya and Maya Histories: Recent Trends and New
         Approaches to Reconstructing Indigenous Pasts in Guatemala. History
         Compass 9(9):701–19.
Carlsen, Robert S.
1997   The War for the Heart and Soul of a Highland Maya Town. Austin: Uni-
         versity of Texas Press.
Carlsen, Robert S., and Martin Prechtel
1991   The Flowering of the Dead: An Interpretation of Highland Maya Culture.
         Man (n.s.) 26:23–42.
Centro de Salud
1991   Unpublished municipal health data, San Juan Comalapa, Guatemala.
1995   Unpublished municipal health data, San Juan Comalapa, Guatemala.
Cervantes, Fernando
1994   The Devil in the New World: The Impact of Diabolism in New Spain. New
         Haven, CT: Yale University Press.
Christenson, Allen J.
2001   Art and Society in a Highland Maya Community. Austin: University of
         Texas Press.
Cojtí Cuxil, Demetrio
1994   Políticas para la reivindicación de los mayas de hoy: fundamento de los
         derechos específicos del pueblo maya. Guatemala: Seminario Permanente
         de Estudios Mayas, Editorial Cholsamaj.
Colby, Benjamin N., and Lore M. Colby
1981   The Daykeeper: The Life and Discourse of an Ixil Diviner. Cambridge,
         MA: Harvard University Press.
Cook, Garrett W.
1986   Quichean Folk Theology and Southern Maya Supernaturalism. In Symbol
         and Meaning Beyond the Closed Community: Essays in Mesoamerican
         Ideas. Gary H. Gossen, ed. Pp.139–53. Institute for Mesoamerican Studies,
         University at Albany, State University of New York.

2000 Renewing the Maya World: Expressive Culture in a Highland Town. Austin: University of Texas Press.

Cook, Garrett W., and Thomas A. Offit
2008 Pluralism and Transculturation in Indigenous Maya Religion. Ethnology 47:45–59.
2013 Indigenous Religion and Cultural Performance in the New Maya World. Albuquerque: University of New Mexico Press.

Correa, Gustavo
1958 Texto de un baile de diablos. New Orleans: Tulane University, Middle American Research Institute, Pub. 27, 97–104.
1960 El espíritu del mal en Guatemala. In Nativism and Syncretism. Munro S. Edmonson, ed. Pp. 39–103. New Orleans: Tulane University, Middle American Research Institute, Pub. 19.

Cortés y Larraz, Pedro
1958 Descripción geográfico-moral de la diocesis de Goathemala. 2 vols. Biblioteca Goathemala, vol. 22. Guatemala: Sociedad de Geografía e Historia.

Cosminsky, Sheila
1976 The Evil Eye in a Quiche Community. In The Evil Eye. Clarence Maloney, ed. Pp. 163–74. New York: Columbia University Press.
1977 Childbirth and Midwifery on a Guatemalan Finca. Medical Anthropology 1:69–104.
1982a Knowledge and Body Concepts of Guatemalan Midwives. In Anthropology of Human Birth. Margarita Artschwager, ed. Pp. 233–52. Philadelphia: F. A. Davis.
1982b Childbirth and Change: A Guatemalan Study. In Ethnography of Fertility and Birth, Carol P. MacCormack, ed. Pp. 205–29. London: Academic Press.
2001 Midwifery Across the Generations: A Modernizing Midwife in Guatemala. Medical Anthropology 20:345–78.

Cresson, Frank M., Jr.
1938 Maya and Mexican Sweat Houses. American Anthropologist 40:88–104.

Csordas, Thomas J.
1990 Embodiment as a Paradigm for Anthropology. Ethos 18:5–47.
1993 Somatic Modes of Attention. Cultural Anthropology 8:135–56.
1994a Introduction: The Body as Representation of Being-in-the-World. In Embodiment and Experience: The Existential Ground of Culture and Self. Thomas J. Csordas, ed. Pp. 1–24. Cambridge, UK: Cambridge University Press.
1994b Words from the Holy People: A Case Study in Cultural Phenomenology. In Embodiment and Experience: The Existential Ground of Culture and Self. Thomas J. Csordas, ed. Pp. 269–90. Cambridge, UK: Cambridge University Press.

del Busto, Inocencio
1961 San Juan Comalapa. Antropología e Historia de Guatemala 13:27–47.

Douglas, Bill Gray
1969   Illness and Curing in Santiago Atitlan, a Tzutujil-Maya Community in the
        Southwestern Highlands of Guatemala. PhD dissertation, Department of
        Anthropology, Stanford University.
Dundes, Alan, ed.
1992   The Evil Eye: A Casebook. Madison: University of Wisconsin Press.
Eber, Christine
1995   Women and Alcohol in a Highland Maya Town: Water of Hope, Water of
        Sorrow. Austin: University of Texas Press.
Edmonson, Barbara
1980   Huautla Nahuatl Texts. Tlalocan 8:83–108.
Edmonson, Munro S.
1997   Quiché Dramas and Divinatory Calendars. Zaqi Q'oxol and Cortés: The
        Conquest of Mexico in Quiché and Spanish; The Bull Dance; The Count
        of the Cycle and the Numbers of the Days. New Orleans: Tulane Univer-
        sity, Middle American Research Institute, Pub. 66.
Esquit, Edgar
2007   Debates en torno a la identidad y el cambio social en Comalapa, una locali-
        dad en el altiplano guatemalteco. In Mayanización y vida cotidiana: La ide-
        ología multicultural en la sociedad guatemalteca, vol. 2: Estudios de caso.
        Santiago Bastos and Aura Cumes, eds. Pp. 235–72. Guatemala: Fundación
        Cholsamaj.
Fabrega, Horacio, Jr., Duane Metzger, and Gerald Williams
1970   Psychiatric Implications of Health and Illness in a Maya Indian Group: A
        Preliminary Statement. Social Science and Medicine 3(4):609–26.
Fabrega, Horacio, Jr., and Daniel B. Silver
1973   Illness and Shamanistic Curing in Zinacantan: An Ethnomedical Analy-
        sis. Stanford, CA: Stanford University Press.
Falla, Ricardo
1971   Juan el Gordo: visión indígena de su explotación. Estudios Centroameri-
        canos 26:98–107.
Farber, Anne
1978   Language Choice and Problems of Identity in a Highland Mayan Town.
        PhD dissertation, Faculty of Political Science, Columbia University.
Farriss, Nancy
1984   Maya Society under Colonial Rule: The Collective Enterprise of Survival.
        Princeton, NJ: Princeton University Press.
Fischer, Edward F.
2001   Cultural Logics and Global Economies: Maya Identity in Thought and
        Practice. Austin: University of Texas Press.
Fischer, Edward F., and R. McKenna Brown, eds.
1996   Maya Cultural Activism in Guatemala. Austin: University of Texas Press.
Fittin, Robert
1993   Some K'ekchi' Beliefs about the Behavior of Women During Pregnancy
        and with Infants. Latin American Indian Literatures Journal 9:135–38.

Foster, George M.
1948   Empire's Children: The People of Tzintzuntzan. Washington, DC: Insti-
        tute of Social Anthropology, Smithsonian Institution.
1976   Disease Etiologies in Non-Western Medical Systems. American Anthro-
        pologist 78:773–82.
Frost, Elsa Cecilia
1993   Indians and Theologians: Sixteenth-Century Spanish Theologians and
        Their Concept of the Indigenous Soul. In South and Meso-American Native
        Spirituality. Gary H. Gossen, ed. Pp. 119–39. New York: Crossroad Publish-
        ing Company.
Frost, Gordon
1976   Guatemalan Mask Imagery. Los Angeles: Southwest Museum.
Fuentes y Guzmán, Francisco
1932–1933 Recordación Florida. 3 vols. Guatemala: Sociedad de Geografía e
        Historia.
Fuller, Nancy, and Brigitte Jordan
1981   Maya Women and the End of the Birthing Period: Postpartum Massage-
        and-Binding in Yucatan, Mexico. Medical Anthropology 5:35–50.
Fundación Centro Cultural y Asistencia Maya (FCCAM)
1990   Algunos conocimientos, actitudes, prácticas y términos que utiliza la
        comadrona maya k'iche' de Chichicastenango en la atención del embarazo.
        Guatemala: INCAP publication C-275.
Furst, Jill Leslie McKeever
1995   The Natural History of the Soul in Ancient Mexico. New Haven, CT: Yale
        University Press.
Gage, Thomas
1958   Thomas Gage's Travels in the New World. J. Eric S. Thompson, ed. Norman:
        University of Oklahoma Press.
García, Hernán, Antonio Sierra, and Gilberto Balám
1999   Wind in the Blood: Mayan Healing and Chinese Medicine. Jeff Conant,
        trans. Berkeley, CA: North Atlantic Books.
García Escobar, Carlos René
1987   Talleres, trajes y danzas tradicionales de Guatemala: El caso de San Cris-
        tóbal Totonicapán. Guatemala: Universidad de San Carlos de Guatemala.
1989   Detrás de la máscara: Estudio etnocoreológico. Guatemala: Universidad
        de San Carlos de Guatemala.
Garzon, Susan, R. McKenna Brown, Julia Becker Richards, and Wuqu' Ajpub'
        (Arnulfo Simón)
1998   The Life of Our Language: Kaqchikel Maya Maintenance, Shift, and Revi-
        talization. Austin: University of Texas Press.
Gerdel, Florence
1949   A Case of Delayed Afterbirth among the Tzeltal Indians. American
        Anthropologist 51:158–59.
Gillin, John
1948   Magical Fright. Psychiatry 11:387–400.

Gobierno de Guatemala, Ministerio de Ambiente y Recursos Naturales, Sistemas
     de Información Ambiental
2010   Información Poblacional de Guatemala 2010, 42. http://www.sia.marn.
          gob.gt/Documentos/InformacionPoblacional.pdf, accessed February 13,
          2014.
Goldman, Noreen, and Dana A. Glei
2003   Evaluation of Midwifery Care: Results from a Survey in Rural Guatemala.
          Social Science and Medicine 56:685–700.
Gordon, Deborah R.
1990   Embodying Illness, Embodying Cancer. Culture, Medicine, and Psychia-
          try 14:275–97.
Gossen, Gary H.
1974   Chamulas in the World of the Sun: Time and Space in a Maya Oral Tradi-
          tion. Cambridge, MA: Harvard University Press.
1975   Animal Souls and Human Destiny in Chamula. Man 10:448–61.
1989   To Speak with a Heated Heart: Chamula Canons of Style and Good Per-
          formance. In Explorations in the Ethnography of Speaking. 2nd edition.
          Richard Bauman and Joel Sherzer, eds. Pp. 389–413. Cambridge, UK:
          Cambridge University Press.
Green, Linda
1998   Lived Lives and Social Suffering: Problems and Concerns in Medical
          Anthropology. Medical Anthropology Quarterly 12:3–7.
Greenberg, Linda
1982   Midwife Training Programs in Highland Guatemala. Social Science and
          Medicine 16:1599–609.
Greenleaf, Richard E.
1961   Zumárraga and the Mexican Inquisition, 1536–1543. Washington, DC:
          Academy of American Franciscan History.
Greenway, Christine
1998   Objectified Selves: An Analysis of Medicines in Andean Sacrificial Heal-
          ing. Medical Anthropology Quarterly 12:147–67.
Groark, Kevin P.
1997   To Warm the Blood, to Warm the Flesh: The Role of the Steambath in
          Highland Maya (Tzeltal-Tzotzil) Ethnomedicine. Journal of Latin Ameri-
          can Lore 20:3–96.
2009   Discourses of the Soul: The Negotiation of Personal Agency in Tzotzil
          Maya Dream Narrative. American Ethnologist 36:705–21.
Guillemin, George F.
1967   The Ancient Cakchiquel Capital of Iximche. Expedition 9:22–35.
Guiteras Holmes, Calixta
1961a   Perils of the Soul: The World View of a Tzotzil Indian. New York: Free
          Press of Glencoe.
1961b   La magia en la crisis del embarazo y parto en los actuales grupos mayances
          de Chiapas. Estudios de Cultura Maya 1:159–66.

Harris, Max
2000   Aztecs, Moors and Christians: Festivals of Reconquest in Mexico and
        Spain. Austin: University of Texas Press.
Hart, Thomas
2008   The Ancient Spirituality of the Modern Maya. Albuquerque: University of
        New Mexico Press.
Hendrickson, Carol
1995   Weaving Identities: Construction of Dress and Self in a Highland Guate-
        malan Town. Austin: University of Texas Press.
Herbruger, Alfredo, Jr., and Eduardo Díaz Barrios
1956   Método para aprender a hablar, leer y escribir la lengua cakchiquel, vol. 1.
        Guatemala: Tipografía Nacional de Guatemala.
Hill, Robert M., II
1992   Colonial Cakchiquels: Highland Maya Adaptation to Spanish Rule, 1600–
        1700. Fort Worth, TX: Holt, Rinehart and Winston.
1998   Anotaciones sobre las morerías kaqchikeles en Chimaltenango en los
        siglos XVI y XVII. Mesoamérica 35:83–91.
Hill, Robert M., II, and Edward F. Fischer
1999   States of Heart: An Ethnohistorical Approach to Kaqchikel Maya Ethno-
        psychology. Ancient Mesoamerica 10:317–32.
Hinojosa, Servando Z.
2002a   "The Hands Know": Bodily Engagement and Medical Impasse in High-
        land Maya Bonesetting. Medical Anthropology Quarterly 16(1):22–40.
2002b   K'u'x como vínculo corporal en el cosmos. Estudios de Cultura Maya
        22:185–97.
2004a   Bonesetting and Radiography in the Southern Maya Highlands. Medical
        Anthropology 23(4):263–93.
2004b   The Hands, the Sacred, and the Context of Change in Maya Bonesetting.
        In Healing by Hand: Manual Medicine and Bonesetting in Global Per-
        spective. Kathryn S. Oths and Servando Z. Hinojosa, eds. Pp. 107–29.
        Walnut Creek, CA: AltaMira Press.
2004c   Authorizing Tradition: Vectors of Contention in Highland Maya Mid-
        wifery. Social Science and Medicine 59:637–51.
2006   Divination Bowls and Blood Simulacra in Colonial and Contemporary
        Mesoamerican Curing. In Change and Continuity in Mesoamerican
        Medicinal Practice. John F. Chuchiak and Bodil Liljefors Persson, eds.
        Acta Americana 13(1–2):79–99.
2011   Ritual Effigies and Corporeality in Kaqchikel Maya Soul Healing. Ethnol-
        ogy 50(1):79–94.
Holland, William R.
1961   Highland Maya Folk Medicine: A Study of Culture Change. PhD disserta-
        tion, Department of Anthropology, University of Arizona.
Hutcheson, Matthew Fontaine Maury
2003   Cultural Memory and the Dance-Dramas of Guatemala: History,

Performance, and Identity among the Achi Maya of Rabinal. PhD disser-
tation, Department of Anthropology, State University of New York at
Buffalo.

2008   Memory, Mimesis, and Narrative in the K'iche' Mayan Serpent Dance of
        Joyabaj, Guatemala. Comparative Studies in Society and History
        51:865–95.

Icú Perén, Hugo

1990   Práctica de traumatología empírica en el area cakchiquel de Guatemala.
        Medical thesis, Universidad de San Carlos de Guatemala, Facultad de
        Ciencias Médicas, Guatemala.

Instituto Indigenista Nacional

1978   Aspectos de la medicina popular en el area rural de Guatemala. Guate-
        mala Indígena 13 (3–4).

Jackson, Michael

1983   Thinking Through the Body: An Essay on Understanding Metaphor.
        Social Analysis 14:127–49.

Jenkins, Janis H., and Martha Valiente

1994   Bodily Transactions of the Passions: *El Calor* among Salvadoran Women
        Refugees. *In* Embodiment and Experience: The Existential Ground of Cul-
        ture and Self. Thomas J. Csordas, ed. Pp. 163–82. Cambridge, UK: Cam-
        bridge University Press.

Jordan, Brigitte

1984   External Cephalic Version as an Alternative to Breech Delivery and Cesar-
        ean Section. Social Science and Medicine 18:637–51.

1989   Cosmopolitical Obstetrics: Some Insights from the Training of Tradi-
        tional Midwives. Social Science and Medicine 28:925–44.

1993   Birth in Four Cultures: A Crosscultural Investigation of Childbirth in
        Yucatan, Holland, Sweden, and the United States. 4th edition. Revised and
        expanded by Robbie Davis-Floyd. Prospect Heights, IL: Waveland Press.

Joyce, Rosemary A.

2000   Girling the Girl and Boying the Boy: The Production of Adulthood in
        Ancient Mesoamerica. World Archaeology 31(3):473–83.

Juarros, Domingo

1981   Compendio de la historia del reino de Guatemala, 1500–1800. Guatemala:
        Editorial Piedra Santa.

Kaufman, Terrence

1990   Algunos rasgos estructurales de los idiomas mayances con referencia
        especial al k'iche'. *In* Lecturas sobre la lingüística maya. Nora C. England
        and Stephen R. Elliott, eds. Pp. 59–114. La Antigua, Guatemala: Centro de
        Investigaciones Regionales de Mesoamérica; South Woodstock, VT:
        Plumsock Mesoamerican Studies.

Klein, Cecelia F.

1990/1991 Snares and Entrails: Mesoamerican Symbols of Sin and Punishment.
        Res 19/20: 81–103.

Klein, Susan
1995   A Book for Midwives: A Manual for Traditional Birth Attendants and
         Community Midwives. Palo Alto, CA: Hesperian Foundation.
Krystal, Matthew
2000   Cultural Revitalization and Tourism at the Morería Nima' K'iche'. Ethnol-
         ogy 39:149–61.
Kurath, Gertrude Prokosch
1967   Drama, Dance, and Music. In Handbook of Middle American Indians,
         vol. 6: Social Anthropology. Robert Wauchope and Manning Nash, eds.
         Pp. 158–90. Austin: University of Texas Press.
La Farge, Oliver
1947   Santa Eulalia: The Religion of a Cuchumatán Indian Town. Chicago: Uni-
         versity of Chicago Press.
Lang, Jennifer B., and Elizabeth D. Elkin
1997   A Study of the Beliefs and Birthing Practices of Traditional Midwives in
         Rural Guatemala. Journal of Nurse-Midwifery 42:25–31.
Las Casas, Bartolomé de
1992a   In Defense of the Indians. Stafford Poole, ed. and trans. DeKalb: Northern
         Illinois University Press.
1992b   A Short Account of the Destruction of the Indies. Nigel Griffin, ed. and
         trans. London: Penguin Books.
Laughlin, Robert M.
1969   The Huastec. In Handbook of Middle American Indians, vol. 7: Ethnol-
         ogy. Robert Wauchope and Evon Z. Vogt, eds. Pp. 298–311. Austin: Uni-
         versity of Texas Press.
Little, Walter E., and Timothy J. Smith, eds.
2009   Mayas in Postwar Guatemala: Harvest of Violence Revisited. Tuscaloosa:
         University of Alabama Press.
Logan, Michael H.
1979   Variations Regarding Susto Causality among the Cakchiquel of Guate-
         mala. Culture, Medicine, and Psychiatry 3:153–66.
Looper, Matthew G.
2009   To Be Like Gods: Dance in Ancient Maya Civilization. Austin: University
         of Texas Press.
López Austin, Alfredo
1988   The Human Body and Ideology: Concepts of the Ancient Nahuas. 2 vols.
         Thelma Ortiz de Montellano and Bernard Ortiz de Montellano, trans. Salt
         Lake City: University of Utah Press.
Luján Muñoz, Luís
1971   Notas sobre el uso de máscaras en Guatemala. Guatemala Indígena
         6:127–47.
1987   Máscaras y morerías de Guatemala/Masks and Morerías of Guatemala.
         Catrin Walters de Vidal, trans. Guatemala: Museo Popol Vuh, Universi-
         dad Francisco Marroquín.

Mace, Carroll E.
1970   Two Spanish-Quiché Dance Dramas of Rabinal. New Orleans: Tulane
         University, Tulane Studies in Romance Languages and Literature, no. 3.
MacKenzie, C. James
1999   The Priest, the Shaman, and "Grandfather Judas": Syncretism and Anti-
         Syncretism in Guatemala. Religious Studies and Theology 18:33–65.
2009   Judas off the Noose: Sacerdotes Mayas, Costumbristas, and the Politics of
         Purity in the Tradition of San Simón in Guatemala. Journal of Latin
         American and Caribbean Anthropology 14:355–81.
Madsen, Claudia
1965   A Study of Change in Mexican Folk Medicine. New Orleans: Tulane Uni-
         versity, Middle American Research Institute, pub. 25, 89–138.
Maloney, Clarence, ed.
1976   The Evil Eye. New York: Columbia University Press.
Manning, Peter K., and Horacio Fabrega Jr.
1973   The Experience of Self and Body: Health and Illness in the Chiapas High-
         lands. In Phenomenological Sociology: Issues and Applications. George
         Psathas, ed. Pp. 251–301. New York: John Wiley.
Markman, Roberta H., and Peter T. Markman
1989   Masks of the Spirit: Image and Metaphor in Mesoamerica. Berkeley: Uni-
         versity of California Press.
Marshall, Lorna
1965   The !Kung Bushmen of the Kalahari Desert. In Peoples of Africa. J. L. Gibbs,
         ed. Pp. 241–78. New York: Holt, Rinehart and Winston.
Maxwell, Judith M., and Robert M. Hill II
2006   Kaqchikel Chronicles: The Definitive Edition. Austin: University of Texas
         Press.
McAnany, Patricia A.
1995   Living with the Ancestors: Kinship and Kingship in Ancient Maya Soci-
         ety. New York: Cambridge University Press.
McArthur, Harry S.
1972   Los bailes de Aguacatán y el culto a los muertos. Guatemala Indígena
         7:117–41.
McKenna Brown, R.
1998   Mayan Language Revitalization in Guatemala. In The Life of Our Lan-
         guage: Kaqchikel Maya Maintenance, Shift, and Revitalization. Susan
         Garzon, R. McKenna Brown, Julia Becker Richards, and Wuqu' Ajpub',
         eds. Pp. 155–70. Austin: University of Texas Press.
Mendelson, E. Michael
1958   A Guatemalan Sacred Bundle. Man 58:121–26.
1965   Los escándalos de Maximón: Un estudio sobre la religión y la visión del
         mundo en Santiago Atitlán. Seminario de Integración Social Guatemalteca,
         Pub. 19. Guatemala: Tipografía Nacional Guatemalteca.

Merleau-Ponty, Maurice
1962   Phenomenology of Perception. James Edie, trans. Evanston, IL: North-
        western University Press.
Merrill, William L.
1988   Rarámuri Souls: Knowledge and Social Process in Northern Mexico.
        Washington, DC: Smithsonian Institution Press.
Metzger, Duane, and Gerald Williams
1963   Tenejapa Medicine I: The Curer. Southwestern Journal of Anthropology
        19:216–34.
Mignone, Javier, Jessica Herrera, Hugo Icú Perén, Carol Couchie, Garry Munro,
        Mélida Jiménez, and Rosa Chex
2009   Strengthening Indigenous and Intercultural Midwifery: Evaluation of a
        Collaboration between Guatemalan and Canadian Aboriginal Organiza-
        tions. Pimatisiwin: A Journal of Aboriginal and Indigenous Community
        Health 7:133–55.
Moedano N., Gabriel
1961   El Temazcal, baño indígena tradicional. Tlatoani 14/15:40–51.
Molesky-Poz, Jean
2006   Contemporary Maya Spirituality: The Ancient Ways Are Not Lost. Austin:
        University of Texas Press.
Monaghan, John D.
2000   Theology and History in the Study of Mesoamerican Religions. In Hand-
        book of Middle American Indians, Supplement 6: Ethnology. Victoria R.
        Bricker and John D. Monaghan, eds. Pp. 24–49. Austin: University of
        Texas Press.
Montejo, Victor D.
2005   Maya Intellectual Renaissance: Identity, Representation, and Leadership.
        Austin: University of Texas Press.
Nash, June
1967   The Logic of Behavior: Curing in a Maya Indian Town. Human Organiza-
        tion 26:132–40.
1970   In the Eyes of the Ancestors: Belief and Behavior in a Mayan Community.
        New Haven, CT: Yale University Press.
Oakes, Maud
1951   The Two Crosses of Todos Santos: Survivals of Mayan Religious Ritual.
        New York: Pantheon Books.
O'Nell, Carl W.
1975   An Investigation of Reported "Fright" as a Factor in the Etiology of Susto,
        "Magical Fright." Ethos 3:41–63.
O'Nell, Carl W., and Henry A. Selby
1968   Sex Differences in the Incidence of Susto in Two Zapotec Pueblos: An
        Analysis of the Relationships Between Sex Role Expectations and a Folk
        Illness. Ethnology 7:95–105.

Orellana, Sandra L.
1987   Indian Medicine in Highland Guatemala: The Pre-Hispanic and Colonial
         Periods. Albuquerque: University of New Mexico Press.
Ortiz Martínez, Lesbia
1993   Máscaras y religión. Guatemala: Subcentro Regional de Artesanías y Artes
         Populares.
Ortiz de Montellano, Bernard R.
1989   Syncretism in Mexican and Mexican-American Folk Medicine. College
         Park: University of Maryland, Department of Spanish and Portuguese,
         1992 Lecture Series, Working Paper no. 5.
1990   Aztec Medicine, Health, and Nutrition. New Brunswick, NJ: Rutgers Uni-
         versity Press.
Otzoy, Irma
1996   Maya Clothing and Identity. In Maya Cultural Activism in Guatemala.
         Edward F. Fischer and R. McKenna Brown, eds. Pp. 141–55. Austin: Uni-
         versity of Texas Press.
Pacheco, Luís
1985   Religiosidad maya-kekchí alrededor del maíz. San José, Costa Rica: Edito-
         rial Escuela para Todos.
Pan American Health Organization (PAHO)
1986   Health Conditions in the Americas, 1981–1984. 2 vols. Washington, DC:
         Scientific Pub. no. 500.
1994   Health Conditions in the Americas. 2 vols. Washington, DC: Scientific
         Pub. no. 549.
Paret-Limardo de Vela, Lise
1963   Original del baile del torito. Guatemala Indígena 3:93–118.
Parsons, Elsie Clews
1936   Mitla: Town of the Souls, and Other Zapoteco-Speaking Peoples of Oaxaca,
         Mexico. Chicago: University of Chicago Press.
Paul, Benjamin D.
1976   The Maya Bonesetter as Sacred Specialist. Ethnology 15:77–81.
Paul, Benjamin D., and Clancy McMahon
2001   Mesoamerican Bonesetters. In Mesoamerican Healers. Brad R. Huber and
         Alan R. Sandstrom, eds. Pp. 243–69. Austin: University of Texas Press.
Paul, Lois
1974   The Mastery of Work and the Mystery of Sex in a Guatemalan Village. In
         Woman, Culture and Society. Michelle Zimbalist Rosaldo and Louise
         Lamphere, eds. Pp. 281–99. Stanford, CA: Stanford University Press.
1975   Recruitment to a Ritual Role: The Midwife in a Maya Community. Ethos
         3:449–67.
Paul, Lois, and Benjamin D. Paul
1975   The Maya Midwife as Sacred Specialist: A Guatemalan Case. American
         Ethnologist 2:707–26.

Pieper, Jim, and Jeanne Pieper
1988   Guatemalan Masks: The Pieper Collection. Los Angeles: Craft and Folk
        Art Museum.
Pitarch, Pedro
2010   The Jaguar and the Priest: An Ethnography of Tzeltal Souls. Austin: Uni-
        versity of Texas Press.
Pop Caal, Antonio
1992   Li Juliisil Kirisyaanil ut li Minok ib': Judeo cristianismo y colonización,
        vol. 2. Guatemala: Seminario Permanente de Estudios Mayas.
Population Reference Bureau
1993   World Population Data Sheet, 1993. Washington, DC.
Quesada, James
1998   Suffering Child: An Embodiment of War and Its Aftermath in Post-
        Sandinista Nicaragua. Medical Anthropology Quarterly 12:51–73.
Ranney, Brooks
1973   The Gentle Art of External Cephalic Version. American Journal of Obstet-
        rics and Gynecology 116:239–51.
Raynaud, Georges
n.d.   Rabinal-Achí: Ballet drama de los indios quichés de Guatemala.
        Guatemala.
Recinos, Adrián, and Delia Goetz, trans.
1953   The Annals of the Cakchiquels; Title of the Lords of Totonicapán. Nor-
        man: University of Oklahoma Press.
Redfield, Robert, and Alfonso Villa Rojas
1971   Chan Kom: A Maya Village. 4th edition, abridged. Chicago: University of
        Chicago Press.
Richards, Michael, and Julia Becker Richards
1987   A Historical, Cultural, Linguistic and Sociolinguistic Overview of the
        Four Major Language Regions of Guatemala. Guatemala: Ministerio de
        Educación, Dirección de Desarrollo Socio Educativo Rural, Programa
        Nacional de Educación Bilingüe.
Robertson, Merle Greene
1972   The Ritual Bundles of Yaxchilan. Paper presented at the Tulane University
        Symposia on the Art of Latin America, New Orleans, April 15.
Roquel Calí, Elva Marina
1995   Conocimientos, actitudes y prácticas sobre el aborto en comadronas
        adiestradas kaqchikeles. Medical thesis, Universidad de San Carlos de
        Guatemala, Facultad de Ciencias Médicas, Guatemala.
Roys, Ralph L.
1976[1931] The Ethno-Botany of the Maya. Philadelphia: Institute of Human Issues.
Rubel, Arthur J.
1964   The Epidemiology of a Folk Illness: Susto in Hispanic America. Ethnology
        3:268–83.

Rubel, Arthur J., Carl W. O'Nell, and Rolando Collado-Ardón
1984   Susto: A Folk Illness. Berkeley: University of California Press.
Sahagún, Fray Bernardino de
1979   Florentine Codex: General History of the Things of New Spain, book 4,
         The Soothsayers; book 5, The Omens. Arthur J. O. Anderson and Charles E.
         Dibble, eds. and trans. Santa Fe: School of American Research.
Saler, Benson
1970   Sorcery in Santiago El Palmar. In Systems of North American Witchcraft
         and Sorcery. Deward E. Walker Jr., ed. Pp.125–46. Moscow: University of
         Idaho Press.
Scarry, Elaine
1985   The Body in Pain: The Making and Unmaking of the World. New York:
         Oxford University Press.
Scheper-Hughes, Nancy, and Margaret M. Lock
1987   The Mindful Body: A Prolegomenon to Future Work in Medical Anthro-
         pology. Medical Anthropology Quarterly 1:6–41.
Scott, Anne Marie
2009   Communicating with the Sacred Earthscape: An Ethnoarchaeological
         Investigation of Kaqchikel Maya Ceremonies in Highland Guatemala.
         PhD dissertation, Department of Anthropology, University of Texas at
         Austin.
Shultze Jena, Leonhard
1954   La vida y creencias de los indígenas quichés de Guatemala. Antonio
         Goubaud Carrera, trans. Guatemala: Editorial del Ministerio de Edu-
         cación Pública.
Simon, Jean-Marie
1987   Guatemala: Eternal Spring, Eternal Tyranny. New York: Norton.
Solien de González, Nancie L.
1963   Some Aspects of Child-Bearing and Child-Rearing in a Guatemalan
         Ladino Community. Southwestern Journal of Anthropology 19:411–23.
Soustelle, Jacques
1962   The Daily Life of the Aztecs on the Eve of the Spanish Conquest. Patrick
         O'Brian, trans. New York: Macmillan.
Stanzione, Vincent
2003   Rituals of Sacrifice: Walking the Face of the Earth on the Sacred Path of
         the Sun. Albuquerque: University of New Mexico Press.
Subcentro Regional de Artesanías y Artes Populares
1992   Danzas folklóricas de Guatemala. Guatemala.
Tedlock, Barbara
1981   Quiché Maya Dream Interpretation. Ethos 9:313–30.
1987   An Interpretive Solution to the Problem of Humoral Medicine in Latin
         America. Social Science and Medicine 24:1069–83.
1992   Time and the Highland Maya. Rev. edition. Albuquerque: University of
         New Mexico Press.

Tedlock, Dennis
1985   Popol Vuh: The Definitive Edition of the Mayan Book of the Dawn of Life and the Glories of Gods and Kings. New York: Simon and Schuster.
2003   Rabinal Achi: A Mayan Drama of War and Sacrifice. New York: Oxford University Press.

Tetzagüíc Guajan, Francisco
1997   Las costumbres del embarazo, parto y crianza infantil en Concepción, Sololá, Guatemala. *In* Informe de las investigaciones etnológicas en el centro y sur de Guatemala, 1991–1994. Proyecto de investigación interdisciplinaria del centro y sur de Guatemala. Pp. 407–12. Tokyo: Museo de Tabaco y Sal.

Thompson, J. Eric S.
1990   Maya History and Religion. Norman: University of Oklahoma Press.

Uzzell, Douglas
1974   *Susto* Revisited: Illness as a Strategic Role. American Ethnologist 1:369–78.

Villa Rojas, Alfonso
1980   La imagen del cuerpo humano según los mayas de Yucatán. Anales de Antropología 17(2):31–46.

Villatoro, Elba Marina, and Joaquín Acevedo
1989   Vida y obra de los curanderos de Todos Santos Cuchumatán, Huehuetenango. La Tradición Popular 74:1–12.

Villatoro, José Luis
1987   Monografía mínima del departamento de Chimaltenango. Guatemala: CENALTEX, Ministerio de Educación.

Vogt, Evon Z.
1965   Zinacanteco "Souls." Man 65:33–35.
1969   Zinacantan: A Maya Community in the Highlands of Chiapas. Cambridge, MA: Harvard University Press, Belknap Press.
1976   Tortillas for the Gods: A Symbolic Analysis of Zinacanteco Rituals. Cambridge, MA: Harvard University Press.

Wagley, Charles
1949   The Social and Religious Life of a Guatemalan Village. Memoirs of the American Anthropological Association, no. 71. Menasha, WI: American Anthropological Association.

Warren, Kay B.
1989   The Symbolism of Subordination: Indian Identity in a Guatemalan Town. Austin: University of Texas Press.

Watanabe, John M.
1989   Elusive Essences: Souls and Social Identity in Two Highland Maya Communities. *In* Ethnographic Encounters in Southern Mesoamerica: Essays in Honor of Evon Zartman Vogt, Jr. Victoria R. Bricker and Gary H. Gossen, eds. Pp. 263–74. Institute for Mesoamerican Studies, University at Albany, State University of New York.

1990   From Saints to Shibboleths: Image, Structure, and Identity in Maya Religious Syncretism. American Ethnologist 17(1):131–50.
1992   Maya Saints and Souls in a Changing World. Austin: University of Texas Press.
Weller, Susan C., Roberta D. Baer, Javier García de Alba, Mark Glazer, Robert Trotter, Lee Pachter, and Robert Klein
2002   Regional Variation in Latino Descriptions of Susto. Culture, Medicine, and Psychiatry 26:449–72.
Wilson, Richard
1991   Machine Guns and Mountain Spirits: The Cultural Effects of State Repression among the Q'eqchi' of Guatemala. Critique of Anthropology 11:33–61.
1993   Anchored Communities: Identity and History of the Maya-Q'eqchi'. Man (n.s.) 28(1):121–83.
Wisdom, Charles
1940   The Chorti Indians of Guatemala. Chicago: University of Chicago Press.
World Health Organization
2007   World Health Statistics 2007. Health Status: Mortality. Geneva, Switzerland. http://www.who.int/whosis/whostat2007_1mortality.pdf, accessed November 10, 2008.
Wuqub' Iq' (José Angel Zapeta)
1997   Christian and Mayan Spirituality: A Dialogue. *In* Crosscurrents in Indigenous Spirituality: Interface of Maya, Catholic and Protestant Worldviews. Guillermo Cook, ed. Pp. 241–60. Leiden: E. J. Brill.
Zavala, Silvio
1991   Repaso histórico de la bula Sublimis Deus de Paulo III, en defensa de los indios. Mexico City: Universidad Iberoamericana, Departamento de Historia; El Colegio Mexiquense.

Index

Page numbers in italic text indicate illustrations.

placenta, 217n2; spirit-owners, 211n20; twitching, 214n2

Christianity: enacting rituals, 222n2; imagery in rituals, 137, 140, 152, 155, 158, 172, 178, 179–80; Maya principles, xxi, 3–7, 46–50, 54–56, 170, 171, 211n18

ch'ulel (body soul): baptism, 221n4; in clothing, 145; fragmentation, 5; location, 6; stillbirths, 221n2

chuq'a'. See soul strength

churches and chapels: *champa*, 154–55, 157–59, 177, 178; in Comalapa, 38–39, 42–43, 45–46, 59; mask ceremonies, 170

Church of Jesus Christ of Latter-day Saints, 46

Chuwa Burro (gorge), 26, 159–62, 197

Chuwi Kupilaj (hill), 22, 23, 25, 26–27, 37

cleft lips/palates, 218–19n12

clinics, 59–60

clothing: confinement practice, 117–18; effigies, 145; infants, 118–19; soul in, 145; sports, 218n10; statues, 73, 74, 214n3; traditional, 41, 117–18

cofradías, *45*; cycles of renewal, 51; divisions over, 42–44; dressing statues, 73, 74, 214n3; popularity, 54, 222n5; as syncretism, 42–44, 48, 54; tradition, 55

cold, 9, 117

colonialism: conquest, 205–6; dance rituals, 170, 171; Maya concepts and principles, xxi, 3–7, 49–50, 54–55

color: eclipses, 218–19n12; rituals, 131–32, 156–57, 167, 184; *ruwa winäq*, 11, 109, 209–10n7

Comalapa: author's visits, ix–x, xvii; economy, 39–41, 207; ethnicity, 36, 39; geography, 3, 37–39; history, 35, 205–7; map, *37*; names, 35, 213n1

community: fright sickness, 147–48; moral framework, 53; *naab'l* (soul concept), 5–6, 18

conception, 108, 112, 113, 214n1

confinement practice, 117–19, 220–21n1

conquest, dance of, 169, 170

continuity thesis, 53–54

Cook, Garrett, 20, 48, 51, 53–54, 169, 182–83

copal, xv, 137, 139, 156–57, 159

coral tree, 209–10n7

corazón. See heart

corrals, 29–30, 177

Cortés y Larraz, Archbishop, 73, 207

cosmic bodies, 107, 218–19n12

costumes, *174*, *185*, *187*; blessings, 155–57, 159–61; descriptions, 172–73; embodiment, 31–32, 51–52, 65, 152, 162, 167; feeding, 67, 68, 73, 75, 160, 161, 164, 167–68, 183–85; grounding, 73–74, 152; Las Delicias vigil, 163–68, 172–78; quality, 156, 164, 199; turning-in, xv–xvi, 192–98

cravings, pregnancy, 70, 108

crops, 39–40

Csordas, Thomas, 68–70

Cúmez, Miguel, 192, 193–94, 196–98

Curruchich, Marco, 177

cycles of renewal, 51–52

dance, *moros*, *165*, *185*, *187*; blessing, 155–57; boundary between soul and body, 64–65, 66; *champa*, 154–55, 157–59, 177, 178; Chuwa Burro, 26, 159–62, 197; connection to spirit-owners, 19, 31–32, 51–52, 65, 70, 75–76, 152, 162, 167, 199–200; corrals, 30, 177; deaths, 31, 170, 178, 212n21; dolls, 67, 191, 193–94; enacting *vs.* presenting, 182; enslavement, 31–32; female dancers, 186, 190, 199, 218n10; finances, 153, 155, 167, 191, 193–94, 195, 222n3; future, 199; grounding, xvi, 63–65, 66–67, 73–74, 75–76, 152, 203; *k'u'x*, 77; Las Delicias, 26, 30, 155, 157–59, 163–68, 172–78; methodology, xvi–xviii, 78, 79–80;

71; community support, 147–48; diagnosis, 9–10, 12; dreams, 32–33; heat, 17, 18; prayers and sacrifices, 66, 147; pregnancy, 8, 109–10, 116, 209nn3–4; soul loss, 10, 14, 109–10; soul strength, 17–18; spirit-owners, 8, 21, 24, 33, 66; symptoms, ix, 9, 17, 137, 209n4. *See also* calling rituals; soul therapists

Fuentes y Guzmán, Francisco Antonio de, 207, 211n18

funeral play, 218n9

ganado, 31–32

gender: dancers, 186, 190, 199, 218n10; hair, 219–20n14; language, 36; numbers, 100–101, 217n4; objects and rituals, 106–7, 218n11; play, 105–6, 218n10; soul strength, 16, 115–16; spiritual enslavement, 31; switching, 107–8, 219n13; umbilical cord, 100–101, 102, 104–5, 217n5; vocational signs, 74, 119–20, 221n3; weaving, 41, 105, 106

geraniums, 132

girls: hair, 219–20n14; numbers, 100–101, 217n4; play, 105; sports, 218n10; weaving, 41, 71, 105

godhead, 16, 77

godparents, 106, 147

gorges: Chuwa Burro, 26, 159–62, 197; as enclosures, 29–30, 177; spirit-owners, 25–26; *ya' son*, 8, 26, 211n19. *See also* Las Delicias (gorge)

grinding stones, 104, 105, 106, 219n14

grounding. *See* spiritual grounding

habitus, 69

hair, 219–20n14

handicrafts, 41

hands as guided, 66, 70–71, 83, 87

hats, 41, 164, 173

health care, 59–61. *See also* midwifery

heart: fetus, 76, 113; placenta as, 76, 100;

soul terms and, 15–16, 76, 77, 210nn10–11

heat: blood connection, 17–18, 58; placenta, 98, 216–17n2; pregnancy, 8, 117, 215n2; *ruwa winäq*, 11, 109; terms, 210–11n12

herbalists, 60, 61

herbs: calling rituals, 140; placenta disposal, 98–99; *uwach winak*, 11. *See also* rue

hexes, 24–25

hills, 22–25, 37, 52, 169–70

horses, 158, 160, 161

hospitals, 59–60, 94–95

Huastec Maya, 218n11

Hunahpu, Chuti', ix

Hutcheson, Maury, 182, 222n3, 222n5

Iglesia Betlehem, 45, 59, 189

Iglesia Elim, 46

illness: call to midwifery, 83, 214n1; diagnosis, 67–68; pulsing, 12–14, 58, 70, 210n9, 214n2; spirit-owners, 52. *See also* fright sickness; *ruwa winäq*; *uwach winak*

images: calling rituals, 137, 140; dance ritual, 152, 155, 158, 172, 178, 179–80; Maya epigraphy, 56–57; theft of, 141–44

incense: calling rituals, 132, *133*, 137, 138; dance ritual, 156, 157, 161, 163, 194, *194*

infants: baptism and presentation, 66, 118, 120–22, 221n4; confinement, 117–19, 220–21n1; mortality, 215n3; *ruwa winäq*, 10–11, 109, 209n2, 209–10nn6–8; soul strength, 16–17; will, 108–9. *See also* fetus; umbilical cord

intestines, 216n6

inversion, fetal. *See* malpresentation

inverted uterus, 90–91, *91*

Ixils and dreams, 213n25

Iximche': clothing of newborns, 119; settling and fighting over, 205–6